Church Flowers

Judith Blacklock

The Flower Press

Published by
The Flower Press Ltd
3 East Avenue
Bournemouth
BH3 7BW

A CIP catalogue record for this book is available from the British Library.

ISBN -13: 978-0-9552391-6-8

Design: Amanda Hawkes

Line illustrations: Peters and Zabransky UK Ltd.

Printed and bound in China by C & C Offset Printing Co., Ltd.

Contents

Introduction

Every week, arrangers across the world celebrate their faith through flowers. Since the beginning of time, flowers have been used to express love of their deity. The Greeks and Romans used garlands. Buddhist priests (originally in India) placed floral offerings to the Buddha, a ritual that expanded to Japan, Korea and other parts of Asia before being taken up by the Christian church in the West as early as the 4th century when monasteries grew flowers for decoration of the church.

Today, there are many areas in the church where flowers and foliage can be arranged simply and easily to great effect. There are other areas where arranging can be testing. How do you present flowers on a sloping window-ledge? How do you decorate a pillar with no features? It is here that a comprehensive knowledge of 'mechanics' or 'how to keep the stems in place' is needed, especially when you want to arrange flowers on a grand scale. You need to know what is available, what can be created, where they can or cannot be used and why. Understanding these factors is as important as knowing how to choose pleasing combinations of flowers.

For larger work in particular, mechanics cannot be whisked out of thin air. They need to be thought out, designed and built. No one should feel inadequate because they are not DIY experts, as this requires specialist expertise. Nails and screws should never be inserted into the fabric of the church without permission from the church authorities. Sometimes it is only being able to do this that will enable you to decorate ledges, pillars and arches. If you know of quicker and easier methods than those described here then do get in touch.

Another major factor to consider is budget. Rare is the occasion when unlimited funds are available. Arrangers usually have to work with what is available and inexpensive. Long-lasting flowers such as spray chrysanthemums and carnations are extremely useful and if arranged with care, they can look absolutely beautiful. This book will show you how to make a little go a long way.

Arranging church flowers is a most creative, absorbing hobby that gives pleasure to all who visit your place of worship and will give rise to many true and lasting friendships. In the space of three days I visited flower festivals in a small local church and one of our largest cathedrals. The fabrics of the two buildings were very different, but both were united in glorifying the different structures. Flowers give beauty, hope and solace and enhance the fabric of the church. They speak of the transience of life. For many faiths, arranging flowers in a place of worship is the giving back of beauty to the One who created us and the medium with which we work.

Judith Blacklock

left Simple and effective placements of spray chrysanthemums, using the advancing colours of yellow and white, fill the space above the hymn books to give a warm welcome at a flower festival.

Church: Cathedral Church of St. Peter and St. Paul, Sheffield
Arrangers: Kath Cottingham, Renee Cuttell, Julia Legg and Valerie North
Photographer: Oliver Gordon

Artistry is advantageous, and some would say necessary, when undertaking church flowers, but very little is achieved in life without efficient organisation. Creating beautiful flower arrangements that are fresh and appropriate Sunday after Sunday, together with taking on the special events in the calendar, requires rigorous organisation, devotion and much hard work allied with a love of flowers. There has to be a clear understanding of what is available from whom, sources of other materials and budgets.

The physical architecture of the church will inspire and yet constrain. Every church is different and will lend itself to different decorative schemes. In your church, you are the expert. The church garden can be a source not just of beauty, but of useful materials. This is especially valuable when budgets are limited – which is usually the case.

The Basics
of
Church
Flowers

1 Organising the Church Flowers

For many centuries, flowers have been used to beautify the fabric of the church. Today, arranging church flowers involves people with a huge range of ability and experience all bound with a common love of flowers and their church.

It is essential to have the supply, arrangement and disposal of the flowers well organised so that the flower arrangers know the procedure and that there is no slip up which may result in a church without fresh flowers.

Organising the church flowers requires a leader and perhaps a Flower Guild or committee. It always needs some enthusiastic flower arrangers.

The Leader

A leader with overall responsibility is necessary to see that everything runs smoothly. Even a small church needs a leader to co-ordinate activities. In bigger churches where there is a committee or Flower Guild, the role is to convene and take the chair at meetings. This can be a most enjoyable and rewarding task, although it can be hard work. Special events, including flower festivals, may be planned and here the leader has a vital role.

left Lime green *Chrysanthemum* 'Shamrock' with *Lilium orientalis* (oriental lily), *Eustoma* (lisianthus) and *Paeonia* (peony).
Photographer: Xander Casey

The Flower Guild or Committee

The Flower Guild is a name often given to a committee of flower arrangers guided by the leader. In many churches, there may simply be a leader and flower arrangers who form the rota.

The Flower Guild should include any experienced flower arrangers, together with people who are not experienced but show interest. Sometimes people are reluctant to join the rota of arrangers on the grounds that they are 'not good enough'. They should be given every encouragement and initially a lot of help. They are doing the work as a service to their church and to the glory of God and not as participants in a floral art competition.

It helps to include one or two members who have facilities for growing foliage and are happy to provide the church with a ready supply. If that is not possible, which is often the case, do not worry. Florists now sell a wide range of foliage. The role of the Flower Guild is to arrange flowers at appropriate times in the church year and to ensure that the flowers are always fresh and in good condition while they are in place so that the responsibility does not always fall on the leader.

Nowadays, Health and Safety regulations are greatly extended and some of the rules may be applicable to the arrangers of church flowers. For example, it may be desirable to check that everyone involved has an up-to-date tetanus injection. The leader should check the health and safety rules and if necessary prepare a handout to give to everyone on the rota.

The Rota

In some churches, a different person arranges the flowers each week. In others, four people each take one Sunday a month, with another person to act as a reserve and to arrange the flowers for any fifth Sunday.

The list can be made at the beginning of each quarter, every half year or annually, unless the flower arranging is always undertaken by one individual or a group working together. A sheet of paper, headed 'Flowers' can be placed in a conspicuous place – usually the porch – with columns showing 'Date' and 'Name'. There could be a space for those who are willing to be called upon at short notice and another for those who may be willing to call in at the church during the week to check the flowers, fill up containers with water, sweep up petals and replace dead flowers. This could be the responsibility of the person who has arranged the flowers, a willing member of the congregation who lives nearby, or the leader.

An additional list can be drawn up of people willing to donate flowers or the money for flowers. They may wish to do this in someone's memory or for other personal reasons. This list may be headed 'Date' 'Donor' and 'Flowers or Money for Flowers' (money is usually preferable). The arranger should know how much has been donated. The name of the donor and the name of the person for whom the flowers are arranged can be included in the weekly leaflet or mentioned by the clergy in 'Notices'.

When the rota is compiled, whether for the quarter or the year, copies should be given to the arrangers and the clergy, as well as posted on the church notice board. If the arrangers need to change duties, they should be asked to keep the leader informed. This ensures that the leader knows at all times the person on duty for any particular weekend. It is essential for the leader to remind the person who has undertaken to arrange the flowers by telephone or email if he or she is not a regular arranger working in a team.

Supply and storage of mechanics

The leader has overall responsibility for making sure that mechanics – foam, tape, containers and so on – are provided and in good order. Facilities for the flower arrangers vary from the dedicated space for storage of mechanics with a supply of water to the situation encountered in many small churches where there may not even be a water supply. In this case, arrangers have to bring in containers, materials and water. This is one small practical area where the relationship with the clergy is particularly important, as sometimes the only place for storage of materials, provision of water and work with flowers is the vestry.

When to arrange the flowers

Friday and Saturday are the best days for arranging the flowers as it is important that they look fresh for the Sunday services. If many people visit the church on Saturdays it is better to arrange the flowers on Fridays. Most flowers cannot last a week without additional water, especially if the church is heated during the week or if sunshine comes through the windows onto the flowers. If the church is kept open, or if there are services during the week, someone should visit the church at least once during the week to check the condition of the plant material. A church looks very uncared for if there are faded or wilted flowers. Some churches do not remain open during the week and flowers are removed after the Sunday services.

right Conditioning and sorting the flowers before arranging.
Church: Chichester Cathedral
Photographer: Christina Bennett

Flower funds

There are various ways of raising funds:

- Members of the congregation or Flower Guild may be happy to donate money or flowers, especially for certain dates that hold particular significance.

- Allocating part of the church collection to the flower fund.

- Keeping back money from the proceeds of a flower festival, coffee mornings and other events.

- Holding special events such as bring and buy or plant sales.

- Placing a box clearly marked 'Flower Fund' near the entrance to the church so that visitors who have enjoyed the flowers may make a contribution. A flower arrangement placed close by looks attractive.

- Reserving an area at the church fair to instruct on making wreaths, handtieds or table arrangements to take home, with the profit going to the flower fund.

below A workshop in St. Mary's Church, Barnes to raise funds.
Photographer: Fenella Deards

In many churches, especially smaller ones, arrangers simply provide the flowers when it is their turn on duty, regarding this as part of their giving. In larger churches, there should be a flower fund budget agreed annually with the church council. It is essential, if flowers are charged to the flower fund, that each arranger knows the maximum to claim. He or she may, from choice, spend more than the allowance but a 'ceiling' sum should be laid down so that the flower fund can be carefully budgeted to last throughout the year. This sum is generally on the low side. The budget for major church celebrations, such as Christmas and Easter, will be greater than that for a regular Sunday. Chapter 4 'Budget Flowers' gives you ideas on how to make a little go a long way.

Making money from arranging the flowers

Some churches are able to make a profit from flowers. One way of doing this is to insist on the Flower Guild doing all the flowers for weddings and funerals. This however can be quite onerous on the Guild. The skill is to work out pricing for the various designs available, such as pedestals, pew ends, archways, that is competitive but fair and to keep to it. The price should be reviewed annually. There are various ways of assessing how to charge:

- Check prices with florists in the neighbourhood. The aim is not to squeeze out the local florist but to offer a price for work that is close to those available from other sources. Flowers may be purchased from the local florist to compensate for any possible loss of trade. Most florists will give a discount if they know there will be regular purchases.

- One way of establishing prices is to double the cost of the flowers and foliage plus 20% to cover miscellaneous expenses.

- Many church flower arrangers charge too little for their work. They forget to include the cost of the foam, the foliage, their petrol and parking and much more. Church flower arrangers do not want to charge for their work but they must remember that the more they receive the more the church will benefit.

Instructions for arrangers

It is very helpful and saves endless repetition by the leader if a set of guidelines is given to each arranger. It should give details of:

- Days and times when the flowers are arranged.
- The allowance (if any) for the flowers.
- When the church will be locked and the location of the keys.
- How to dispose of rubbish.
- Where to find water, containers, mechanics and floral foam.
- Contact details of the leader and alternative email and telephone numbers.
- What to do with the previous week's flowers.
- The positions where the flowers are needed.
- Names and contact details of those who will look after the flowers throughout the week.
- Any special rules applicable to the church such as flowers being allowed on the altar.
- The liturgical colours for the seasons of the church's year which will determine the colour of the altar frontals and vestments. The list should be agreed with the clergy for each year.
- Information on how to condition the flowers.
- Suggestions for flowers that last well.
- Sources of supply for flowers and foliage.
- How the money should be claimed back and to whom receipts should be given.

Flowers for weddings and funerals

It is advisable to have a clear policy on flowers for weddings and funerals. Some churches insist on the Flower Guild always being responsible and a charge is made. These are however the exception and usually the wedding or funeral party organises its own flowers. In this case, the leader needs to find out their plans for the flowers after the service and sometimes has to show outside arrangers where to find containers, water and other necessities. It is often desired to take away pew ends or windowsill arrangements after the service and this should not cause difficulties. If there is a pedestal beside the altar or communion table it should be suggested that this stays in the church. Most people are glad to agree. The flower arranger on the rota should be informed of the situation and told whether flowers will be available for the Sunday.

Disposal of flowers

Dead flowers should be placed in a bin provided for this purpose. Ideally, every church with a garden, however small, should have a compost heap (see page 47). When churches are kept open all week the flowers are usually left in place after the Sunday services. If the church is closed during the week the flowers are often taken to sick, elderly or bereaved members of the congregation after the last service on the Sunday.

The church magazine

It is helpful to have a column in the church magazine, leaflet or newsletter to give information about flowers. It can contain acknowledgements for flowers, the rota, helpful hints on conditioning and picking, a list of flowers that are needed for various weeks or for special occasions, possibly an article on flower arranging or the legends of flowers. Mention could be made of easy-to-grow flowers, information on flower arranging generally, flowers in season and those which have special significance. There could be a list of impending festivals, both locally and further afield.

Donated flowers

If flowers are being donated, they should be sent to the church at a specified time – on Friday or Saturday morning if they are already conditioned. If not, they should be received earlier so that they can be placed in water overnight. Flowers from the florist will have already been conditioned. Unless from a known, reliable source, the arranger should not rely totally on what may turn up. It is best to have a good idea of what will be arriving as someone else's choice of flowers may not be that of the arranger!

For events such as Christmas and Harvest, donations for extra flowers to supplement the purchases made by the leader or Guild are very welcome.

Classes

Most flower arrangers benefit from classes from time to time regardless of whether or not they are experienced. A day could be arranged with a tutor when everyone does a practical arrangement and receives kindly assessment and constructive suggestions. Alternatively a demonstration could be given. A series of classes may be organised and the local flower or garden club may be able to suggest a tutor. It is also sometimes possible to arrange a course through a college of further education. The head of the department concerned may be able to find a flower arranging tutor. It could add to the interest to have a minister to teach subjects such as church architecture, the church year and so on.

Classes are a great incentive for encouraging more people into helping with the church flowers, especially those who feel they are not good enough and are intimidated by the whole idea.

left Flowers ready for transporting to the church hall.
Photographer: Judith Blacklock

Children

Children love flowers and enjoy being involved. They can be made responsible for the flowers in the children's corner of the church. These children may well grow up to be the church flower arrangers in future years. It would prove useful to link up with one of the NAFAS Junior Flower Clubs which are available throughout the United Kingdom. NAFAS Headquarters would be happy to provide information on these Clubs (see page 406).

Classes in basic floral design could be given by a member of the Flower Guild or a teacher from a local flower club who is used to working with children. Meetings could be held in the church or in a home for an hour or so at weekends. Little expense need be incurred, because simplicity is the secret of stimulating interest. The position of the flowers can be discussed as well as lessons on flowers for special occasions and on the legends of flowers. Occasions such as Easter and Christmas are especially interesting to children.

It is important that each child is assigned a Saturday on which to arrange the flowers for Sunday services in this special children's area. Whoever is responsible for the children's work should give some help the first time. It may be difficult to stand back and allow the child to arrange the flowers alone but this is important if the child is to feel the work is his or her own. Perfection is not as important as stimulating enthusiasm to learn and participate.

left **Children's Cross**
Church: Holy Trinity Church, Princeton, NJ
Arrangers: The children of Holy Trinity Church
Photographer: Beth Walker

right **All Things Bright and Beautiful**
A large piece of hessian was the base of this design. The top border was hemmed to take a length of dowelling which fitted the hanging space. Chicken wire, sprayed gold, was wired to the hessian. Six long stems of artificial foliage were purchased and these were manipulated to create a 'tree' which was wired onto the chicken wire. Test tubes were covered in gold sisal, filled with flowers and wired to the frame.
Church: Paisley Abbey
Arrangers: Jackie Boy, Joy Bruce, Ellen Craig, Margaret Cumming, Val Miller, Pat Mories and Margaret Morrison
Photographer: Bob Brown

2 Practicalities

This chapter covers the procedures and practices that will enable your flowers to last longer. It also discusses the items that should be found in a well-stocked flower room or cupboard. Finally it informs on some practical techniques needed to create designs effectively.

Flowers and foliage

Picking flowers and foliage

If picking from the garden, cut the stems in the cool of the day and place the cut stems immediately in a bucket of tepid water. If picking from the wild, place the plant material in a damp plastic bag and blow air into the bag before sealing and taking home.

Turn to page 50 on restrictions for picking from the wild.

left In the cloisters – arrangements of flowers ready for installation in the catering marquee in the grounds of the Cathedral.
Church: Salisbury Cathedral
Arrangers: Broadstone and Corfe Mullen Flower Club
Photographer: Oliver Gordon

Where to buy flowers and foliage

Every part of the world is different for the purchasing of flowers. I would however suggest that wherever you live you establish a good relationship with one, two or three suppliers of flowers depending on the amount you buy. If you scatter the purchasing too widely, you run the risk of not getting preferential treatment or discounts.

Flower stalls and florists often have an excellent range of quality flowers and most will allow you to order any particular requirements. Trade markets are for the professionals who buy regularly in bulk and you may find that instead of getting bargains you pay more because you are having to buy a greater quantity of flowers than you need. Flowers sold at the flower market are in boxes, bunches, bundles or sold as full buckets. Some of the more expensive flowers, such as *Hippeastrum* (amaryllis) or *Cymbidium* orchids, are sold by the stem. There is little or no negotiation on price unless you buy regularly and in volume.

The quality of the flowers sold in supermarkets varies considerably. Buy from the one where the buckets always contain water and the stem ends are immersed, as customers tend to replace bunches haphazardly. It needs a diligent team and a good manager to keep them in prime condition.

Conditioning flowers

Conditioning means the preparation of flowers and foliage so that they last for the maximum amount of time. It is more about common sense than high technology. When purchasing flowers, the following procedure should be followed:

- Remove foliage from the bottom 50–60% of the stem.
- Carefully remove any thorns without scraping and damaging the stem.
- Cut 5cm (2in) off the bottom of short/medium stems and 10cm (4in) off longer stems. Cut at a sharp angle to expose more of the inner stem. It is the inner part that takes up the majority of the water.

- Place the stems immediately in a clean bucket or container of clean, tepid water.

Tips

- Cut flower food, which comes in a sachet and dissolves in water, is sold under various brand names. In the tests I have done, cut flower food does extend the life of flowers. The buds develop fully and the leaves and stems retain freshness (which is not the case with other additions to the water).
- I do not add bleach and sugar to water, as it is extremely difficult to get the balance right. I do however add a drop of bleach to a bucket of water for gerberas as they are particularly vulnerable to bacteria.
- Mature foliage can be left under water for an hour or so to condition. Do not however immerse grey foliage as the hairs that create the 'greyness' quickly become waterlogged and the colour is lost.
- The toxic sap in the stem of daffodils is detrimental to other flowers. Once the daffodils have been conditioned in their own containers or have had special food added to the water they may be used with other cut flowers but do not re-cut the stems.
- Wide hollow stems such as *Hippeastrum* and *Delphinium* can be filled with water and then plugged with cotton wool to keep the water in the stem. A stick may be inserted up the stem of these flowers to give more rigidity in arrangements.
- Tulips continue to grow once cut. The leaves do not. A test for freshness is to check that when purchasing the top leaves are at a similar height to the flowers. If the tip of the flower is much taller than the leaves then the flowers are a few days older than you would like.
- Flower stems, which contain a milky substance called latex, such as poppies and *Euphorbia pulcherrima* (poinsettia), can have their ends burnt in a flame for a few seconds and then placed in water. They will last longer when treated in this way.

Transporting the flowers

Many church flower arrangers prepare the flowers at home and then transport them to the church. Here are six ways of transporting the flowers so that they arrived in prime condition.

Method 1

Long cardboard boxes of the kind used to transport flowers to florists are excellent. They can be placed in the boot or on the back seat of the car. (A florist will probably be happy to give you one or more of these boxes.) Cut a black plastic bag and line the box. Arrange sheets of damp newspaper over the plastic as it can sweat in a hot atmosphere. Place the flowers and foliage in the box. Add a second layer of damp newspaper and fold excess bin liner over the top.

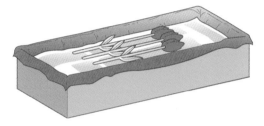

Method 2

Cut the tops off water or soft drink bottles. Seal the cut ends with tape to avoid cutting yourself or damaging the stems. Place the bottles in a water or wine carrier, fill each with water and add your flowers.

Method 3

Use cream Dutch buckets (see page 18) if travelling by car. They are more stable than round buckets.

Method 4

Cut a board to fit the inside of your car and wider than the circumference of a standard bucket. Fit uprights, of a height that will safely hold the bucket.

Method 5

In the USA, there is a special support that you can place in the car boot – it is a black grid, adjustable in size. You can sit large buckets or large arrangements on the grid and use PVC plastic pegs to keep them in position. They can be shipped around the world. Contact *www.seminoleds.com*

Method 6

If you walk to the church, or travel by bus or public transport, then place well-conditioned foliage in a plastic bag. Blow into the bag so that it is filled with air and seal the top.

Watering the flowers after they have been arranged

If there are weekday services or if the church is to be open during the week, it is important to have someone (or a team) who will visit the church during the week to give the flowers water, to remove any wilted or dead flowers and foliage and to sweep away any fallen petals.

It is a good idea to leave a few flowers or foliage in a bucket in a chosen place so that gaps left by dead plant material can be filled. If it is just foliage, this can be left outside.

The church flower cupboard or flower room

In many churches, the arrangers use their own supplies and bring everything along when they are arranging the flowers. In the ideal world however every church would have a flower room but as many of you know this is not always available. A cupboard can usually be adequately equipped for flower arranging in the vestry or a convenient room.

The leader should see that the flower room/cupboard is kept tidy, well equipped and has careful, listed instructions for the care and use of equipment displayed on the wall or cupboard door. A corridor which is seldom used can act as a flower room. A narrow shelf could be installed at an appropriate height.

If money and space were unlimited, the items below would be found in every well-stocked cupboard or flower room. It is essential that all equipment is kept scrupulously clean to avoid the spread of bacteria that shorten the life of flowers.

OASIS® Auto Corso

The OASIS® Auto Corso is available in two sizes. Both are covered with plastic caging with a suction device on the base. The smaller is domed shaped and the larger is a square. They can be fixed and removed from clean, dry surfaces such as glass, windows and mirrors. The foam can be replaced so that they can be used time and time again.

Buckets

It is helpful to have several buckets especially for the church flower arrangers. The most easily available are round, black buckets about 40cm (16in) high. They are sometimes given away by florists or at the flower market. If you can, try and obtain 'Dutch' buckets from your florist or wholesaler but these will have to be purchased. They are cream coloured and have a stable rectangular base. You can also purchase an extension that fits in the top of the bucket to give taller sides.

Candlecups

Candlecups are plastic or metal round containers with a protrusion which fits inside a candlestick or an altar vase with a narrow opening. It is a good idea to fix the candlecup firmly into the candlestick with floral fix and then to fix a plastic holder into the candlecup, before putting in the foam. An inexpensive alternative is to glue a cork to the bottom of a round plastic dish.

Candles

Candles are regularly used in church. Your church will have a specialist provider of thick, white candles of all heights and dimensions. To secure candles in foam, turn to page 28. There is now an amazing range of imitation candles available which are very realistic and are extremely useful for placing in inaccessible places where safety could be an issue.

Chicken wire

Chicken wire (or wire netting as it is also known) is a meshed wire essential for many aspects of flower arranging. Some arrangers do not like to use foam to support stems as it is non bio-degradable. For them chicken wire is ideal, as unlike floral foam, it can be reused many times. It is more cost effective to buy chicken wire by the roll and not by the metre or foot. Store in a clean, dry place. Chicken wire can be purchased in different gauges – the most useful gauge has holes of about 3.5cm (1$\frac{1}{2}$in). If it has a smaller gauge it can be difficult to insert stems through the holes.

Chicken wire can be used:

- Wrapped round foam to create a parcel that can be suspended. Stub or reel wire can be used to attach the parcel in a specific position, for example along a baton or hooked onto masonry hooks or nails.

- As a cap over foam, thus giving extra support. The wire should lie so that it does not cut into the foam. Heavy stems often need this extra support. A length of reel wire can attach a heavy stem to the chicken wire.

- Crumpled into several thicknesses and used on its own as a support, or in conjunction with a pinholder. You will need large gauge netting for this – no smaller than 5cm (2in) – so that when crumpled, stems can still be threaded through the holes.

Tip

Chicken wire can be covered with decorative material such as ribbon, sisal, fresh or preserved leaves and used decoratively in contemporary designs. A smaller gauge wire is often used in contemporary work. There is one, available from large DIY stores, which is made of a very shiny silver wire. It is however much more expensive.

Biodegradable copper-mesh wire is also available and much used in innovative design.

Decorative coloured chicken wire 'Deco-net' is also available for inclusion in modern design work.

Cones

Cones are used to raise the height of plant material. Today they are made of plastic or metal. The plastic cones are easier to clean but do not last as long. A cone may be used on its own – simply place the pointed tip of the cone into the foam. To give extra height, you can tape one or more cones onto a cane. Chicken wire or foam in the cones helps to keep the stems in place. They are particularly useful in pedestal designs.

Containers

Plastic containers are easy to clean, inexpensive and easily hidden by plant material. Round plastic bowls are available in a range of sizes and are available from garden centres, DIY centres, craft stores and some florists. It is useful to have several of each size. These containers can be used to hold arrangements of all kinds and sizes from a small table design to a large pedestal.

Glass containers give a contemporary feel to an arrangement, especially if the flowers are arranged within the container. They need to be kept spotlessly clean which is difficult if the vase is large. You can tape a brush to a long pole to remove any stains. Do take care when carrying glass vases full of water – they are very heavy.

Ceramic, stone and fibreglass containers, such as urns, always look lovely with flowers. Place a smaller plastic container within these more decorative containers so that you do not need as much foam and they are easier to clean. Fibreglass containers are good to look at and light to transport.

Tip

When carrying a glass vase never hold it by the rim as this is its weakest area and is therefore more likely to break.

Cowee sticks

Cowee floral picks and stakes are essential tools of the trade, helping floral designers to keep stems in place as the square pick shape does not turn or twist. Cowee's signature product, the wired floral pick, can be used for:

- securing stems in floral foam
- bundling and supporting dried materials
- wrapping and securing bows, ribbons and pine cones
- securing fruits and vegetables

They come in many different lengths colours and styles, from tiny double-pointed picks to standard wired floral picks to extra long plant stakes. They are widely available in the USA and Canada. For more information and where to purchase *www.wjcowee.com*.

OASIS® Dekorette

A caged piece of foam with holes in the sides of the plastic base so that it can be firmly stapped to a surface.

Dust pan and brush, mop and bucket, clean rag, dusters, kitchen towelling

It is essential that the church must be left immaculately clean after preparing the flowers. A mop is ideal for dealing with any major spillages and kitchen towelling for smaller spills.

Tip

If you have a spillage and no mop to hand, use a block of unsoaked floral foam to absorb the water.

Floral foam

There are various brand names for foam. The market leader is many countries is OASIS® but you can also purchase a brand called Trident Foam (*www.tridentfoams.co.uk*) and one by Val Spicer called Florafoam (*www.valspicer.co.uk*). In the USA, there are two other excellent brands of which I am aware. Syndicate Sales offer a foam called Aquafoam and there is a brand called Artesia® Floral Foam distributed by the FloraCraft Corporation.

In Europe, Smithers-Oasis sells three different types of foam bricks which at the time of writing are called:

- *Classic:* a soft foam perfect for stems such as daffodils and anemones which can be inserted easily.
- *Ideal:* for general use whatever the time of year.
- *Premium:* a dense foam suitable for strong stems such as branches of blossom and exotic plant material.

OASIS® *'Jumbo'* is a foam of Premium density but instead of being the usual 20 bricks to the single box there is a choice of either three or one large blocks to the box. This foam is perfect for church pedestals and other large designs as it holds tall stems more securely. It can be carved into small pieces with a long bladed knife.

In the USA, OASIS® is sold as Premium or non Premium.

Premium Foam
- Springtime (light density) suitable for flowers with hollow, delicate stems such as most bulb flowers.
- Standard (medium density) – perfect for everyday designs.
- Instant (medium density) – standard floral foam punched with holes for faster water absorption.
- Deluxe (heavy density) ideal for larger-stemmed flowers, especially tropicals.
- Instant Deluxe (heavy density) – deluxe foam punched for faster saturation.
- Designer Blocks (heavy density) – equal in size to six standard size bricks.
- Grande Brick (heavy density) – equal in size to two standard size bricks.

Non Premium Floral Foam Bricks
ADVANTAGE Plus – An all purpose economy foam punched with holes for faster water absorption for the price conscious – a light to medium density foam with average stem grip.

On a personal note, having worked with various foams in the USA, I would personally avoid the cheaper foams. I find light density and non Premium bricks too soft for many stems. For only a little more you can purchase really good, easy to use foam.

www.smithersoasis.com will gives details of products currently in production.

Florette/OASIS® FLORACAGE

These are spray trays filled with foam that are covered with a plastic cage. The handle bears a hole to make suspension easy. In the USA and Canada, they are called FLORACAGE and in Europe, OASIS® Florette. The only difference is that the Florette has bevelled sides. They are available in two sizes. The cages can be opened and the foam replaced. They are more expensive than the basic spray trays but are very easy to use.

Florists' fix

This is a green, putty-like substance that is used in conjunction with a foam holder or frog to keep foam in place. It can also be used on the base of a pinholder to hold it secure or to fix a candlecup to a candlestick. It can be used to adhere any two clean, dry items together. It is rather like Blutac® or indeed chewing gum.

Florists' tape / pot tape / anchor tape

This is a strong adhesive tape used to tie foam down to secure it to the container. If you have a choice of purchasing different widths I find the wider one better as it remains in good condition longer and provides more security.

Foam holders or frogs

Foam holders are light plastic discs with four prongs. They can be purchased in two sizes – small and large. They are ideal for keeping small pieces of foam in place when used in conjunction with florists' fix, Blutac® or similar.

Foam rings

Foam rings have a diameter of between 20cm (8in) and 40cm (16in). They can be purchased with a plastic or polystyrene base. They are useful for door hangings, Advent rings, at Easter to surround the Paschal candle and on many other occasions.

Garland mechanics

OASIS® Garland consists of 12.5cm (5in) cylinders of foam held together with nylon netting which can be cut to any desired length. They can be arranged to fit any desired space including doors and gazebos or to create a floral archway.

Trident Foams 'Ultra Garland' is comprised of 12 plastic cages holding foam, each with interlocking hooks for ease and flexibility. They are ideal for garland making and are reusable. They can also be used singly to create swags and balls of flowers.

Le Clip®

This is a product by Smithers-Oasis which is a domed piece of foam encased in plastic with a flexible curved handle which can be lengthened. It is more expensive than a spray tray but the foam can be changed. It is ideal for hanging over pew ends with a straight top or any other straight slim projection such as a chair back.

Life extender spray

In the UK this product is called Glory® produced by Chrysal. Other manufacturers have a similar product. If sprayed lightly over the flowers it will extend their life. It does seem to work.

Mist spray

This is a plastic or metal container which will deliver a fine spray of water. This should be used after completing or when refreshing an arrangement. A well-washed bottle of kitchen cleaner can be adapted for use in this way.

Pedestal stands/plinths

It is most helpful if the church is equipped with one or two pedestals or plinths. If acquiring these for the first time avoid very flimsy decorative ironwork pedestals as they can look inadequate if supporting a large arrangement of flowers and foliage. Stronger versions may be initially more expensive but they usually look better and give surer stability. Perhaps someone could be persuaded to donate a pedestal or a gifted craftsman in the congregation would make a good plinth. Solid plinths give a more contemporary feel, are visually larger and for large designs these work well. An urn on a pedestal gives gravitas to the arrangement and it also raises it higher. Fibreglass urns and plinths are excellent as they are light, stable and look extremely good.

Pinholders

A pinholder consists of numerous pins embedded in a lead base that is designed to support stems that can be used again and again. They are ideal for woody and hollow stems. Pinholders come in a range of sizes and shapes although the circular 6cm ($2^{1}/_{2}$ in) pinholder is the most commonly available and the most useful. They are sometimes referred to as 'frogs'.

Plastic sheet/black plastic bags

These are needed for rubbish. I like to hook a big black bag over a chair or the end of a pew. Alternatively, use a cotton or plastic sheet flat on the floor and scoop the rubbish away when you have finished.

Tip

If the church has a compost heap, waste or faded flowers and foliage can be added to it. If the local authority provides special dustbins for waste plant material, care should be taken to put the rubbish into the correct one.

OASIS® Raquette

This is a length of foam covered in perforated film which minimizes water evaporation. It can be easily penetrated by hard stems. It comes in three sizes – small, medium and large. If you do not have the budget for this product then wrap foam (ideally a piece from a denser quality 'Jumbo' block) in cling film.

Scissors for flowers and foliage

These should be clearly labelled with distinctive tags. Alternatively, issue every new arranger with a pair of scissors for which they have responsibility. In the hands of an expert a knife is the best tool for cutting stems but for the less experienced scissors (and secateurs for heavy woody stems) are best. Do not cut wires with scissors or secateurs, use wire cutters. Have a notice on the wall of the flower room and be firm to the point of being difficult on this subject as scissors are quickly ruined if they are used to cut wires.

Secateurs

A good pair of secateurs is essential for cutting branches and strong stems. They need to be of a size that fits the hand comfortably. Make sure they are safely closed when not in use.

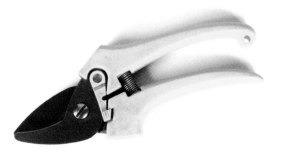

Sisal

Sisal is produced from the leaves of *Agave sisalana* a native plant of Central America and Mexico and comes in many colours. It gives excellent texture and easy cover. It can be secured to foam with mossing (German) pins. It is not an essential for the flower room but gives decorative interest.

Spheres

Foam spheres are available encased in green nylon netting. Wire or twine can be used to suspend the sphere to create a hanging ball of flowers.

Spray trays

Sometimes known as pew ends or shovels these rectangular plastic trays with a handle are invaluable for arranging flowers in a church. They are similar to the Florette/OASIS® FLORACAGES but are considerably less expensive. The hole in the handle means that they can be easily suspended to decorate the pews, the walls or used to create columns of flowers.

Stem cleaner

An inexpensive, round, yellow plastic disc manufactured by OASIS® is one of the latest products on the market to remove leaves and thorns from stems. It is gentle on the stems and very effective. Do not use metal strippers. They damage the stem and therefore allow bacteria to enter.

Stem tapes

These are florists' tapes that stretch and adhere to the stem or wire if pulled tightly. They help to keep the moisture in the stem and to give a more decorative finish. I prefer the plastic Parafilm® but many people find Stemtex® easier to use. Stemtex® is like crepe paper and slightly sticky to the touch if the temperature is high.

Watering can with a long spout

A watering can with a long spout is essential to add water to your flower arrangements on a regular basis – at least once a day for a large design.

Wires

There are many different gauges or weights of wire used in floral design. The heavier the wire the heavier the stem it will support. In general church work it is not necessary to have a large selection of wires but I would suggest the following:

a) Stub wires – these are available in many different gauges. If you want four weights that will be suitable for most work consider these:

  - 1.25mm (18 gauge) for supporting heavy stems
  - 0.71mm (22 gauge) for general wiring. These are good for making into hairpins of wire.
  - 0.46mm (26 gauge) for wiring light stems
  - 0.32mm or 0.28 mm (30 or 32 gauge) for very delicate wiring

There are other types of decorative wire and there is always something new and exciting coming on to the market. These wires are used more in contemporary and wedding work to give shine and interest as well as binding.

e) Paper covered wire or bind wire
   This is ideal for hanging arrangements where wire would slip or cause damage. It is also used for binding together branches and twigs securely and unobtrusively and for creating structures where the binding is made into a decorative feature.

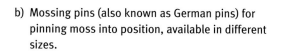

b) Mossing pins (also known as German pins) for pinning moss into position, available in different sizes.

c) Reel wire (called spool wire in the USA) – this comes on a reel. For fastening moss onto a frame 0.56mm (24 gauge) wire is ideal. Finer reel wire 0.32mm or 0.28mm (30 or 32 gauge) – either green or silver – is also useful, particularly for wedding work.

d) Decorative wire
   Decorative wire comes in many colours such as:
   - thick aluminium wire
   - light aluminium wire on a reel
   - boullion/bullion crinkly wire on a reel

Techniques

Reviving wilted plant material

Flowers wilt if water is not reaching the flower head. If the flower is fresh this is usually because a blockage has occurred in the bottom 15 percent of the stem. Remove this amount with a clean cut at a sharp angle and then either:

a) Place the stem end in 5–10cm (2–4in) of hot water for 60 seconds. Protect the flowering head, if the stem is short or the flower delicate, with tissue or a paper bag.
If the stem is soft, use water of a lower temperature.
Transfer the stem to deep tepid water and leave in a cool place for 12 hours.

   or

b) Immerse the stem and flower lengthways in a basin of water for at least 30 minutes.

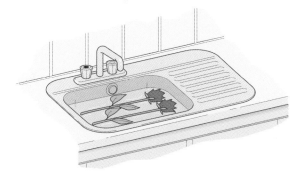

left A magnificent pedestal design of foliage and fruit. The large green apples at the focal area are highlighted and framed by smooth textured *Bergenia* leaves. See page 29 on how to secure fruit in arrangements.
Church: Southwell Minster
Arranger: Alan Smith
Photographer: Toby Smith

Preparing wet foam

a) Cut the piece of foam you require and let it sink under its own weight, horizontally, in water that is deeper than the piece of foam you are soaking. Do not push the foam down into the water. As a guideline for time a brick will have fully absorbed water in 50 seconds. Premium foam, OASIS® Rainbow® foam and some branded foams take a little longer to soak. All foam is fully charged with water when the colour of the entire piece has changed to a darker colour.

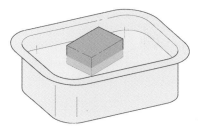

b) Store unused foam that has been wetted in a tied plastic bag. In this way, the foam will remain wet and keep for up to a year. If foam that has been wetted is left in the open air it will dry out and never again retain water with the same efficiency. You can try pouring boiling water, to which a little liquid soap has been added, over used foam that has dried out.

c) Do not leave foam in water – it will become spongy. Consequently it will be difficult to insert stems cleanly.

d) Discard foam with lots of holes. It is false economy to keep on trying to use foam that has had heavy use as the entire design could well fall to bits just as you are trying to place the final stem!

Using a pinholder

a) Place a coil of florists' fix or several small pea-sized blobs on the base of the pinholder and press down firmly in the container. Alternatively cut a piece of rubber, or the packing that is placed under packaged meats from the supermarket, to fit under the pinholder.

b) Cut stems at a sharp angle. For woody stems make one short slit up from the base. The angled cut of the stem should face away from the direction in which the branch is to lean. Tie thin-stemmed material, such as freesias, together with wool before placing on the pins.

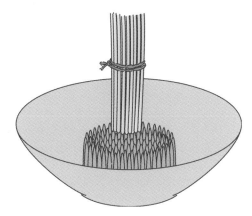

Securing candles

Secure your church candle in the foam by:

a) Placing 3, 4 or 5 cocktail sticks or short lengths of wire bent into hairpin shapes, on a piece of florists' tape with the tip of the stick rising just above the tape.
b) Wrapping the tape tightly around the candle so that the tape is at the bottom of the candle.
c) Inserting the ends of the sticks in the foam.

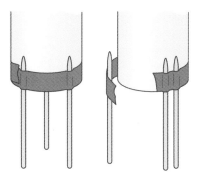

Alternatively, for thicker candles, you can heat the ends of three heavy gauge wires (1.25mm/18 gauge) and then ease these into the base of the candle. The heat will soften the wax and allow easy insertion of the wires into the foam.

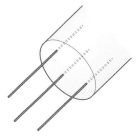

Tip

When relighting a candle remove the end of the wick with scissors as it is the carbon on the wick that generates smoke.

Wiring

Wiring a small cone

a) Take a medium gauge wire and bend the wire round the scales of the cone at the lowest possible point.
b) Pull tight. Twist and take the wires under the cone to the central base to form a stalk.

Wiring a large cone

a) Take two medium gauge wires and thread each halfway round the circumference of the scales.
b) Twist the wires together at each side and bring them down under the base of the cone.

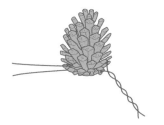

Extending a stem with a single leg mount – suitable for lighter stems

a) Take a medium gauge wire and bend approximately one fifth of the way along the wire.
b) Place the bent wire against the stem you wish extended so that the short leg extends to the end of the stem.
c) Wrap the longer wire round the shorter wire and the stem three times leaving one wire end free for inserting in your foam. Cut to the length required.

Extending a stem with a double-leg mount – suitable for heavier stems

a) Take a medium wire, or a heavier one if the stem or branch is heavy, and bend so that one end is about 20% longer than the other.
b) Place the stem on top of the wire so that both ends are parallel with the stem and project well beyond the end.
c) Wrap the longer wire around the shorter wire and the stem three times with equal space between each wrap.
d) Pull the wires down straight in line with the stem.
e) Use Stemtex® or Parafilm® to cover the stem and the wires.

Wiring fresh fruit and vegetables

There are two ways of doing this – with wires or with sticks. Wires are flexible but it does mean that you cannot use the fruits or vegetables afterwards. With sticks you can but you do not have as much flexibility.

a) Take a medium (0.71mm 21 gauge) or heavy-gauge wire (1.25mm 18 gauge) through the fruit and out the far side, about one third of the way up the fruit.
b) Repeat with a second wire at right angles to the first.
c) Bring the wires down and twist together to create a stalk.

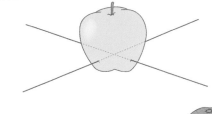

Alternatively, insert wooden cocktail, barbecue sticks or Cowee picks into the base of the fruit.

3 The Church Garden

Most churches have a churchyard. If the churchyard is also a garden then there are opportunities for the church flower arranger to grow plants from which foliage can be pruned for arranging. Many shrubs have lovely flowers and berries that can also be used. If possible try to have one plant coming into flower as another plant fades. Evergreens are an especially good choice as they are available all year round. Native species always do best.

Useful shrubs and perennials and why

On pages 32–42 I offer a list of shrubs and perennials that I have found useful when creating designs in church together with suggestions as to how they can be used to advantage.

There are entire books written with detailed information on these plants. Here I give a brief summary of the plants I feel will be of most value to the arranger. They are easy-going in many soils, aspects and climates although do check with your local horticulturalist or garden centre if in doubt. All these foliages last well in water when mature.

The plants are listed according to their botanical name. A common name, where appropriate, follows in brackets.

> E – evergreen
> D – deciduous
> SE – semi-evergreen

left A peaceful spot in the church garden.
Church: Church of St. Mary the Virgin, Mortlake
Photographer: Judith Blacklock

Acacia (wattle, mimosa) – spring flowering shrub that lasts well once cut but must not be allowed to dry out. Most forms are extremely fast growing and do best on sandy soil. If you have heavy clay soil then plant them young so that they spread their roots before they grow too high. The balls of yellow flowers are slightly fragrant and a favourite with many. (E)

Aspidistra (cast iron plant) – incredibly long-lasting plant but slow to grow. The leaves are enjoyed by slugs and snails so it is best grown in a pot. *Aspidistra* is slightly tender to frost. The leaves are good-natured and can be manipulated into many forms to give interest. They can be wired along the back rib to give strength and then manipulated into a 'wave' or loop. They work well in pedestal designs. (E)

Abelia – small dainty pale pink flowers in the summer. Good in small and medium designs although the flowers do tend to drop quite quickly. (SE)

Alchemilla mollis (lady's mantle) – a well-known perennial that is easy to grow and much loved by flower arrangers. Useful frothy lime-green flowers in summer. Grows in sun or shade and is useful ground cover. Let it seed itself. This wonderful plant material can simply be massed in vases or mixed with any other flower to great effect. Try positioning vases in a line along a window ledge and fill with *Alchemilla mollis* in the summer and Queen Anne's lace in the spring. (D)

Amelanchier – small tree with lovely cream blossom in spring with bronze young foliage. It provides good arching sprays for large arrangements. The foliage is also useful when just beginning to colour in autumn. It is tolerant of sun or semi-shade. (D)

Aucuba japonica (spotted laurel) – long-lasting berries and leaves, it can be grown just about anywhere. It absorbs pollution and is therefore useful grown close to a busy road. Short sprays can be used quickly and easily to hide mechanics. The variegation may dominate the leaf or be barely seen according to the variety. (E)

Bergenia (elephant's ears) – large smooth textured leaves ideal for large designs. It is tolerant of sun or shade, as well as dry soil. Some varieties have red-bronze leaves in the winter when grown in direct sun. (E)

Buxus (box) – small leaved, long-lasting foliage but slow to grow. Good as cut foliage for covering long-lasting floral carpets, garlands and swags in areas where it is difficult to add water. (E)

Camellia – the most wonderful evergreen with long-lasting shiny leaves that is excellent in all designs. They can be used all year round and the flowers are an added bonus. The only downside is that it grows slowly and prefers an acid soil. (E)

Centranthus (valerian) – pink or white flowers in the summer. A very tolerant perennial which will cope with shade and very dry soil. Seeds aggressively so remove the dead heads unless you want a colony! It is attractive to bees, a pretty sight in the church garden and useful in arrangements generally. (D)

Choisya ternata (Mexican orange blossom) – a prolific grower with radial leaves that are ideal for covering foam at a low level. It is tolerant of most conditions. The golden leaved form 'Sundance' looks healthier in semi-shade. (E)

Clematis tangutica – an autumn flowering clematis with small yellow flowers. It provides long flowing sprays for September arrangements. It is particularly useful because of the lovely silvery seed-heads very like the wild clematis known as old man's beard. Prefers a neutral or slightly limy soil. (D)

Acacia

Aspidistra

Abelia

Alchemilla mollis

Amelanchier

Aucuba japonica

Bergenia

Buxus

Camellia

Centranthus

Choisya ternata

Clematis tangutica

Conifers – most have useful evergreen foliage whose value should not be underrated. Many varieties are available so the most important thing to bear in mind when planting is the final size. Anything too vigorous can become quickly unmanageable and anything too small will not provide enough material. Conifers are ideal for covering foam and are particularly useful during the winter months. (E)

Cornus (dogwood) – invaluable for their colourful stems which must be cut back hard in the spring. Grow *C. sericea* 'Flaviramea' for yellow-green stems, *C. alba* 'Sibirica' for red, *C. alba* 'Kesselringii' for deep red-black and *C. sanguinea* 'Midwinter Fire', 'Midwinter Flame' and 'Magic' for shades of yellow-red. The stems can be used to create colourful structures which are fantastic in contemporary designs. (D)

Cotinus (smoke bush) – stunning shrubs with rounded leaves and plumes of airy flowers in mid-summer. Many varieties have deep red-purple foliage and spectacular autumn colour. Only use when the new foliage is mature, generally from mid June onwards. Good in pedestals. (D)

Cytisus (broom) – beautiful sprays of bright yellow, white or pink flowers in late spring and summer with curving sprays of foliage all year round. It is useful in most designs especially *Cytisus battandieri* (pineapple broom) – a small tree providing long sprays of silvery foliage that can be used all year round. It conditions easily when mature and lasts well into the autumn. The flowers smell delicately of pineapple. (E/D)

Daphne – produces small highly scented flowers in late winter. They are best planted close to the church door to take advantage of the fragrance. The best and most easily grown is *D. odora* 'Aureomarginata'. It does very well in shade or semi-shade. As daphnes do not grow prolifically use short sprigs in smaller designs. (SE)

Elaeagnus pungens 'Maculata' – green leaves splashed with gold – a marvellous plant to fill the church garden with bright colour during the winter months. The stems are rather rigid and suit larger designs where they will give a big splash of colour, particularly useful if you have only a few flowers. The variegation can be a good substitute for flowers. Other attractive *Elaeagnus* plants are *E. x ebbingei* 'Gilt Edge' and *E. x ebbingei* 'Limelight'. (E)

Epimedium – tough long-lasting leaves that are happy in semi to deep shade. Bold, useful foliage on wiry stems. The leaves can be cut back in late winter to allow the beautiful flowers to be seen. However it is the foliage that is loved by flower arrangers. (E)

Escallonia – branches of delicate pink, white or red flowers in June and July. *Escallonia* is a very pretty shrub but the flowers drop quickly so use for a wedding rather than for a pedestal that has to last a full week. It is especially useful in seaside gardens. (E)

Euonymus fortunei (winter creeper) – useful evergreen foliage that looks fresh all year round. The plants sprawl but are easily clipped into shape. If grown against a wall they will climb, like ivy. They are tolerant in sun, shade or even dry shade. 'Emerald 'n Gold' and 'Silver Queen' are good varieties. Good filler foliage for all designs. When on a budget the variegation can take the place of flowers. (E)

Euphorbia – many varieties are useful. Most have long-lasting heads of lime-green bracts with tiny flowers from late winter to midsummer but one or two (*Euphorbia griffithii* 'Fireglow' and *E. g.* 'Dixter' have lovely red bracts and reddish stems (depending on variety). Easily grown but looks best in full sun. The foliage is evergreen and useful. Beware of the white sap (latex) as this can cause a skin rash on contact. It seeds itself when happy. (SE)

Fagus sylvatica (beech) – mature beech provides one of the best outline foliages for large pedestals. The young growth is soft and wilts quickly but from July to October nothing is better. Small plants keep their leaves throughout the winter. These leaves are dead but are copper coloured and very beautiful. These are excellent in autumnal designs and can be sprayed gold for Christmas. (SE)

Fatsia japonica (Japanese aralia) – easy to grow shrub that provides large architectural leaves for pedestals. It is best grown in shade for the best leaf colour or if grown in sun it can look bleached. Useful varieties are 'Variegata' with cream edges to tips or leaves, 'Aurea' with yellow variegations, 'Annelise' with green edged yellow leaves and 'Spider's Web' – filigree white markings on green background. (E)

Fatshedera x *lizei* – larger leaves than the ivy but smaller than the *Fatsia*. Excellent bold, dependable leaves for medium sized designs. (E)

Garrya elliptica (silk tassel bush) – tough reliable evergreen that produces long tassels during the winter months that look lovely in larger designs but the leaves are rather dull. It glycerines beautifully if cut when the tassels are about 4cm (2in) long. The upper side of the leaves goes a very dark brown, almost black, and the underside and the tassels go a soft velvety grey. Choose 'James Roof' (male) for the longest tassels. (E)

Griselinia littoralis – good near the sea, its lovely lime green leaves are easy to use in pedestals. This shrub is extremely useful for many designs. It can be slow to get going and the soft growth in the spring wilts easily. There are several beautiful variegated forms which add interest and lightness both to flower arrangements and in the garden. (E)

Hebe – good natured plant that comes with a variety of leaf shapes and colours. Choose one that has a neat leaf structure. (E)

Hedera (ivy) – one of the most useful plants in the church garden. The trails, the individual leaves, the strong variegated *Hedera colchica* 'Dentata Variegata' and *Hedera helix* 'Luzii' and the bushy *Hedera helix* 'Arborescens' are invaluable. Ivy grows particularly well on box tombs, especially modern brick tombs where it can be allowed to grow in long 'loops'. The trails can be used to create outlines, the individual leaves to give bold smooth texture in small designs and the simple dark green glossy leaves and fruits of the more bushy form (which occurs when the ivy leaves the support up which it is climbing) can be used in just about any design. (E)

Helleborus – strong, leathery leaves that support pretty unassuming flowers from winter through to spring depending on variety. The flowers stay on the plants for a long time. When the stamens in the centre of the flower have given way to seed they will last well once cut and are delightful in small to medium designs. (E)

Hosta (plantain lily, funkia) – beautiful bold, flat leaves. There are many varieties available with lovely variegation. They are prone to snails and slugs so it may be best to grow the thicker-leaved cultivars such as *H.* 'Krossa Regal' and *H.* 'Sum and Substance'. The grey-blue hostas tend to get spoilt by rain which washes off their lovely bloom. They are perfect for giving interesting bold form, colour and texture. (D)

Hydrangea – an essential shrub for the church garden. Most types flower only on old wood and are best pruned lightly after flowering. Newer varieties flower on new growth. They all grow quite fast but most prefer some moisture. Plant the mop head hydrangea not the lace cap. Flowers are superb in pedestal designs for late summer and autumn. Their size fills the design quickly and easily and they give colour, form and texture. (D)

Hypericum (St. John's wort) – nondescript leaves that produce brilliant yellow flowers followed by berries. The new varieties give a good range of colour and are a wonderful addition to any flower design. (SE)

Ilex (holly), *I. aquifolium* 'Golden King' (green-margined gold leaves) and *I. a.* 'Silver Queen' (silver-edged leaves) are superb in Christmas designs. The plants grow very slowly so let them be among the first to be planted. For yellow berries select *I. a.* 'Bacciflava' and small bluish leaves *I.* x *meserveae* 'Blue Prince'. (E)

Laurus nobilis (bay) – dark green leaf, not greatly exciting but easy and quick to grow in most normal to dry soils in sun or shade. Useful in pedestals when there is nothing else! Golden variety *L.n.* 'Aurea' is useful. (E)

Fatshedera x lizei

Garrya elliptica

Griselinia littoralis

Hebe

Hedera (foliage)

Hedera (berries)

Helleborus

Hosta

Hydrangea

Hypericum

Ilex

Laurus nobilis

Lavendula (lavender*)* – an essential for every church garden. Lavenders only grow well in full sun or they become stringy. *L. angustifolia* (English lavender) is hardy and long-lived and the best choice for more permanent plantings. Many varieties are available but *L. a.* 'Hidcote' is a classic choice. All prefer dry soils. Lavender is easy to propagate by taking cuttings. Use in small designs, perhaps at the entrance table where the fragrance can be appreciated. (SE)

Ligustrum ovalifolium 'Aureum' (golden or Californian privet) – in many areas evergreen all year round. Young foliage is soft in the early spring but long-lasting later in the year. Pretty white flowers in early summer followed by black berries. The berries are particularly useful in autumnal designs. (SE)

Lonicera (honeysuckle) – a fragrant shrub excellent for growing against a church wall. Its perfume is irresistible. It grows well in sun or part shade but can become very twiggy eventually. The flowers do not last long but look wonderful trailing through pedestal designs during the summer months. Also useful is *L. nitida* (box honeysuckle) with tiny leaves and cream flowers in spring. Its trailing stems make good outlines for classic work. (SE or D depending on variety)

Magnolia grandiflora (bull bay) – strong glossy large leaves often with rust-coloured felted undersides. During the summer months the magnificent white flowers give beauty in the garden. In cooler climes they develop well when planted near a wall. The flowers do not live long but the foliage is bold and good-natured and lasts well when cut. Perfect for large pedestals. (E)

Mahonia (holly grape) – perfectly happy growing in sun or shade, providing foliage throughout the year as well as yellow flowers in winter or spring (depending on variety). *Mahonia x media* 'Charity' is perhaps the most popular, flowering in late winter. This shrub has a spiky, structural form that can be difficult to use in classic designs. When used with a few flowers in a contemporary design it can be stunning. All varieties of *M. japonica* glycerine well, giving dark brown leaves which will last for years. (E)

Myrtus (myrtle) – long-lasting small leaved shrub that is slightly tender to frost but tolerant otherwise. It enjoys a sunny position. Its wonderful autumn berries are very suitable for autumnal designs. Like box it is suitable as ground cover in swags and garlands as the form is neat and regular and can last well without copious amounts of water. (E)

Paeonia (peony) – many flower arrangers think of peonies as one of their favourite flowers. The plant provides sumptuous but short-lived flowers on long-lived plants that thrive in sun but tolerate partial shade. They are best planted and left alone as they have very large deep roots. The foliage is also superb and from June until the hard frosts can be used in medium to large designs. (D)

Parthenocissus tricuspidata (Boston ivy) - invaluable deciduous climber with glossy three pointed leaves that last well from late June until the hard frosts. Do not plant its cousin *Parthenocissus quinquefolia* (Virginia creeper) which is difficult to arrange. The leaves on their strong wiry stems are invaluable in smaller designs giving smooth bold texture and neat form. (D)

Phormium (New Zealand flax) – tough sword-like leaves that can be manipulated and last out of water. Best varieties *P.* 'Dazzler' (red), *P.* 'Firebird' (red fading to bronze-purple), *P.* 'Bronze Baby' (bronze-purple), *P.* 'Yellow Wave' (yellow and green) and *P. cookianum* 'Tricolor' which has green and cream striped foliage. (E)

Photinia x *fraseri* 'Red Robin' – a must for many gardens. The young foliage is bright red and matures quickly. Excellent in late spring for pedestal outlines if conditioned well. (E)

Phyllostachys (bamboo) – a large genus of bamboos with many being suitable for the garden. The foliage looks good all year, perhaps less good in early summer when some leaves are shed. Beware however as *Phyllostachys* can spread at the root even if the label says they do not and established clumps are very hard to lift. They are not suitable for the smaller English churchyard. The black (*P. nigra*) and yellow (*P. aurea*) stemmed bamboo, when defoliated, give straight stems ideal in contemporary work. (SE)

Physocarpus – an excellent shrub for sun or semi-shade, giving wonderful arching stems of green or purple, depending on variety. The variety 'Diabolo' is particularly valuable for its strong purple foliage. The shrub can grow quite large but is easily kept to size and shape. It has pretty cream/pink flowers in late spring/early summer. (E)

Pittosporum – easy to grow shrub that grows into a tall tree if left unattended. It has a shallow root structure so plant near the church for shade, foliage and interest. (E)

Polypodium (fern) – looks particularly good in autumn and winter. These evergreen ferns are drought-tolerant and give an exciting, almost exotic look when cut long. Use in medium and large designs and pedestal arrangements. (SE)

Prunus laurocerasus (cherry laurel) – not one of the most exciting additions to the church garden but reliable and easy to grow. They can get very large if left unpruned. The individual leaves can be removed from the main stem and used out of water to create interesting designs as they last well once cut. For a marbled look try *P. l.* 'Castlewellan' (marbled white). (E)

Rhododendron (azalea/rhododendron)– tough evergreen foliage ideal for pedestals in winter and early spring. Flowers are usually produced in late spring. Needs an acid or neutral soil. *Rhododendron* foliage provides an excellent structure for winter and spring pedestal designs. (E)

Ribes sanguineum (flowering currant) – easy to grow shrub that is early to leaf and one of the last to fall. Round, long-lasting foliage with flowers that are loved or hated. The smell of the flowers does dissipate after several hours in water. Ideal for outline foliage. (SE)

Rosmarinus (rosemary) – easy to grow shrub that likes full sun and is not fussy about being watered. It is especially lovely when added to wedding bouquets giving fragrance and interesting texture. (E)

Rumex crispus (curled dock) – this will frequently be found growing as a weed but should be encouraged as the flowers and seedheads are beautifully coloured with reds and browns later in the season. *Rumex* is one of the best discoveries in the flower arranging world. It is useful in all stages in parallel designs and in pedestals. It glycerines well if cut before the flowers are fully open. (D)

Sarcoccoca (Christmas or sweet box) – fragrant, non-showy flowers that bloom during the winter months, it is an ideal shrub to have close to the church door. Grows well in sun or shade and dry soil. It is often planted in dry shade but they look better if planted in moisture-retaining soil. Use small sprigs in arrangements at the entrance or in pew end designs. (E)

Senecio/Brachyglottis – this shrub provides grey leaves that are long-lasting when cut. The shrub creates a low rounded form which must be pruned regularly to stop it going leggy – all the better for the flower arranger! (E)

Skimmia japonica – bright green evergreen foliage and red berries if male and female are planted together. There are also varieties that are bi-sexual. Shade suits them well. This long-lasting foliage is excellent in most designs and the berries provide colour during many months of the year. (E)

Sorbus aria (whitebeam) – deciduous but early to leaf tree with silver green foliage that is best in the sun. It becomes a reasonably large tree in time. It is ideal for creating the outline of pedestals from May until the frosts. This tree has a beautiful, graceful form and is an ideal choice for the larger church garden. (D)

Pittosporum

Polypodium

Prunus laurocerasus

Rhododendron

Ribes sanguineum

Rosmarinus

Rumex crispus

Sarcococca

Senecio/Brachyglottis

Skimmia japonica
(berries)

Skimmia japonica
(flowers)

Sorbus aria

Sorbus aucuparia (mountain ash or rowan) – a lovely small-medium tree with hanging clusters of orange fruits in autumn and winter and ash-like leaves in the summer. It provides ideal outline material for autumn pedestal designs. (D)

Syringa (lilac) – useful shrub/small tree for the flowers in spring. The foliage should be removed if the flowers are to last once cut. Cut when some of the flowers on each stem are open and give it a good drink. (D)

Tamarix ramosissima (tamarisk, salt cedar) – shrub/small tree with delicate upright branches and small narrow leaves. It is not fully hardy and will not flourish high above sea level or in gardens where the temperature is very low. (E)

Trachelospermum jasminoides (star jasmine) – an evergreen climber that needs a support and is best grown up a warm wall for maximum flowering although, for the arranger, it is the leaves that are valuable. It is reputedly slightly tender and often grown in conservatories but it is hardy in much of the UK.

The plants grow faster with lots of water in the summer but need a soil that is acid-neutral. The leaves turn bronze in winter and are suitable for designs all year round. (E)

Viburnum tinus (laurustinus) – pretty white flowers with a tinge of pink late winter / early spring followed by black berries. The form *V.* 'Eve Price' is compact and free-flowering. Shade tolerant and drought-tolerant. It is exceptionally useful in all arrangements from October through to spring. The foliage, without flowers or berries, is uninspiring. (E)

Weigela florida (evergreen weigela) – useful shrub that produces arching sprays of foxglove-like flowers in early summer. *Weigela florida* 'Variegata' is very floriferous and has good foliage with creamy-yellow margins. Needs sun. (D)

Tips

- When planting, check how big the plant will be in seven years and leave space accordingly.
- Young, healthy plants are easier to establish.
- A calendar can be made of the shrubs, plants and bulbs which flower during each of the twelve months so as to highlight any gaps.

below **Garlanded arch in churchyard**
A long rope was wound round the arch and anchored firmly at each end. A good handful of moss was tied with twine at intervals onto the rope. *Rumux* (dock), *Solidago* (immature golden rod) and sprays of tiny white chrysanthemums were pushed into the moss.

Church: St. Mary the Virgin, Mortlake
Arranger: Caroline Edelin
Photographer: Judith Blacklock

Other considerations

Plants with Biblical associations

There are about 100 species of plants mentioned in the Bible. Of these only about half are cultivated. There is the pink flowering *Cercis siliquastrum* (Judas tree), *Crataegus monogyna biflora* (Glastonbury thorn) as well as *Helleborus orientalis* (Christmas and Lenten roses), *Lilium candidum* (Madonna lily) which is associated with many paintings of the Annunciation, and *Rosmarinus* (rosemary) for remembrance. There is barley, figs, flax, olives, vines and wheat. The ash tree, bay, box, chestnut, hemlock, mulberry and pomegranate are all mentioned.

Flowers of the Bible include crocus, iris, lilies, myrtle, roses and tulips but the flower translated as 'lilies of the field' is probably the iris.

Scented and aromatic plants

Fragrance is an important part of a garden. The scent of foliage and flowers can lift the spirits. It also encourages insects, butterflies and bees. *Myrtus* (myrtle) could be planted by the vestry door and sweet-smelling *Sarcococca* (Christmas box) and winter honeysuckle close to the pathway. Aromatic rosemary and lavender, old fashioned musk roses, pinks and oriental lilies give fragrance to fill the air on summer days.

left A design using a glorious mix of flowers from the church garden including tree ivy, *Echinops*, *Hydrangea,* marigolds and thistle. Most of these flowers will dry in situ if harvested in late summer/early autumn when they are mature.
Church: Tewkesbury Abbey
Arranger: Hazel Green
Photographer: Lynn Keddie Photography

In warm climates

Plants for church gardens in the Caribbean, Africa and other warm climates could include orange trees, oleanders, palms, pomegranates and olive trees. Other plantings could include *Agave*, *Banksia*, *Callistemon*, *Cassia*, *Ficus*, *Grevillea*, *Cycas*, *Leucadendron*, *Leucospermum*, *Metrosideros*, *Musa*, *Protea*, *Pseudopanax* and *Strelitzia*.

Labour-saving gardens

Churchyards are often maintained by volunteer parishioners as money is usually scarce to pay for extra labour. Every effort should be made to choose plants needing minimal maintenance. Those needing staking, cosseting or special soil should generally be ruled out. Wherever possible select plants that have been awarded the FCC (First Class Certificate) or AGM (Award of Garden Merit) from the Royal Horticultural Society. These have been chosen as garden-worthy and dependable, as well as being attractive in their own right.

Help in the garden

A successful, productive garden needs a hard-working leader with knowledge of horticulture or gardening. Work parties need to be planned. Sunday afternoons are often a good time.

Donor scheme

A donor scheme can be set up for parishioners who wish to give money for commemorative shrubs. The person in charge of the garden can draw up a list of shrubs which parishioners can choose to buy so ensuring the suitability of gifts to the overall scheme and avoiding a confusion of colours and forms.

Memorial gardens

In many parts of Europe memorial graves are tended regularly and lovingly and planted with seasonal plants and vases of fresh flowers. This is a habit one would love to see more widespread.

Photographer: Judith Blacklock

Composting

Composting is a natural process that occurs in nature. It transforms previously living material into a valuable soil conditioner.

Every church garden will benefit greatly from a compost bin. Spent church flowers, trimmed stems and even paper wrapping are all sources of organic matter which, when composted, will create a useful material for the church flowerbeds. It is the ideal way to reduce impact on landfill and recycle. For the best results choose a dedicated area that can be confined, covered to insulate the contents and open at ground level to allow worms and beneficial mini-beasts and microbes to move in and do their magic.

Secrets of success

Good composting is not shrouded in mystery. You simply need to follow some basic rules. The most important one is to ensure that any wet, leafy material is alternated with equal quantities of dry, woody material. It is like making a cake. If you add too much liquid (wet material) it results in a stodgy mess and conversely too much flour (dry material) and it just does not cook properly. You need to mix the ingredients well and keep them as balanced as possible for the best results.

- Flower stems, spent flowers and foliage should be cut up if possible to increase their surface area. This will speed the composting process.

- Woody material, paper, cardboard and compostable Cellophane should be shredded or cut into smaller pieces together with shredded paper from the church office.

- Make sure that lawn clippings are not dumped into the heap without the corresponding amount of shredded, woody prunings or shredded paper.

- If the heap is too wet, add more dry material and cover with old carpet to protect it from rainfall.

- If the heap is too dry, add water or leafy material and spent flowers from weddings and festivals.

How to make a compost system

You can either confine your compost heap to a secluded corner and build a wooden bin from old pallets, or invest in dedicated plastic bins. It does not matter too much what materials you use, the object is to confine the contents to a neat area, protect it from extreme weather and to make sure that it is open at the base for excess liquid to drain away. It is important to make sure each bin is at least the size of large dustbin so you achieve a critical mass of microbes to do the actual composting.

- Add the waste in layers to the bin, alternating between wet, green, flower and leafy waste, and dry, shredded, woody waste or paper.

- If you need to add grass mowings in abundance then make layers of grass 10–15cm (4–6in) deep, with two or three layers of flattened cardboard boxes in between.

- If vermin are an issue then build a base layer of loose bricks and stand the bin on this – the thin gaps between the bricks will allow beneficial creatures such as worms to enter the heap and facilitate excess fluid to escape, while preventing unwanted visitors burrowing up through the bottom. Regular turning of the heap will deter vermin from setting up home in your compost.

What to compost

You can compost pretty much anything that was once living such as flower debris, plants, fruit and vegetable waste, tea bags, shredded newspaper, cardboard and grass cuttings in moderation.

- Avoid composting flowering / seeding weeds, perennial weeds, plastic, cooked food, meat, metal, fat and thorny prunings. Dispose of them otherwise.

- Be careful to follow the local authority's rules about what can be put into the plant recycling dustbin.

4 Arranging on a Budget

A limited budget is an issue that needs ingenuity and helpful guidance. The good management of funds is an essential part of church flower arranging and there are many tricks to make a little go a long way. Creating something special with only a small allowance is challenging, creative and rewarding.

Growing your own foliage at home or in the church garden

Unless you have a large, well-managed garden I would limit growing flowers for cutting to an essential few. Flowers in the florists and supermarkets have been treated in a silver nitrate solution after cutting. This inhibits the production of ethylene gas (which shortens the life of plant material). They will consequently last longer than those cut from the garden. If you have a small garden you may wish to leave the flowers growing, to give longer lasting pleasure.

What is important, whatever your size of garden, is the cultivation of shrubs and other plants for foliage for these are invaluable all year round. Many shrubs also have lovely flowers and berries that can be used in church arrangements.

Shrubs are of course not instant and they should be planned with a long-term view. The church garden can be used as a cutting garden but primarily for foliage rather than flowers. See chapter 3 'Church Gardens' for more information.

left The beauty of garden foliage creating an impressive design with a minimum of material.
Church: Southwell Minster
Arranger: North Hykeham Flower Club
Photographer: Toby Smith

Plant material from the wild

The flowers that grow in abundance vary wherever you are in the world. Use what is available whether from the roadside verge or the garden. Condition well, keep the water clean and your flowers will look good for longer. Simple flowers can often be the best.

It is essential to remove excess foliage and to give the cut stems a long drink in a cool place before arranging.

Warning

In the UK, under the Wildlife and Countryside Act 1981 and subsequent legislation, it is a criminal offence to pick or transplant many wild plants. Schedule 8 to the Act contains a list of specifically protected plants but even when picking plants not specifically protected only pick those growing in abundance.

Here are some of my favourites.

- *Aesculus hippocastanum* (horse chestnut) – bowls of chestnuts, together with some of their shells are lovely on the entrance table in the autumn.
- *Anthriscus* (Queen Anne's lace) – abounds in the spring and is fabulous massed on its own or to give delicacy in mixed designs.
- *Astilbe* – grows in profusion in many parts of the world in damp and shady places.
- *Astrantia* – long-lasting when mature and dries well.
- *Chrysanthemum* – the ox-eye daisy is a delight to use during the summer months.
- *Digitalis* (foxgloves) – attractive line material in pedestal arrangements during the summer months.
- *Fagus* (beech) – excellent for outlines for pedestal arrangements. Pick when mature from mid summer onwards.
- *Hedera* (ivy) – whether short or long this foliage is useful for just about every design.
- *Rumex* (dock) – grows rampantly throughout the UK and many parts of the world. The seeds turn from green in the summer to rich red brown in the autumn. The seeds stay well on the stem and are useful in both seasons. It also glycerines

exceptionally well if picked while still green and provides linear material throughout the later part of autumn and winter.

- *Tilia* (lime) – stripped of its leaves, the branches of green keys last well and provide a wonderful outline for large arrangements and pedestals in late spring and their fragrance is an added attraction.
- *Typha* (bulrushes) – take care they are not too mature or they may explode once they are taken into a warm atmosphere. They can be kept stable by spraying with hair spray.
- *Viburnum opulus 'Roseum'* syn. 'Sterile' (guelder rose) has black berries which give long-lasting colour and do not drop easily.
- fir cones – invaluable. Position a bowl full of cones at the church entrance. Cones can be wired and used together with other plant material in autumn and Christmas arrangements.
- catkins of alder, hazel and willow. Display these on their own in spring and use in pedestals at Easter. Alternatively, add a few branches to a bowl of flowering bulbs. It will give the impression of the flowers growing under a 'tree'.
- rowan berries – magnificent in summer and autumn arrangements of all sizes.
- wild rose hips – strip their thorns before using.
- heather – can be easily preserved in glycerine and the flowers will retain colour well.
- hawthorn – branches covered with white flowers which abound in the spring.

Tip

Most wild flowers are annuals – they flower and die in one year. They are stronger later in the year and consequently will last longer if cut at this time.

right A mass of *Anthriscus* (Queen Anne's lace), arranged in water. The container was a plastic bucket covered with sheet moss, held in place with florists' wire.

Church: St. Mary's Church, Barnes
Arrangers: St. Mary's Flower Guild
Photographer: Judith Blacklock

Flowers in season

In the shops and at the flower markets, flowers in season are less expensive. Think of daffodils and tulips in the spring, phlox, peonies and sunflowers in the summer, hydrangeas, dahlias and *Solidago* (golden rod) in the late summer and autumn and anemones, fragrant narcissi, winter hellebores and *Hippeastrum* (amaryllis) in the winter. Use with variegated foliage to create impact at little expense.

Sourcing locally grown flowers

Local flowers will not have been flown in from distant parts. They will also be less expensive. In the UK, *Zantedeschia* (calla lilies) and *Narcissus* are wonderful in the spring. *Antirrhinum,* lavender, peonies, phlox, stocks and sweet peas can be found during the summer months. In the autumn dahlias, *Hydrangea*, *Physalis alkekengi* var. *franchetii* (Chinese lanterns) and *Solidago* (golden rod) are superb value. Try your local allotment society and see if they have any ideas on where to buy or if any of the allotment holders would be willing to sell or contribute excess flowers.

Neighbours' gardens

Many a time I have resisted the temptation to wait until dark to 'borrow' a few stems of foliage. I have however found that when I have knocked at the door and asked permission to cut for the church I have usually been granted permission cheerfully and positively. Try it and see!

right Seasonal flowers are often the best option both for price and longevity. At the base of the choir stalls stripped, dried stems of *Cornus*, *Hedera helix* (ivy),*Garrya elliptica*, *Rubus tricolor* and *Salix* are interwoven and held in place with paper covered wire to provide a long-lasting structure for *Crocosmia*, *Parthenocissus tricuspidata* leaves, *Sandersonia*, berries and terracotta mini *Gerbera* 'Choco'.
Church: Southwell Minster
Arrangers: Sue Timpson and Jean Wilson
Photographer: Toby Smith

Purchasing quality flowers

Fresh quality flowers last longer so try and find a good reliable source of flowers. Unless you are buying on a very large scale it is best to create a good relationship with a florist or stall holder rather than going to the flower market where purchases have to be made in bulk and a refund can be difficult unless purchases are made on a very regular basis.

There are a number of wholesalers who are happy to deliver flowers direct to a non-commercial address if the order is over a certain amount and requested on a regular basis. Check in magazines such as 'The Flower Arranger' for details.

Preparing the plant material

If treated correctly, flowers and foliage will last much longer. Details of how to prepare flowers and foliage so they last longer is covered in Chapter 2 'Practicalities'.

You should:

- arrange the flowers in the medium that suits them best – such as placing spring flowers in shallow water – with or without a support of chicken wire
- water the flowers at least once a day if the weather is hot (if not twice) and leave a reservoir of water in the bottom of the container
- treat the finished arrangement to a fine mist spray of cool water
- position the arrangement where it does not receive direct sunshine
- if the position for the flowers is in a draft only use robust flowers and foliage. Rapid transpiration caused by cold draughts of air causes rapid moisture loss and this shortens the life of the flower.

Dried and preserved plant material

Dried plant material is particularly useful in late autumn and winter. Rather than purchasing dried flowers from the florist try drying them at home by hanging. Many flowers such as *Angelica*, *Allium*, *Delphinium*, *Dipsacus* (teasels), *Cortaderia* (pampas grass), *Hydrangea*, *Lavendula* (lavender), *Lunaria* (honesty seed pods), *Nigella* (love-in-a-mist) and *Physalis alkekengi* var. *franchetii* (Chinese lanterns) can be preserved by suspending them in an airy room. Bracken dries extremely well if placed between newspaper and then tucked under a heavy rug for a few weeks.

Dried material is always quite fragile and the colour will fade over time. It is best to consider dried material as 'long-lasting' rather than 'eternal' so do discard once it is past its best or use a spray paint to re-vitalise the colour. Preserved material is longer lasting than dried plant material as the water, as it evaporates, is replaced by glycerine and the plant material is consequently not as brittle.

There are different ways of drying and preserving plant material and over the following pages I have described the most popular methods.

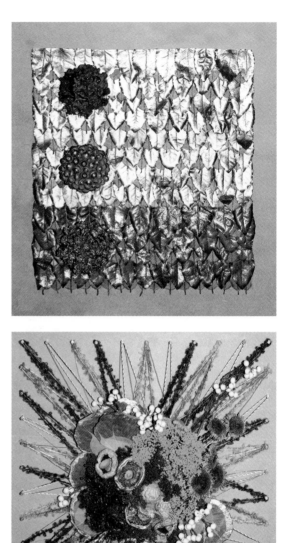

far right This delicate design of dried, preserved and artificial materials, reflecting the muted colours of the 17th century altar frontal, was created from three foam wreaths 30cm (12in), 35cm (14in) and 40cm (16in) suspended on long cup hooks on an upright post in a paint tin filled with concrete. Newspaper was packed between the two containers and then covered with reindeer moss. The wreaths were created on wet foam rings as dry foam wreaths were unavailable. The plant material included dried wheat, hydrangea heads, teasels, gold sprayed fir cones and blue statice, glycerined *Pittosporum*, reindeer moss and two sizes of cream and bronze artificial rose-buds. The bows of wired edged ribbon was inserted as the final touch.

Church: Salisbury Cathedral
Arrangers: Rosemary Allen, Jenny Harrison, Bridget Trump, Margaret Clark and Jenny Hexter, Members of the Mothers' Union
Photographer: Oliver Gordon

above Glycerined, dried, preserved twigs, leaves and flowers in tints, tones and shades of brown, highlighted with cream and yellow in these two screens.

Church: Southwell Minster
Arranger: Diana Knight and Margaret van Oudheusden
Photographer: Toby Smith

Drying by hanging

This is an inexpensive way of preserving plant material. Strong colours preserve best. Light colours will go paler and dark colours darker during the drying process.

below Dried flowers, from left, clockwise, *Scabiosa, Lavendula, Hydrangea* and poppy seedheads.

Photographer: Judith Blacklock

Method

1 Choose your drying time carefully. A hot dry summer spell is ideal. A damp November is not. Plant material should be picked when it is dry. Do not pick flowers when the dew is still on the ground, or after a rain shower. If you have no alternative but to pick flowers with moisture still on the flower head, place them in a vase with their stem ends in water until the flower heads are dry. Avoid picking in the mid-day heat as the flowers may wilt before you are in a position to dry them. Process as soon as they have been picked. If you are drying for scent, pick before the sun is high as it breaks up the flowers' fragrant chemicals.

2 For dry air to penetrate to the centre of your flowers there needs to be maximum air movement, not only between the flowers as they hang but in the room in which they are hanging. The flowers should be tied in small quantities. Most of the foliage should be removed and the flower heads slightly staggered. Bunch only a few flowers together – the amount will vary according to the size of the flower head. As a rough guide, about 30 stems of lavender, five roses, or just one spike of delphinium.

3 Tie the stems together tightly as shrinkage occurs during the drying process. A tight hold will also allow the heads to splay out. Elastic bands, garden twine or stem tape work well. An excellent, inexpensive medium is a strip cut from a pair of used stockings or tights. About 30 ties can be made from just one pair.

4 If the correct conditions are met your flowers should dry quickly with good colour retention. A rose will take about seven days, smaller flowers a little less time, larger ones a little more. You will know that they are ready once they feel completely dry to the touch. You can break one of the stems to see if it snaps easily. If they have been dried in an unheated garage or shed they should be removed before the damp weather sets in. They should also be removed from direct sunlight which fades the colour.

5 Keep the flowers in a cool dark place until you want to use them.

Preserving with glycerine

Glycerine is suitable for foliage rather than flowers as the addition of glycerine causes the colour to change. This gives a range of colour from black through to brown to pale cream. Glycerined foliage provides an excellent foil to brightly coloured flowers. *Fagus* (beech) – the green rather than the red – is the ideal foliage to treat in the summer months. It only takes days for treatment to be complete so that it can be used for the rest of the year. Few flowers preserve well with glycerine on a non-commercial level.

Evergreens can be preserved throughout the year except when putting on new growth in the spring as this new growth wilts too easily. Tree ivy is excellent preserved in this way. Deciduous foliage, that loses its leaves during the winter, must be preserved at the height of its strength not when the leaves are newly formed in the spring or in the late summer when the stems are preparing to shed their leaves for the winter. Timing will be different according to geography but generally late June or early July is ideal.

Method

1 Remove any damaged leaves and those near the bottom of the stem. Cut the stem ends on the slant to allow the easy intake of liquid and place in water in a cool place for several hours so that the plant becomes turgid with water. This will mean that plant material, especially the leaves furthest from the stem end will be less likely to wilt before the slower moving glycerine and water mixture arrives. Do not crush the stem ends. This only damages the stem and causes bacteria to multiply rapidly.

2 Fill a jam jar about a quarter full with glycerine. Add double the amount of very hot water so that the jar is three-quarters full. Stir well so that the glycerine and water form a mixture. If you wish to add colour to your plant material add a few drops of dye in the colour mix of your choice. You may need to experiment a little to get the exact colour required.

below A garland of long-lasting glycerined foliage highlighted with the addition of cream artificial flowers and muslin loops. The garland was made to commemorate John Wesley's 300th birthday anniversary.

Church: Guisborough Methodist Church
Arrangers: Stokesley and District Flower Club
Photographer: Paul Stenson

3   Place the plant material to be preserved in the jam jar containing the mixture. It should rise approximately 8–10cm (3–4in) up the stem. If the stems are long, place the jam jar in a bucket so that the stems can rest against the rim and thus avoid the risk of falling over. Heavy textured leaves can be wiped with glycerine before the stem ends are placed in the mixture. Ivy leaves and small sprays of leaves respond well to being totally submerged in the mixture.

Glycerine and water mixture

4   Place the plant material in a dry area and monitor the progress of the glycerine mixture climbing the stem and entering the leaves. You will notice some degree of colour change as the mixture moves upwards.

5   The stems can be removed when the entire stem and leaves have received the mixture. Add more glycerine mixture, in the same proportions as step 2, if all is taken up by the stem before preservation is complete. Do not leave the foliage in the mixture once it has changed colour, especially if it is going to be left in a humid atmosphere, as the glycerine will ooze out of the leaves. This is particularly disastrous if dye has been used. If the leaves are slightly greasy wash them in soapy water. Rinse, allow to dry on a piece of kitchen towel and if not being displayed immediately store in a dry place.

6   The glycerine mixture can be reused again and again. Pass the used mixture through muslin or a fine sieve to remove any bits. If you find the mixture becomes mouldy add a drop of bleach to minimise the risk of this recurring.

7   Do not store the glycerined plant material in plastic bags as the glycerined stems and leaves will sweat. Place in cardboard boxes.

above Glycerined plant material, from left, clockwise, *Fagus* (beech), *Magnolia grandiflora* leaves, *Stachys byzantina* syn. *S. lanata*.

Photographer: Judith Blacklock

Preserving with a desiccant

A desiccant is a substance that absorbs moisture. If flowers are covered by a form of desiccant and left there for a short period of time – a few days to a few weeks – they will be preserved in their three-dimensional shape for a considerable period of time, if kept dry and out of direct sunlight. They are most suitable for use in smaller designs such as on an entrance table.

The advantages of this method of preserving are that the shape and the colour are kept virtually the same as when fresh. The disadvantage is that a flower preserved by this means is brittle and therefore easily damaged. To keep good colour the flowers will need to be kept out of strong sunlight.

Although sand, borax, alum and even soap powder can be use as a desiccant there are two mediums easily available that perform well. These are silica gel and a product called 'Flower Dry'. Excellent instructions are enclosed with the product. Silica gel is available from larger pharmacists and Flower Dry may be obtained from the supplier mentioned on page 406. If silica gel is sold in large grains it is easier to use when ground into small particles.

Preserve large single-petalled or deeply volumetric specimen flowers such as daffodils, lilies and iris just prior to maturity and only select perfect plant material that is dry.

Method

1   Cut off the stems to within approximately 2.5cm (1in) of the flower head.

2   Add a false stem of wire by inserting a wire up the stem using a gauge sufficient to support the weight of the flower.

3   The process can be speeded up by placing the flower on a little desiccant in a non-metallic container in a microwave. Do not wire before microwaving. If you are using a microwave leave a short stem or pierce a hole in the plant material for wiring after drying. Timing will depend on the microwave you are using.

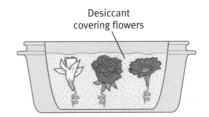

Desiccant covering flowers

4   Place the flower face up, with the stem twisted or coiled, on a bed of desiccant. Gently pour desiccant around the flower and then between the petals. Add desiccant until no part of the flower is showing. Do not crowd flowers together in the container.

5   Leave the container open if left in a warm dry place. If there is any likelihood of damp add a lid.

6   Leave the box in a warm, dry place such as an airing cupboard for as long as necessary. Keep checking every few days.

7   When dry, pour off the desiccant in a steady stream with one hand below the container to catch the flower. You can use a sieve.

8   The flowers should be sprayed with a sealant to help them to last longer.

9   All desiccants need to be dried out thoroughly before re-using.

Retarding flowers

It is helpful sometimes to be able to hold back the development of flowers, especially if they are required later in the week. It is also useful to bring some buds into flower and hold others back when a bunch of flowers is purchased with all at the same stage of maturity.

Place the stems of flowers such as daffodils, gladioli and peonies in a box on a stone floor in the coolest part of the church and you will be able to hold them back about five days. If you buy tulips with the white part still at the end of the stems you will be able to store these without water for a much longer period.

Smaller flowers may also be retarded by placing them in the refrigerator after they have been conditioned. I wrap the flowers in damp tissue paper and spray them lightly with water. I then place a plastic bag over the flowers and secure the end of the bag so that the flowers are in their own mini eco system and put them in the vegetable compartment. Do not have the temperature in the fridge too low or you will freeze the flowers.

Long-lasting flowers

Flowers in church should always look fresh. For reasons of economy of money and time it is not always possible to renew the flowers during the week. It is therefore worthwhile knowing which flowers will last at least a week and may perhaps also be used for a second week. Factors such as heat, draughts, dry atmosphere and lack of water contribute to the length of a flower's life but the following last especially well. It is essential however to buy fresh flowers of a good quality.

Alstroemeria
These flowers can last up to three weeks. They are reliable, good-natured and not expensive. They are easy to grow in the garden where they will flower for many weeks and spread wonderfully.

Anthurium
Anthurium come in a wonderful range of colours – white, cream, lemon, orange, brown, red and many more. The paler colours bruise more easily so be sure to purchase unblemished flowers.

Cymbidium orchids
In the UK orchids from Asia are at their most inexpensive during the winter months. British grown *Cymbidium* are in season during the summer. These flowers are less expensive than many people think and give an exotic flavour to arrangements.

Dianthus (spray carnations and single blooms)
With their strong round form, wonderful colours from the palest of pastels to vibrant multi-colours the carnation is the stalwart of the flower arranger. If purchased fresh they will last for up to three weeks. A fresh flower should have no stamens visible at the centre.

Chrysanthemum
Spray *Chrysanthemum*
As a budget flower there is none to beat the spray chrysanthemum. With most of the leaves removed and mixed with interesting foliage the humble spray chrysanthemum becomes radiant. In the summer single white spray chrysanthemums have a thousand uses and are wonderful in garlands and topiary. They will last for weeks.

Bloom *Chrysanthemum*
Large bloom chrysanthemums give strong, long-lasting form and texture and are ideal in large scale pedestal arrangements. Fresh flowers should have good quality, strong leaves. These will last for two weeks or longer.

Hydrangea
Hydrangeas are invaluable in large scale designs. They are easy to grow in many parts of the world but they will only be sure to last if harvested late summer to late autumn. They should be firm to the touch, not soft and be cut on the stem produced the previous year (this will be brown rather than green). When pruning never cut away more than half the blooms. If you cut all the flowers you will have none the following year although some new varieties are being developed that produce flowers on new growth.

Lilium
In some respects lilies can be difficult. However, there is no other bold, flower that lasts so long, has fragrance and elegance and is not particularly expensive most months of the year. When purchasing check that the stem stands upright if you are holding just the bottom of the stem as this means it has a strong stem. If some of the flowers are opening check that all the petals on each flower are opening at the same time.
There are four types of lilies available – the fragrant Oriental lily, the trumpet-shaped *L. longiflorum*, the inexpensive Asiatic lily and LA lilies, the heads of which have a good form and strong stems. LAs are a hybrid (cross) between *L. longiflorum* and the Asiatic lily.

Protea
a) *Leucadendron*
Leucadendron 'Safari Sunset' is a deep red and is very long-lasting. Its deep tones give depth in arrangements of pastel flowers and calm in those of hot colours. The green variety is also useful.
b) *Leucospermum* (pincushion protea)
Wonderful colourful flowers from South Africa that last and last. They are available during the spring, autumn and winter in the northern hemisphere but are relatively difficult to find in the summer months. They are available in orange, red and yellow.

Alstroemeria

Anthurium

Cymbidium

Spray Dianthus

Dianthus

Bloom Chrysanthemum

Spray Chrysanthemum

Hydrangea

Lilium orientalis

Lilium longiflorum

Leucadendron 'Safari Sunset'

Leucospermum

Pot plants

Pot plants are invaluable in providing long-lasting plant material and living colour. They are particularly effective when grouped or when placed in a row thus creating good design through repetition. You might use poinsettia plants at Christmas and hyacinths in the early spring. Succulents need practically no attention and their thick fleshy leaves provide a different texture and look.

One of the most effective displays of flowers I have ever seen was in a church in Italy where about 20 bright red *Pelargonium* (geranium) pot plants were placed on the reredos at different levels providing a bright long-lasting arrangement that was spectacularly beautiful.

below *Hydrangea* and foliage plants surround the baptismal font which is adorned for the annual Cathedral Festival of Flowers.

Church: The Cathedral of St. Mary of the Assumption, San Francisco, CA
Arranger: Darrell Charm
Photographer: Jocelyn Knight Photography

Care should be taken to place the pot plants in a more attractive outer container than their original plastic holders. One easy way to do this is to place double-sided tape around the plastic holder and to adhere long-lasting leaves such as *Prunus* (laurel) or *Cocculus* onto the tape so that they overlap but this does take time.

Another way to use pot plants is to group them together in a large, lined basket, being careful to consider form, texture and colour. In many parts of Europe a basket is frequently placed close to the altar for weddings. The basket is then removed after the ceremony and taken to the reception.

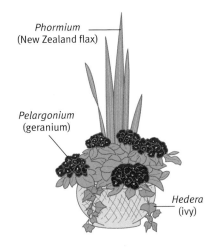

Phormium (New Zealand flax)

Pelargonium (geranium)

Hedera (ivy)

top right A simple display of *Pelargonium* (geranium) plants in a church in the Italian Alps.

Photographer: Judith Blacklock

bottom right Pot plants in an ancient church in Tuscany, Italy.

Photographers: Elisabetta Andolfi and Riccardo Troiani/iStockphoto.com

Some long-lasting and easy to care for plants are:

Anthurium
This is a brilliant flowering plant which will endure neglect and poor conditions. If the leaves go limp, just water and leave the plant in a bowl of water for a few hours and it will usually recover.

Aspidistra
Aspidistra is a very useful plant that thrives in poor light. The leaves can be cut and used in both classic and contemporary designs.

Ferns
They come in a wonderful variety of forms and textures. Try frothy *Asparagus setaceus* or *A. densiflorus* Sprengeri group with delicate branches of bright green needle-like leaves. Then there is the delicate, light fronds of *Adiantum* (maidenhair fern), the strap like leaves of *Asplenium* (bird's nest fern) and the wiry stems with dark green button leaves of *Pellaea* (button fern). They are great for a shady position.

Pelargonium (geraniums)
Available during the summer months these easy to care for plants can be transferred to the garden if they show signs of needing sunshine.

Phalaenopsis (moth) orchids
These will flower for up to three months. They need a few drops of water each week. They will flower again if treated with care but do remove them to the vestry or home in their dormant period as they can look rather sad when not in flower.

Euphorbia pulcherrima (poinsettia)
With their flaming red bracts, poinsettias are the Christmas pot plant although other colours such as orange, pink and lemon are also now available. Avoid purchasing if they are being sold outside the shop as they are particularly vulnerable to draughts.

Sansevieria
Considered virtually indestructible these plants are commonly known as 'mother-in-laws' tongues'.

Schlefflera (umbrella plant)
Tall plant – long-lasting and easy to care for.

Tip
If you are looking for plants that will survive well in poor light then purchase those with dark, plain green leaves. Variegated leaves contain less chlorophyll and therefore need more sunlight to photosynthesize.

Using fruit and vegetables

Fruit and vegetables provide form, colour and texture dramatically and inexpensively. Think how many flowers you would need to take the place of a marrow or a melon!

When creating with fruit and vegetables it is important not to clump fruit and vegetables at the foot of any arrangement or it can become bottom heavy. If possible, they should be raised so that they integrate into the design. They can be linked into the arrangement by angling stems of trailing plant material such as ivy or blackberries over them.

Fruit can be placed in designs by giving them stalks of wire, cocktail or kebab sticks, Cowee picks or lengths of strong woody stems.

The more linear forms of vegetables such as celery, bananas, rhubarb and carrots should be used at the extremities of the arrangement with the more rounded forms such as apples and melons and oranges at the centre. Aim at contrasts of colour and texture and shape and use leaves 'tucked in' to soften their appearance.

Tip
It must be recognised that fruit and vegetables are detrimental to the life of flowers. The ripening of vegetables produces a gas called ethylene and this causes flowers to age rapidly, particularly roses and carnations. Consider this before you arrange your fruit and vegetables with flowers.

Branches

In spring, branches with the first leaves to bud are wonderful in designs. Later in the year many branches, with or without flowers, look most effective.

- For spring: pussy willow, hazel, alder, cherry blossom, *Photinia* x *fraseri* 'Red Robin', *Sorbus aria* (whitebeam)
- For summer: beech, lime or any branch with blossom
- For autumn: larch, beech, copper beech or *Cotinus* (smoke bush)
- For winter: holly, pine, cypress, rhododendron or Douglas fir

Tip

If a branch of *Forsythia*, *Ribes* (flowering currant) or cherry blossom, showing only a small amount of green bud, is placed in water in a warm room it will develop and bloom within two or three weeks and look most attractive whilst developing. If *Ribes* come into flower indoors it tends to loose its pungent fragrance which is not always to everyone's taste.

below Branches can create a large design on their own or with the addition of a few bold flowers, positioned in the central area of the design.

Church: The Cathedral of St. Mary of the Assumption, San Francisco, CA
Arranger: Darrell Charm
Photographer: Jocelyn Knight Photography

Altar gardens

Laura Iarocci from The Cathedral of St. Philip in Atlanta tells us how pot plants are used to create altar gardens in the United States of America.

An interesting and long-lasting alternative for flowers in worship spaces is to create a garden using potted plants assembled with natural elements. Altar gardens can be placed on a retable or in front of an altar. This type of an arrangement can be a very cost effective way to decorate an altar that is not in service as it will last for many weeks if watered. It is also a very effective arrangement during holidays when volunteers are scarce. The arrangement can be changed seasonally.

Step by step

Altar garden

You will need
- thick black plastic such as part of a dustbin bag
- plastic pot liners to go under all the plants
- interesting natural materials such as rocks and branches with lichen moss – use mood (bun) and sheet (flat) moss
- 5–8 potted plants depending upon the size of the area. Longer lasting potted plants such as orchids, chrysanthemums, and bromeliads are the best choice.
- 3–5 ferns. Choose a variety of different forms and sizes.
- small pots of ivy – variegated ivies are particularly useful

Method

1 Line the area to be decorated with thick black plastic. Add a second layer for extra security against water leaks.
2 Place larger garden elements, such as a big rock, log or garden statue, in position. These will be the focal areas of the arrangement.
3 Place potted flowering plants in a staggered arrangement. For additional height, elevate pots at the back with empty pots or blocks.
4 Place ferns between the flowering plants.
5 Tuck smaller natural elements into empty areas in order to hide the bottoms of the pots.
6 Cover remaining gaps with moss. Sheet moss covers pots nicely. Bright green mood moss creates interest and texture. Moss can be reused for months.

At Easter, children enjoy the addition of stone bunnies and eggs along with potted, blooming spring bulbs. The photograph above shows an altar with this technique using a collection of inexpensive orchids, moss and potted ferns. Rocks and sticks with interesting lichen that have been collected over time are also added.

above

Church: The Cathedral of St. Philip, Atlanta, GA
Arranger: Victoria Denson
Photographer: George Westinghouse

Artificial flowers

I am a great believer in using a few artificial flowers if:

- budgets are tight.
- there is a paucity of flowers around.
- used for festivals where a certain flower is appropriate but out of season such as Remembrance Sunday when fresh poppies are unavailable. 'Haig' poppies can be purchased in various sizes and are very effective both for their visual impact and as a reminder of the occasion. A few artificial blooms amongst living foliage fulfil the symbolism perfectly and can be used year after year.
- placed in inaccessible parts of the church, such as high up a pillar, where watering would prove a nightmare.
- in areas close to valuable vestments, marble or wood where water could create permanent water marks.

above Artificial plant material, from left clockwise, *Lavendula, Chrysanthemum* 'Shamrock', *Lathyrus* (sweet pea), poppies and *Eucalyptus* foliage.

Photographer: Judith Blacklock

right A niche holds an arrangement in an urn of dried *Magnolia grandiflora* leaves with some added artificial flowers for long term effect. Stacked dry foam, carved into a conical form is the base of the design.

Photograher: Judith Blacklock

Other factors

Using space

Over the past 10 years there has been a trend in many design styles to limit space to the minimum. Space however is free and the more space between the flowers the larger the design for the smaller of budgets.

Placement

Do not try and make a small budget provide flowers throughout the church. Decide on the key areas where the flowers will have maximum impact.
A pedestal design, close to the altar, usually has the greatest eye pull and is often the only arrangement needed for most occasions.

Variegated foliage

Variegated foliage is a wise way to make your flowers go further. They give a splash of colour which if linked to the colour of the flowers give the impression of doubling the number of flowers used. Some useful shrubs and plants that have varieties with useful variegated foliage are:

* *Aspidistra*
* *Astrantia major* 'Sunningdale Variegated'
* *Aucuba japonica*
* *Elaeagnus*
* *Euonymus*
* *Fatsia*
* *Hebe elliptica*
* *Hedera*
* *Hosta*
* *Ilex*
* *Pittosporum*
* *Prunus*

Advancing colours

Using advancing colour also creates a greater sense of abundance because the flowers are more noticeable, see Chapter 5 'Arranging the Flowers'.

Moss

Moss is an inexpensive way of making plant material fill a large area effectively. The following mosses are all useful.

Leucobryum glaucum and *Grimmia pulvinata* (bun or mood moss) – this has the appearance of mini hilly hummocks. It is a rich green, gorgeous, full of depth and texture and is immensely decorative.

Plagiothecium undulatum (flat or sheet) moss – thin pieces of green moss ideal for covering large areas decoratively and inexpensively.

Cladonia rangiferina (reindeer moss) – A soft spongy moss that has usually been treated with a softening agent. They cover quickly so give an interesting soft texture. Various dyed colours are available.

> ### Tip
> If your moss dries out and turns dull green or light brown, pour boiling water over the moss and it will often regain its green colour.

Sisal

Sisal is dyed in a wide range of colours – some more natural than others. It is a natural product and covers large areas quickly and inexpensively. It can be re-used many times. It can be held in place with long hairpins of florists' wire or German pins.

right The variegation on the *Aucuba japonica* provides additional interest to this simple arrangement of lilies.
Photographer: Xander Casey

5 Arranging the Flowers

Those of you who are new to flower arranging will find this chapter important as it explains the essential basics of design. These are referred to as the elements and the principles and will help you to understand good design for both classic and contemporary arrangements.

Detailed information on how to arrange flowers in specific situations and with appropriate mechanics is given elsewhere in this book. Reference to these guidelines will enable you to assess your work and discover how it may be improved.

The information below is essentially for classic arranging but once this is understood it can be easily adapted to contemporary design. This chapter also describes the differences between the two styles.

The elements of design

The elements indicate how you should choose and combine your flowers and foliage.

Form

Form is the word used to describe the three dimensional shape of flowers and foliage. Most flowers can be categorised as one of these three forms.

- Round – such as *Gerbera*, *Helianthus* (sunflower) and *Hydrangea*
- Spray – such as *Alchemilla mollis*, *Gypsophila*, *Hypericum* and spray carnations
- Line – such as *Delphinium*, *Digitalis* (foxgloves) and *Gladiolus*

left A magnificent pedestal design using round, spray and line flowers.

Church: St. Paul's Church, Knightsbridge
Arranger: Neil Birks
Photographer: Xander Casey

Round flowers

This is the most dominant form in any group of mixed flowers. At least one flower with this form should be included in any arrangement of mixed flowers. The eye rests longer on a round form as the eye is drawn into the centre of the flower where it lingers. The larger the flower and the more advancing the colour the more dominant these flowers will be.

Line flowers

In large-scale, classic designs (such as pedestal designs) they are important for taking colour from the edges of the arrangement into the centre. In landscape and contemporary designs, they are used to give strong vertical direction.

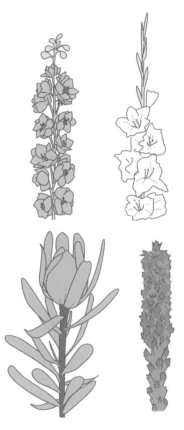

Spray flowers

Spray flowers give interest and variety when added to a composition of round flowers. They can be said to be the supporting actors to the principal players.

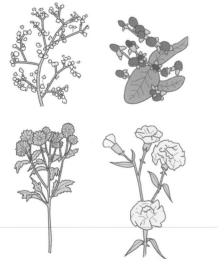

right Roses give the round form, *Leucadendron* 'Safari Sunset' and *Delphinium* the line and *Symphoricarpos* (snowberry), *Alstroemeria* and fynbos from South Africa offer a spray form.

Arranger: Judith Blacklock
Photographer: Judith Blacklock

59

Texture

Texture in flower arranging means how we imagine plant material will feel to the touch. It is 'visual' texture rather than 'actual' texture. Interest in an arrangement is created by the use of different textures which contrast with each other. Smooth texture can hold together all the other elements of design.

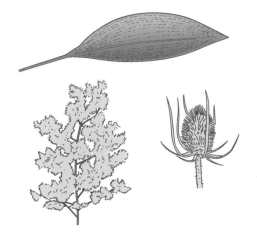

Arrangements where texture is of particular importance
- Monochromatic designs using tints, tones and shades of one colour.
- An arrangement of dried plant material as the drying process reduces many flowers to a similar texture.

> ## Tip
> Try and include foliage with a smooth visual texture such as *Aspidistra*, *Bergenia*, *Eucalyptus*, *Fatsia* or a flower with round form and smooth petals such as open roses, *Gerbera* and sunflowers in every design.

above Crinkly, rough and velvety textures combined with the smooth texture of the lily petals and mini *Gerbera*.
Arranger: Judith Blacklock
Photographer: Judith Blacklock

left Textural contrast at the most skilful of levels is seen here to complement the Roman Plaster. The base was a tree trunk with three shelves inserted at appropriate levels. Supermarket meat trays were used as containers for large pieces of 'Jumbo' foam. Textural contrasts were given by the grainy slices of bark, the woolly *Amaranthus,* the shiny *Anthurium,* glossy *Hypericum* berries, the feathery pampas grass and the smooth raffia drink mats which became exotic flowers. The *Corylus avellana* 'Contorta' picked up the tracery of the Plaster.
Church: Southwell Minster
Arranger: Ian Buxton
Photographer: Toby Smith

Colour

Although the appreciation of colour is subjective, it is important to understand the basics of colour theory to create successful arrangements. Colour in the spectrum of refracted light is best understood if viewed as a wheel. The colours appear in a full circle, merging with each other through the full range.

What follows is colour theory particularly relevant to designing with flowers.

Terms

- **Hue** – another word for colour
- **Tint** – a colour to which white has been added sometimes referred to as a pastel colour
- **Shade** – a colour to which black has been added
- **Primary colours** – blue, yellow and red
- **Secondary colours** – created when two primary colours are mixed together: purple (blue and red), green (yellow and blue) and orange (red and yellow)

Colour Schemes

- **Monochromatic** – a colour scheme using tints and shades of one hue, such as pink, red and maroon. This is a safe, pleasing scheme with gentle contrast.
- **Adjacent** – a colour scheme which uses up to one third of the colour wheel, the colours all being found next to each other. Again it is a colour scheme that is easy on the eye, without strong contrast. An example would be blue-green, green, green-yellow and yellow.
- **Complementary** – the use of two colours opposite each other on the colour wheel, such as blue and orange, red and green, purple and yellow. This combination is dramatic and shows each colour at full intensity. Consider using a tint or tone of one colour, rather than two at full intensity, to create interesting colour schemes.
- **Polychromatic** – a scheme using many colours together. This is particularly lovely in late summer and autumn when rich tones of every hue are mixed together. Be careful adding a tint to a mix of strong colours.

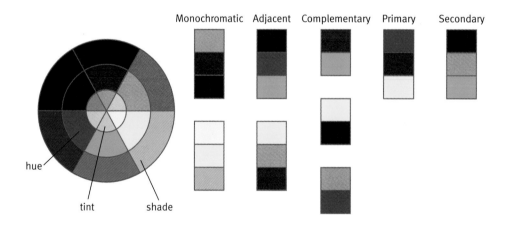

following pages This glorious arrangement could not fail to lift the spirits. *Molucella laevis* (bells of Ireland), peonies, roses, tulips, *Viburnum opulus*, and fragrant *Polianthes* (tuberose) arranged on the reredos behind the altar.

Church: St. John's Episcopal Church, Georgetown, DC
Arrangers: Stephen McLeod and Laura Scanlon
Photographer: Mark Finkenstreadt

right Gentle tints of purple against a stained glass window create a stunning monochromatic design. Tones of purple, which is a recessive colour, would disappear at a distance and would therefore not be appropriate.

Church: All Saints' Church, Banstead
Arranger: Margaret Trepant
Photographer: Mike Pannett

Tips

- Link diverse colours by using lots of mid to dark green foliage.
- Lime green gives freshness and looks good in virtually all arrangements.
- In an arrangement of dark colours adding a tint of a colour – that is used in a deeper shade – gives vitality.
- In a design using tints, the addition of a dark colour gives depth.
- English seasonal colours are blue, yellow and pink in the spring; mixed colours in the summer; orange, pink and terracotta in the autumn and red, green, white and gold for the winter months. Using these colours is very evocative of the time of year.

- Reds, oranges and orange-yellows, are warm colours and are good together. Blues, purples and green-yellows are cool colours and work well together. Sometimes surprisingly beautiful colour schemes can be achieved by blending tints and tones of opposite hues from the colour wheel.
- Consider the colour of the container. If it is white, incorporate some white or cream flowers in the arrangement so that it does not dominate the flowers.
- Blues and purples are recessive colours and disappear at a distance especially in a large or dark building.
- Grey foliage is a useful complement to pinks, creams and lighter tints of blue.

above A design of hot orange roses, *Zantedeschia* and green *Cymbidium* orchids is set on a red carpet to emphasize the mood.

Church: St. Peter's Church, Inkberrow
Arranger: Jean Hogg
Photographer: Chrissie Harten

right A splendid example of a polychromatic colour scheme. These horizontal installations consist of metal grids through which flowers are suspended, reflecting the colours of the stained glass windows beyond. The stem ends of the flowers are held in individual tubes covered in sisal to create a contemporary design with a difference.

Church: Salisbury Cathedral
Arrangers: Churches in the Salisbury diocese – St. Mary's, Milston; St. Georges & Zeals, Parish of Upper Stour; St. Catherine's, Netherhampton; St. Clement's, Parkstone; St. Mary's, Drimpton St. John's; Wimborne and the Milbury Group
Photographer: Ash Mills

Space

Solid is the opposite of space. Without space there is no form. Space can be incorporated into a flower arrangement in the following ways:

Within the arrangement

Classic design incorporates space between the plant material using a greater amount of space at the limits of the design, rather than at the stronger focal area which is generally positioned just below the centre of the arrangement.

In a contemporary design using limited material, space can be used to balance form, colour and texture. Space can have as much eye-pull as a solid form, usually when enclosed by manipulated loops of leaves, cane or raffia. Remember space costs nothing.

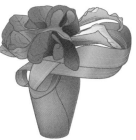

left In the refectory, adjacent to the cloisters at Salisbury Cathedral, a few flowers in pastel colours create an impact through the use of enclosed space.

Church: Salisbury Cathedral
Arrangers: Members of St. Bartholomew's, Wootten Bassett
Photographer: Oliver Gordon

In a massed contemporary design, there is little space within the design. Space however can be incorporated by placing plant material at varying levels or by using 'bridging' material such as driftwood or manipulated foliage.

Underneath the container

In both classic and contemporary designs, space underneath the container can be used to give a sense of lightness and grace.

In the setting

It is vital to position your arrangement so that it is surrounded by space.

The principles of design

The principles indicate the correct way in which the elements of design should be used.

Rhythm

Rhythm means that the arrangement attracts lasting attention as the eye moves through it and back again. Think of music – a rhythmic tune holds the attention. Rhythm can be achieved by:

- **Repetition**
  The repetition of colours, forms and textures takes the eye through the design smoothly. The repetition of repeated designs also creates good, easy rhythm.

- **Transition**
  The gentle graduation of size, form and texture leads the eye in and out of the arrangement.

- **Radiation from a central core**
  Lines that flow from a central point give a feeling of movement. This feeling is dispelled if any of the lines cross as the rhythm is interrupted.

right Ecce Homo – bold the Man, echoing the words of Pontius Pilate when he handed over Jesus to the high priests after his trial, even thought he could not find him guilty of anything under Roman Law.

The strong vertical lines of the statue of Jesus by Peter Ball are repeated in this sympathetic design of lime and orange against the sandstone background. The mechanics were a bamboo screen cut into two thirds and one third with the smaller placed to the fore. Dried plant material created the horizontal placements. The fresh flowers are in tubes or from a brick of foam at the base. The zigzags were created from bent *Phormium tenax* sprayed black which actually give extra strength to the bamboo screen.

Church: Southwell Minster
Arranger: Lynn Wherrett
Photographer: Toby Smith

left Rhythm is created by the arched *Equisetum* repeating the shape of the arch and the repeated use of *Aspidistra, Hydrangea*, lotus seed heads and *Phormium tenax* to create a long low design.

Church: Lichfield Cathedral
Arrangers: Rita Cole and Christine Taylor
Photographer: Tom Allwood

Contrast

Contrast is a vital principle, without it a design will fail to have any impact. Contrast is the difference shown when objects are placed next to each other. When using different forms and textures the contrast will be obvious but there is also contrast when a mass of flowers of the same variety are placed in a vase. The contrast is then based on the different length of the stems and the flowers in their various stages of development. If you are using just one type of flower angle them in different directions to add interest.

- **Contrast of form**
  When using more than one type of plant material try to find materials that contrast well with each other, in form, texture or colour. Try to use at least one type of flower with a round form.
- **Contrast of colour**
  Complementary colours make the strongest contrast. If the colours have gentle contrast strong contrasts of form and texture are often needed.
- **Contrast of texture**
  Contrast of texture is particularly valuable in monochromatic designs and dried flower arrangements.

below A long-lasting arrangement of *Anthurium* and *Leucospermum*. Note how the *Anthurium* have been placed at different angles to create interest and contrast.

Church: St. Peter's Church, Inkberrow
Arrangers: Gill Eley and Joyce Lampitt
Photographer: Chrissie Harten

Dominance

If an arrangement contains two equal and therefore competing attractions there may be discord. Dominance gives a sense of order, unity and harmony. It is often linked to proportion. In classic flower arranging, one element should be more dominant than the surrounding elements. This can be achieved by the following:

- **Dominant texture**
  A smooth shiny texture is more compelling than a rough texture.
- **Dominant size**
  A larger flower is more dominant than a smaller one.
- **Dominant form**
  Round is the most dominant form.
- **Dominant colour**
  Pale colours are usually more dominant than darker colours. Advancing colours are more dominant than recessive colours.

Anything that is visually dominant will be visually heavy. In order to have a well balanced design these strong round flowers need to be placed more centrally rather than at the outer edges of the design. Angling round flowers to show an oblique or side view reduces their visual impact and adds to their interest.

Scale

Scale means the relationship in size between different, individual elements of the design: each individual piece of plant material.

- It is important to consider the size of each flower and stem of foliage in relation to each other.
- The size of the container should be in scale with the flowers.
- Consider the setting. A large space such as a church needs an arrangement with large-scale plant material. A tiny area needs an arrangement of smaller plant material.

Volume

When you have a mass of plant material think in terms of volume: that is the relationship between the plant material and the container. The volume of the container to flowers should be 1.5 : 1 (one and a half to one) or 1 : 1.5 (one to one and a half). It should not be equal.

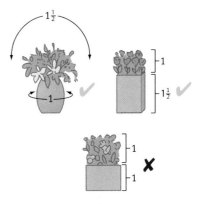

Tip

As a guideline to the good use of scale, no flower should be more than twice the size of the one closest to it in size.

Proportion

Proportion is the word that describes the relation of one part of your arrangement to the other parts and to the arrangement as a whole.

In western art and architecture, rules for good proportion (the Golden Mean) were formulated by the ancient Greeks, and have constantly been applied in the visual arts ever since. They are useful guidelines in flower arrangement, as in any other art form. To simplify the rules think in terms of 1.5 : 1 (the exact proportions are 1.67 : 1 but this can be harder to evaluate).

right In this simple arrangement of tulips the proportion of flowers to vase is one and a half to one.

Church: St James's Episcopal Church, Knoxville, TN
Arranger: Becky Wade

- **Height and width**
  If your container is tall and if you are only using a few flowers, a useful guideline is to make sure that the height of the flower arrangement is not less than one and a half times the height of the container (1.5 : 1). If your container is wide and low, and again you are only using a few stems, a similarly useful guideline is to make sure that your tallest stem is not less than one and a half times the width of your container (1.5 : 1).

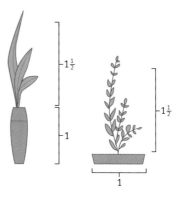

Tip

When any arrangement has been completed the arranger should stand back from it and walk from side to side and then from any point from which the visitors might see it to ensure that it is in the best position in relation to the background and presenting its best aspect.

left Contemporary proportions of 1.5 : 1 with the container having a greater volume than the flowers.

Church: Church of Alden Biesen, Bilzen, Belgium
Arranger: Stef Adriaenssens
Photographer: Judith Blacklock

Balance

Symmetric balance

Many of the classic designs illustrated in this book show symmetrical balance. This means that if you were to take an imaginary line through the centre of the design, down from the tallest stem to the base, one side would be approximately equal in visual weight to the other. Symmetrical arrangements are used in a setting where the areas exposed on each side are similar, such as the centre of an altar or communion table, within an arch or against a column in a church.

below The cross, the candelabras and the two asymmetric designs create overall symmetric balance through their placement.

Church: Grace Episcopal Church, Charleston, SC
Arrangers: Members of Grace Church Flower Guild
Photographer: Wally Breidis

Asymmetric balance

Asymmetric design is where a line taken from the tallest stem down to the bottom of the design shows unequal balance, in terms of visual weight, on either side of this axis. The flowers and foliage are different on each side of the central axis. Balance is achieved by its placement within its setting. An example could be placement of an asymmetric arrangement to one side of a table near the church door where association with objects, such as a collection plate, donation box, hymn books, magazines or leaflets for distribution or indeed a second design, will provide balance.

Two asymmetrical designs – for example one each side of the altar – can balance each other through an overall symmetric image.

Whether your design has symmetrical or asymmetrical balance it should have physical and visual balance. It should be balanced from side to side, top to bottom and front to back.

- **Physical balance**
  Physical balance means that the arrangement must not fall over.

- **Visual balance**
  If your arrangement looks as if it might fall over the visual balance needs adjusting. The arrangement will only be pleasing if there is stability and does not make you feel anxious.

Tip

Visual weight increases:
- the further the materials are from the central axis
- the stronger the colour
- the larger the form
- the more advancing the colour
- the shinier and smoother the texture
- the rounder the form

left An exciting contemporary asymmetric design. Good balance is created by the positioning of the cushion and Bible on the right to balance the cascade of flowers. The mechanics were a ceramic dish about 5cm (2in) deep, filled with two bricks of foam. Fresh, contorted willow (which was easy to manipulate) and hazel were bound with paper-covered wire to create the framework. The flowers were white calla lilies, green and white bloom chrysanthemums in orchid tubes covered with brown architect's tape (this tape is sticky and works well but you could also use brown Stemtex).

Church: Salisbury Cathedral
Arrangers: Lindsey Cobb and Lesley Rann, Damerham Flower Group
Photographer: Oliver Gordon

Design points of special interest when working in a church

Flower arranging in a church is different from flower arranging at home for the following reasons.

Scale

The space is much larger so arrangements need to be bigger. The scale of the plant material needs to be much greater. This means larger flowers and leaves and longer stems than you would use at home rather than just more plant material. Containers need to be larger and more substantial mechanics are needed.

Height

The flowers need to be placed higher than usual so that they can be seen above the heads of people, whether standing or seated. This can be achieved through the use of pedestals, plinths and containers and using flowers and foliage with longer stems. Sometimes arrangements can be placed on permanent features in the building such as high shelves or the top of a screen when there is a ledge running across the top.

Viewed from all angles

Many designs are seen from more than one direction. Pedestals are usually seen from three sides unless right up beside the altar. An arrangement as you enter the church is often seen from all angles as you walk to your seat.

Colour

The colours of the church flowers should be brighter or more luminous because they are seen from a greater distance and in dimmer light. The windows in a church are often relatively small and stained glass further reduces the light. The eastern, or altar end of the church is often in a dark situation and these areas need strong bright colours. The richest and the brightest colours are required for shadowed areas and pure hues of red, blue, yellow, green and white – which may be quite overly strong in ordinary light – are harmonious and beautiful in semi-darkness.

The most effective colours in a dark setting are the following in order of importance:

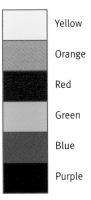

Yellow
Orange
Red
Green
Blue
Purple

At a distance, yellow will advance and be enjoyed by the viewer even from the entrance whereas blues and purples will disappear and give the appearance of black holes.

Complementary colours are red and green, blue and orange, yellow and purple. These colours are at their most intense when placed with each other. This means that if you have a purple background yellow flowers will be at their most powerful. Similarly, blue with orange and red with green have dramatic effect.

left Flowers complement the Kelham Madonna through the powerful use of balance. The tall slim design of lilies on the left reinforces the upright figure of the Madonna. The lower design on the right follows the line of the cradled infant Jesus.

Church: Southwell Minster
Arranger: Sandra Snell
Photographer: Toby Smith

Backgrounds

The interior of the church or cathedral will present arrangers with a variety of backgrounds against which they want their arrangements to look their best.

Here are some aspects to consider.

- **Sandstone walls**
  Warm colours such as red and orange and yellow will be harmonious and give warmth.

- **Wooden panelling**
  Avoid dark colours such as deep red which will blend into the wood.

- **White walls**
  White flowers disappear against a white background unless you use lots of plain green foliage as a backcloth. Strong coloured flowers look best and most effective against a white wall.

- **Ornate and multi coloured elements**
  The colour of the flowers should be complementary and used in large groups. Small flowers increase the fussiness and their impact is lost against the multi coloured or ornate background.

- **Grey walls**
  Grey and in particular grey stonework is the best background of all – every colour will look good. It is hard to go wrong!

- **Stained glass**
  Flowers are often wasted in front of a stained glass window and also distract the eye from the window itself. A possible solution is to avoid arranging on the ledge in front of the window and to hang a swag beneath it from two small arrangements at either end of the window thus achieving both decoration and leaving the glory of the stained glass to be seen.

- **Clear glass windows**
  In front of clear glass windows the outline of the flowers is important and the detail and colour less so. Think of the lacy effect of *Ammi majus* (Queen Anne's lace) or the strong silhouette of budding branches or those bearing blossom.

- **War memorials**
  If a war memorial is to be decorated try to make sure that no part of the arrangement obscures any of the names.

- **Statuary**
  Do not obscure the faces of statuary.

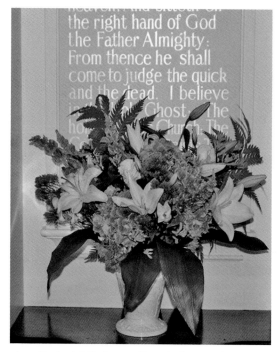

above The backcloth of green allows the flowers to be seen and appreciated against the predominantly white background.

Church: St. Michael's of the Valley Episcopal Church, Ligonier, PA
Arranger: Kathryn Dybdal Mellon
Photographer: Ron McIntosh

right A tall arrangement complements the sandstone colour of the courtyard and the dark wood door behind. An ornate brass pedestal container holds bronze chrysanthemums, soft pink and coral roses, dried hydrangea and a rich variety of garden greenery.

Church: The Cathedral of St. Philip, Atlanta, GA
Arrangers: Laura Iarocci
Photographer: George Westinghouse

- **Elaborate background**
  There may be elaborate carvings or perhaps a mosaic, a brocade or embroidered hanging behind where you plan to place your design. In these circumstances it is best to use some solid foliage to create a background against which the flowers can be seen.

- **Dividing lines**
  When the arrangement is in front of stone blocks, divided by lines of strongly visible mortar, consider how this may affect the positioning of the flowers in the arrangement.

- **Strong vertical columns**
  When the background is composed of strong vertical columns then a tall 'thin' arrangement may be most suitable.

above This is an excellent example of what to do if your background is elaborate and multi coloured. The designers have created a bold design within a contained framework using selected advancing colours of white, green and yellow. The design is seen in its own right but complements rather than overpowers this important hanging in the cathedral.

Church: Chelmsford Cathedral
Arranger: Maldon Flower Arrangement Club
Photographer: David Lloyd

Classic or contemporary?

As with any art form, new techniques and ideas change the established order. Flower arranging is no exception and the inspiration of different designers from all over the world over the past 50 years has led to the development of contemporary design.

Although it may be said that classic designs are best in a traditional church and contemporary in a modern church, I believe there is no hard and fast rule and that good design can be enjoyed anywhere. Detailed step-by-step instructions, for both styles of arranging, are contained within the chapters that follow.

below Classic design – an arrangement by Sheila Macqueen arranged in her 92nd year at Chichester Cathedral. The stacked alabaster vases (you only see the bottom one clearly) were her own and her flowers include the St. Richard of Chichester rose.

Church: Chichester Cathedral
Arranger: Sheila Macqueen
Photographer: Michael Chevis

Characteristics of classic design

- All stems radiate or appear to radiate from a central core.

- Foliage is an essential part of the design to create a strong structure and to provide a neutral colour against which all other colours look great.

- The different designs are loosely based on a geometric form.

- There is a more dominant area at the base of the tallest stem, approximately two thirds of the way down the design. This can be achieved with round, larger, or stronger coloured forms.

- Recessing some of the plant material by placing flowers closer to the foam gives a strong 3D effect.

- Plant material is traditionally scattered through the design but grouping (placing several or many flowers together to give a bolder design) gives a contemporary edge to a classic design.

- There is space between the elements to show each and every form to advantage. Reduction of space between the plant material also gives a contemporary feel to the design.

- All arrangements of mixed plant material should include some with a smooth texture such as *Anthurium, Aspidistra, Fatsia* or *Hedera* (ivy).

- A round form is essential in every design of mixed flowers to hold the design together.

Tips

- Do not insert the stem too deep in the foam. Placing the stem too deep will cause the foam to break up and also give a stiff, contrived look to the arrangement. Foam however dries at the outer edges first, so if you are unable to water the arrangement regularly insert the stems more deeply.

- Angle plant material down over the rim of the container to hide or break up the rim otherwise your design will appear to be sitting on the container and be in two halves.

- For good visual balance stronger larger forms should be lower in the design but not so low that they appear to be falling out. A bold form, such as a rose, needs to have a leaf positioned under it or it will look as if it is falling out.

left A seasonal pedestal design using line, spray and round forms.
Church: Bothwell Parish Church
Arranger: Anne Protheroe
Photographer: Anne Protheroe

right Visitors to the Cathedral often compliment Christine Powell, head of the Salisbury Cathedral Flower Guild, on the arranging of flowers in the classic style reminiscent of the Constance Spry era.
Church: Salisbury Cathedral
Arranger: Denise Watkins – Salisbury Cathedral Flower Guild
Photographer: Oliver Gordon

Characteristics of contemporary design

- Plant material sometimes radiates from the central area but frequently the stems have their own individual point of origin.

- Where a lot of plant material is used the plant material is grouped rather than scattered.

- Plant material is blocked where a flower or leaf is not seen individually but as part of a mass of colour, form and texture.

- The container is often strong and sculptural and constitutes an essential part of the overall design.

- Colour is often bold and striking.

- Mechanics are innovative – test tubes, chicken wire, grids are used in novel and interesting ways.

- Leaves are manipulated to change their form to give space, volume and excitement. They can be woven, plaited, twisted, split or curled.

- Accessories such as metal, glass and wire are used to give texture, form and interest.

- Bold, exotic plant material is used extensively.

It could therefore be said that of the designs described in this book – the pedestal, table and ledge arrangements – follow the criteria for classic design and that the landscape designs and those shown on pages 89 and 185 are contemporary. When you feel confident with the classic style then that is the time to develop and experiment with contemporary ideas but always within the boundaries of good design.

right Contemporary design in a Baroque setting. Rhythm and cohesive design is created through the repetition of colour and the use of square containers in varying heights and sizes, interspersed with those of a round form to give contrast and variation. The horizontal placements of the twigs link the containers and are sympathetic with the lines of the altar.

Church: Chapel at Chatsworth
Arrangers: Sheffield Floral Art Club
Photographer: Oliver Gordon

above A low design on the stone floor creates rhythm through the sinuous use of manipulated *Cornus* that encapsulates space.

Church: Westminster Abbey
Arranger: Christina Curtis
Photographer: Judith Blacklock

left Contemporary flowers arranged in a contemporary church. Glass vases contain flowers placed symmetrically to highlight the impressive bronze sculpture above.

Church: The Cathedral of St. Mary of the Assumption, San Francisco, CA
Arranger: Roberto Ponce
Photographer: Jocelyn Knight Photography

right Rebuilt and modified since Saxon times, the Cathedral Church of St. Peter and St. Paul has always been a parish church. The Crypt Chapel of All Saints houses wonderful contemporary stained glass and the vases holding stems of *Lilium longiflorum* fit the mood of the architecture perfectly.

Church: Cathedral Church of St. Peter and St. Paul, Sheffield
Arranger: Alma Kitchen
Photographer: Oliver Gordon

Churches vary so much in their layout that the placement of flower
arrangements will depend on the situation in each individual church.
Many Roman Catholic churches and those belonging to the Anglican communion
(the Church of England, US Episcopalian and the Scottish Episcopal Church,
for example) will have a layout similar to medieval cathedrals. Usually from
west to east you will observe an area immediately inside the porch, a central
aisle (with perhaps side aisles in larger churches), an area called the choir or the
chancel, and a sanctuary where the altar is to be found. However, many
churches of other traditions including most non-conformist churches (including
Baptist, Methodist and Presbyterian) do not conform to this pattern.
Most of the suggestions in this book are for the decoration of churches in the
traditional linear form. I invite flower arrangers with other layouts to adapt the
suggested ways of approaching church flowers to their own needs.

Around
The Church

6 The Approach

The approach to the church is its public face. It is an opportunity to say "This is special. Come on in". Whatever the individual case, the arranger can create an immediate, public impact.

A lovely feature of many mediaeval churches is the lychgate which begins the approach to the church. It may well lend itself to adornment for flower festivals or weddings. Churches without one may still have decorative ironwork gates and a pathway leading to the main entrance door and what follows can be adapted for these even where there is no actual lychgate.

A pathway can be made beautiful (and perhaps provide some foliage) by careful year-round planting to lead the eye pleasantly to the porch of the church.

Floral arches are always popular for flower festivals and weddings. The mechanics can be a bit tricky, but once they have been constructed they can be used time and time again.

The lychgate

The lychgate is a covered open structure. It normally consists of four or six oak posts embedded in the ground in a rectangular shape. It is usually located next to the street or road. It was traditionally a resting place for coffins on their way to and from the church.

The roof structure is typically of oak. Over the years, many have had nails embedded in the wood so that garlands or swags of flowers can be easily attached for special occasions. A swag may be created in one of several ways.

left Every spring there is a blaze of glorious daffodils along the path leading to the church entrance.

Church: St. Mary's Church, Staveley-in-Cartmel
Photographer: Judith Blacklock

left The mechanics for this delightful swag were three home-made cages of plastic strawberry netting. Each held almost a full brick of foam. They were joined together with small hanging basket 'S' hooks and secured to the wooden pillars in several places with wire. The flowers used were *Aster, Eustoma* (lisianthus), oriental lilies and roses.

Church: Holy Trinity and St. Constantine, Wetheral
Arranger: Patricia Howe
Photographer: Patricia Howe

right Low square trays on the grass filled with a tapestry of plant material lead the eye along the path to the church.

Church: Dyrham Church, near Bath
Arrangers: Bradford on Avon and District Flower Club
Photographer: Judith Blacklock

Swag

Swags are vertical or horizontal arrangements of flowers and foliage on a suspended background which is concealed. The background is not meant to be part of the design. The following construction methods all work well. The decoration with flowers and foliage is the same for all four. Firstly cover with foliage and then add your flowers.

Method 1

Take a thin rectangle of pegboard of the desired size and glue or tape narrow rectangles of foam onto the board. Create a hanging loop by passing wire through one of the central holes.

Method 2

Take a length of carpet grip and firmly strap rectangles of foam onto the larger nails with florists' tape. Attach a hanging wire round one of the larger nails left exposed.

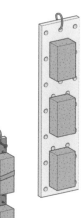

Method 3

Place rectangles of soaked foam on 2.5cm (1in) gauge chicken wire of the required length. For larger swags use a larger gauge netting. If you wish, cover the foam lightly with moss. If you do not have moss you could cut some long grass with scissors and use this instead. This will help prevent the chicken wire cutting into the foam. Wrap the chicken wire firmly around. Create a loop, attached to the chicken wire, for hanging. Cover the back of the swag with a piece of black bin liner, using hairpins of wire or mossing (German) pins to secure. This will protect the post from water damage.

Method 4

Use a spray tray and create a swag/pew end design as illustrated on page 156, ensuring that the tray is well hidden.

Tip

Swags without a rigid back structure, can be attached to decorative ironwork gates or grids and decorated so that the design is attractive from both sides. If the back is rigid, you need identical mechanics on each side so the mechanics are hidden front and back.

The pathway

One of the most charming ways to decorate the approach to the church is to plant bulbs, annuals or flowering shrubs for year round interest. Bluebells, *Crocus*, daffodils, *Forsythia* and tulips in the spring, *Hosta* and *Phlox* in the summer, *Hydrangea*, *Nerine* and *Physalis* in the autumn and *Helleborus*, *Viburnum tinus* and snowdrops in the winter provide regular but changing delight. In addition, hardy and shade tolerant plants such as *Bergenia* and *Fatsia japonica* may be invaluable to people who might otherwise be reluctant to help on the flower rota because they are without access to foliage.

The rails

Some porches have steps leading up to them with handrails. Often an urban church has no pathway, but opens directly onto the street so the steps and rails are the first opportunity for decoration. A simple design can create a delightful effect. You could perhaps take long trails of *Danae racemosa* (soft ruscus) or ivy, condition them well by submerging under water for several hours and then twine them around the rails. If there are spearheads at the top of the railings, foam can be impaled on some of them and flowers arranged around. If there is a low wall to the side of the top step, an arrangement could be placed here.

The doorway

The doorway lends itself to decoration of all sorts and is a favourite place for photographs at weddings. Here are some of the ways to make a statement.

below Simple but effective – flowers on the rail leading to the church finished with a tie of ribbon.

Photographer: Xander Casey

below The colours of late summer/early autumn are prominent in this delightful design of garden plant material. The flowers include roses, *Sedum, Buddleja, Rudbeckia* (coneflower), *Dahlia, Nandina, Hydrangea*, quaking oats, *Miscanthus*.

Church: Tabor Presbyterian Church, Crozet, VA
Arranger: Beverley W. Hereford
Photographer: Judith Blacklock

Topiary

Topiary is one of the most effective designs for the entrance and it is easy and inexpensive to create. Topiary trees can be placed on each side of the main door or several can be lined up to create a floral corridor, either inside or outside of the church.

above A line of topiary ready to be placed in position for a Flower Festival. The size of the container to the volume of plant material is equal to give pleasing proportions.

Church: Paisley Abbey
Arranger: Flora Minno
Photographer: Bob Brown

Tip
Berried foliage such as holly and *Skimmia* look effective in topiary trees at Christmas.

Step by step

Topiary tree

You will need
- straight birch branch (or similar) about 1m (3ft 4in) in height and 5–10cm (2–4in) in diameter
- plaster of Paris or quick drying cement
- stones for ballast
- spirit level or plumb line
- plastic bucket
- outer decorative container
- thick rubber band
- half a brick of foam or a square of OASIS® 'Jumbo' foam if this is available
- mixed foliage to give contrast of colour, form and texture
- 10–12 stems single spray chrysanthemum (white single flowers give a lovely effect)

Method

1 Take the length of branch and hold vertically in the centre of your plastic bucket. Place stones in the bottom of your bucket around the branch. This provides weight, thus making the topiary more stable and less likely to blow over.

2 Mix the plaster of Paris or quick drying cement with water to create a smooth batter. Pour over the stones and fill the bucket about two thirds full. If you do not trust your eye, then use a spirit level or plumb line to ensure that the branch is vertical. Leave for 10 minutes until firm. It will take longer if you are using quick drying cement than if you are using plaster of Paris.

3 Place the plastic bucket into a more decorative outer container such as a terracotta pot.

4 Place the thick rubber band over the top of the branch and slide it down 5cm (2in).

5 Soak the foam. Cut the edges from the foam to give an overall form that is more round than square. Push the foam down over the branch until it meets the rubber band. This will prevent the foam from sliding further down the branch.

6   Place a stem of foliage vertically in the top of the foam and a second stem vertically down out of the bottom of the foam. Your objective is to create a ball of flowers and foliage that is approximately the same size as the outer container. If it is larger, the topiary will appear top heavy. If it is smaller than the container it will appear bottom heavy.

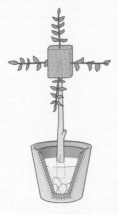

7   Place four stems of foliage horizontally out of the centre of the foam at equal intervals, angled neither upwards nor downwards. Angle further stems out of the foam. Each stem should appear to radiate from the very core of the foam and should be approximately the same length.

8   Create the sphere of plant material by radiating more foliage from the centre until it is difficult to see the foam.

9   Add your flowers. I have tried many flowers but spray chrysanthemums work best whatever your budget. They have round dominant flowers on strong secondary stems and last well outside whatever the time of year. White, single-petalled spray chrysanthemums are particularly effective.

right A delightful but inexpensive topiary of mixed foliage and peach spray chrysanthemums made festive with the addition of waterproof florists' ribbon.

Arranger: Ann-Marie French
Photographer: Judith Blacklock

Pedestal design

A pedestal works well in this position, but ensure that the pedestal or plinth will withstand gusts of wind.

Arch

There are various ways of creating an archway over the door to the porch.

Full arch

- **Using plants**

  Take climbing or trailing plants such as *Clematis*, ivy or jasmine growing in two separate containers. Add a metal arch, placing one end in each of the two containers positioned at a suitable distance from each other. Untangle lengths of foliage from the plant (there are usually plenty on a good quality plant) and wrap around the arch. If this is not possible add extra strands of well-conditioned cut stems.

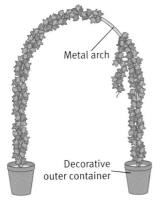

Metal arch

Decorative outer container

left These two pedestal designs, arranged in solid stone urns on plinths, would withstand almost any gusts of wind.

Church: St. Paul's Church, Knightsbridge
Photographer: Toby Smith

Using trees

Use flexible trees such as birch or willow at least 2m (7ft) tall and tie the tips at the top to form an arch. To give colour, wrap moss around large plastic orchid tubes and bind on with reel wire. Fill the tubes with water and add your flowers. Bind to the tree with wire and then place flowers of your choice in the tubes.

right Two birch trees were planted in pots and positioned either side of the entrance to the church. The tips were bent over and secured together. Tubes were wrapped in moss and attached to the trees at intervals. Cut roses were then placed in the tubes.

Church: St. Paul's Church, Knightsbridge
Photographer: Judith Blacklock

- **Using spray trays or OASIS® Florette cages**
  This is perhaps one of the easiest ways, but again you will need nails in the masonry. You can use inexpensive spray trays containing foam that have been strapped in securely with florists' tape or OASIS® Florette cages. Simply hook the hole in the handle of each tray or cage over the nails at regular intervals and arrange your flowers and foliage. At the top of the arch keep your plant material long and angle it to follow the arch.

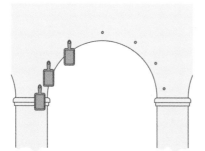

- **A bespoke wooden frame**
  A purpose built timber frame needs to be made by a carpenter as this requires the skills of an experienced person. Parcels of foam are covered with cling film and taped to the frame and then decorated with foliage and flowers before the frame is put in place. When complete the frame is tied to the hinges of the door with florists' ribbon.

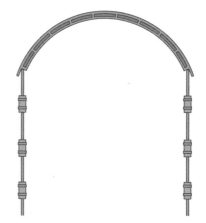

I have also seen a trellis frame made to fit in the indentation of the arch, again created by an experienced professional. Small blocks of soaked foam were encased in sandwich bags and placed on long nails embedded in the trellis frame. Chicken wire was stapled over the foam.

left In this shortened arch foam cages were attached to nails and hooks on the face of the porch. A base of foliage was created with, *Euonymus*, *Photinia* and *Pittosporum* and decorated with *Alstroemeria*, orange and yellow mini *Gerbera*, spray chrysanthemums, *Eryngium* and purple *Trachelium*.

Church: All Saints Church, Banstead
Arranger: Margaret McFarlane
Photographer: Mike Pannett

right A purpose built timber frame made by a carpenter is the base of this magnificent arch of flowers.

Church: St. Mary's Church, Innishannon, Ireland
Arranger: Dympna Murphy and Mary O'Keeffe
Photographer: Mary O'Keeffe

- **Using foam wrapped in chicken wire**

  This method only works if nails are already in the masonry or you have permission to put them there. Pieces or entire bricks of soaked foam are wrapped in chicken wire and the chicken wire hooked over the nails. The gaps between the 'parcels' are linked with plant material. On a small to medium sized arch, garlands can be created using the OASIS® Garlands or Trident Foam Ultra Garland (see page 22). This also creates a half arch.

- **Using lengths of wood and pipe lagging**

  This method, which was devised by John Chennell, works particularly well. The mechanics can be stored and used time and time again. See the step by step design below.

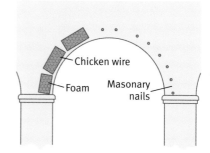

right A full arch

Church: St. Paul's Church, Knightsbridge
Arranger: John Chennell
Photographer: Lyndon Parker

Step by step

Full arch

> **You will need**
> - two lengths of wood 5cm square (2in x 2in), the same length as the height of the doorway
> - 6 sturdy shelf brackets with screws
> - branches such as willow or hazel which are thick but easily bendable
> - pipe lagging
> - florists' tape

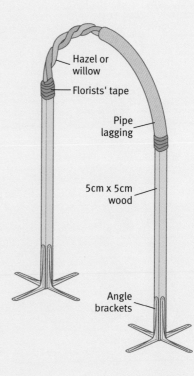

Method

1 Screw three brackets to the sides of the base of each length of wood.

2 Attach the branches of willow or hazel to the top of one of the lengths of wood with florists' tape. Wind together, then curve them over and attach to the other piece of wood.

3 Wrap the lagging around the top of the arch so that it covers the join and reinforces the willow. The arch should now stand steady and secure.

4 You can now attach foam to the vertical structures – either by wrapping it in chicken wire or plastic film and taping it securely, or by taping on spray trays filled with foam.

5 Cover with foliage to give a good cover but not so tightly that it is difficult to find space for the flowers. Use flowers with strong stems.

Half arch

To decorate the top of an arch you could adapt some of the methods described for a full arch or you could create the following using a wooden frame. Before proceeding you will need to get the approval of whoever is responsible for the fabric of the church to provide the supports that a wooden frame will need. This will involve drilling into the fabric to take screw eyes into wall plugs or exposed lathes. If this is prohibited then it is unlikely that a frame can be mounted and it needs to be free standing.

If you are not competent with DIY, you need to ask the local carpenter or find a willing volunteer who can create such a frame for you. It needs to have three rings attached – one at the top and one at each side. These can then be hung over the embedded support. The frame itself needs nails at regular intervals around the shape over which chicken wire, filled with foam, or covered in moss, can be hooked.

This mechanic requires a significant investment in time and trouble but is well worth the effort as it can be used time and time again.

Step by step

External half arch using a wooden frame

You will need
- screw eyes
- large sheet of wood or plywood
- nails
- bricks of foam
- sphagnum moss
- chicken wire

Method

1 Make a template of the shape of the arch to be decorated. You could use tracing paper or measure the arch using a tape measure if you are confident to do this.

2 Cut a support from the wood or plywood using the template to give the dimensions (or employ someone to do this for you).

3 Drill screw eyes into the wall plugs in the appropriate places. Wrap each brick of foam in the chicken wire and nail these at regular intervals along the wooden arch.

4 According to the weight that the supports can bear you can:
a) Cover the frame with a thick covering of damp moss. Keep this in place with a cap of chicken wire. Use flowers with strong stems so that they can be pushed into the moss without breaking.

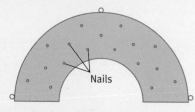

Nails

b) Place pieces of foam at regular intervals along the frame. Cover lightly with moss. Attach a cap of chicken wire over the foam and moss. Your flowers will last longer as it has a direct source of water, but the weight will be greater and will consequently need stronger support than (a). You will also need to keep changing the foam as once foam has dried out it will not re-take water.

5 Hook the rings on the wooden arch onto the screws.

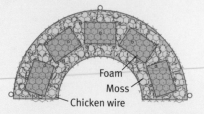

Foam
Moss
Chicken wire

Hanging arrangement

If the arch is high enough, a sphere covered with plastic netting or a piece of foam wrapped in cling film surrounded by chicken wire can be suspended from the central point of the arch.

Attach wire for hanging from the netting or chicken wire. The plant material can then be arranged out of the foam to create a circular design in a similar way that you decorate the top of a topiary tree.

Tip

- If the porch is facing south and the weather is warm, ensure that the flowers are not put in place too far in advance, that they are sprayed well with water and that the flowers used are robust.

right A ball of flowers hanging from the centre of an arch.

Church: St. Mary's Chapel, Raleigh, St. Mary's School Campus, NC
Photographer: Lee Thompson

The mechanics were plastic cages called 'Simply Garlands' which at the present point in time are no longer available. (I am hoping they will soon be back in production.) As an alternative, use chicken wire wrapped around soaked floral foam or the new garland mechanics produced by Smithers-Oasis. Use nails to suspend the cages or chicken wire.

The central arrangement is created on a spray tray placed in position first and suspended from a nail with plastic garden wire. To give additional security it was attached at a second point with waterproof florists' ribbon. You have to take extra special care when arrangements are hanging above people. Wendy has given a great tip – "The fabric of old churches is prone to crumble. To repair gather the crumbling bits that have fallen to the ground. Mix with water and push back in place with a strong thumb action."

Church: St. Peter's Church, Inkberrow
Arranger: Wendy Smith
Photographer: Chrissie Harten

Tips

- Wet foam is weighty and if your mechanics are not generously supported, you will have problems and it would be better to use wet moss and no foam.
- The foam and moss will drip after you have inserted the flowers. It is therefore recommended that you arrange the flowers, in position, well in advance. Drips from garlands, wreaths, pew ends and other designs cause a lot of anxiety both to arrangers and to the church authorities. Less-tutored flower arrangers need to be warned about the problem in a very positive way and advised how to overcome it.

7 The Entrance

Once one has penetrated the doorway, there may be a porch and an inner door which can be decorated. There is certainly an area where worshippers are welcomed and where first impressions are gained. This is an opportunity to decorate, in a modest way, without detracting from the centrality of the altar and pulpit.

Spiritual entrance to the church at baptism is via the font. To enhance this symbolism, from the early days of the Christian church, the font was usually placed in the entrance area (if not actually in a separate baptistery).

In modern times, and in many non-conformist churches, a portable font is sometimes used so that baptisms take place in front of the congregation. In these cases, the suggestions below for decorating the font should be adapted where necessary.

The porch

A ledge in the porch lends itself to a display of flowers whatever the time of year. If there is a notice board above the ledge take care that you do not obscure the messages. If there is a shelf in the porch, or a long seat or bench, then a suitable design would be a landscape arrangement running its length.

left A handsome low pedestal design in the porch using flowers and seedheads from the riverbank close to the church with Canterbury bells, *Hydrangea* and foliage from the churchyard. The twisted *Dracaena* (lucky bamboo) was used to interpret the spiral stairs for which money was being raised to restore access to the top of the tower.
Church: St. Mary the Virgin, Mortlake
Arranger: Susie Lansbury
Photographer: Judith Blacklock

following page Inside the door, this landscape design was created in flat black dishes raised on bricks to give space beneath the arrangement and additional height.
Church: All Saints Church, Banstead
Arrangers: Monica Gerlach and Margo Hall
Photographer: Mike Pannett

The door

Wreaths

A seasonal wreath is a lovely way to welcome people into the church. They are especially effective at Christmas, Easter, Harvest and Thanksgiving. There are many ways to create wreaths and you will find instructions for some of these below.

Ready made wreath

These can be purchased inexpensively out of season and stored until required. The decoration on the wreath can be easily changed to give a fresh look the following year – simply remove and add your own cones, seedheads and flowers (dried, artificial or fresh in tubes) to the base.

Using garden plant material

This is another way to benefit from a church garden.

> ## Tip
> If you add a couple of stems of artificial berries or colourful autumn foliage, intertwined between the natural plant material, few will be any the wiser!

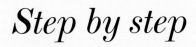

Step by step

Wreath using garden plant material

You will need
- about 6m (20ft) of stripped climber such as *Akebia, Clematis, Convolvulus* (bindweed), *Hedera* (ivy), *Meuhlenbeckia, Parthenocissus, Rubus* (ornamental bramble) or *Salix* (willow)
- raffia covered wire, reel wire or garden twine

Method

1 Wrap the stripped climber around so that it is entwined and creates a circle.

2 Use short lengths of twine, paper covered wire or wire to fix the stems securely in place.

3 Decorate with dried or preserved plant material. Alternatively attach orchid tubes, wrapped in leaves or sisal, into which you can insert fresh flowers.

top left Trailing *Amaranthus* and loops of *Phormium* extend this textured design to fill the length of the porch. The mechanics are hidden with a palisade of twigs.
Church: Dyrham Church, Dyrham
Arrangers: Wootten Bassett Flower Club
Photographer: Judith Blacklock

left The porch in Wordsworth's church in Grasmere had this wonderful Easter arrangement of daffodils in jam jars with raffia, eggs, moss and a simple message.
Church: St. Oswald's Church, Grasmere
Photographer: Judith Blacklock

Wreath on a Styrofoam or plastic base

These pre-made foam bases are a more expensive
option but are very easy to use.

Step by step

Wreath on a foam ring

You will need
- foam ring in a size of your choice
- garden twine or paper covered wire for hanging
- foliage – you can use either a mixture or just one variety such as tree ivy
- flowers of choice

Method

1 Soak the ring for about 60 seconds under water, immersed at a slight
   angle.

2 Wrap garden twine or paper covered wire around the ring, knot and
   make a loop for hanging. Allow any excess water to drip from the ring.

3 Cover 70–90 percent of the foam with your foliage. Make sure that
   foliage is angled down over the edges of the ring, both on the inside
   and on the outside.

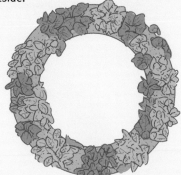

4 Add your flowers. Keep the stronger, rounder forms more central, rather
   than at the edges of the ring in order to keep the movement circular.
   Do, however, give interest to the inner and outer edges with less dominant
   flowers and berries.

right A colourful welcome wreath of late spring and early summer flowers in a foam base.
Photographer: Lee Thompson

Wreath using moss on a wire frame

Although more labour intensive, this wreath will last for many weeks and is ideal for Christmas.

Step by step

Mossed wreath

You will need

a) for the basic structure
- a wire ring – 25–30cm (10–12in) gives a good sized ring. If the door is large, use a 35cm (14in) ring.
- strong reel wire or garden twine (the text will refer only to reel wire but strong garden twine will work well)
- approximately 8 large handfuls of *Sphagnum* moss
- 2 large branches of blue spruce or long-lasting foliage of choice such as tree ivy, conifer, *Skimmia*, box
- garden twine or paper covered wire for hanging

b) for decoration
You will need a selection of the following
- pine cones
- hard fruits such as lemons, limes, tangerines
- vegetables such as chilli peppers (avoid contact with the eyes), small aubergines, whole cloves of garlic
- large poppy seedheads
- cinnamon sticks
- dried lavender
- dried orange slices
- walnuts (which have a soft opening at the base for a strong wire or cocktail stick)

Method

1 Attach one end of the reel wire to the point of a 'V' in the wire frame.

2 Spread the moss out on a clean surface. Remove any twigs, stones and sharp objects. Fluff up the moss. Take handfuls of the clean moss and manipulate into tight, hard balls. Each complete ball will be approximately the size of a medium sized orange. You will need about 12–15 for a 30cm (12in) ring.

3 Starting where the wire is attached place the first ball on the wire frame and push the second ball tightly up against it. Take the reel wire around the frame and the moss at approximately 5cm (2in) intervals, pulling tightly. Repeat until the frame is fully covered. Do not cut the reel wire.

4 If you are using spruce, cut all the secondary stems off the main stem. You will find that you have really good pieces, not so good pieces and poor pieces.

5 Place a 'good' piece on the top of the ring and wrap the reel wire tightly around the stem end twice. Place the 'second quality' stem on the outside of the wreath, slightly further to the right (or left) and pass the reel wire around two times so that three-quarters of the stem is free. Avoid capturing any outward secondary stems from the previous placement. Wrap round twice. Take a 'third quality' stem and place on the inside, slightly to the right (or left) and capture with the wire. Wrap round twice.

6 If you are using mixed foliage cut each type of foliage into lengths of about 75cm (3in). Bundle 3–5 lengths together with wire to secure. The number of lengths in each bundle will depend on the plant material used. Lay the bundles on the moss and wrap in with reel wire in the same way as suggested for the spruce.

7 Continue until the wreath is complete. Overlap each piece by about half to make the wreath thick and lush. Make sure that the foliage is evenly spread and that there is plenty of freedom of movement. Cut your wire with a long end. Thread through the wreath and out the other side. Push the end back in to secure.

8 To decorate, use your imagination and add ribbon and other accessories to make your wreath unique. You could also:

a) To secure fruit and vegetables use wooden sticks. Cocktail sticks will probably not be long enough so use lengths of kebab or garden stick. In the USA, Cowee sticks are available and these are custom made for this purpose. Insert the sticks firmly into the wreath.

b) Thread a wire through a few orange slices, close to the pith. Twist the wire close to the skin leaving a wire stalk.

c) Bundle dried lavender and/or cinnamon sticks and wrap with wire leaving a 'stalk' to insert in the wreath.

9 Wrap the ribbon or paper covered wire twice round the part of the wreath you have selected to be the top, knot and then make a loop for hanging.

above A floral wreath in a foam frame using lotus seed heads, *Euonymus*, *Viburnum tinus* fruits, *Diplocyclos* fruits, flat shells and David Austin fragrant roses.

Church: St. Paul's Church, Knightsbridge
Arranger: Judith Blacklock
Photographer: Judith Blacklock

Tip

If you cannot find a wire wreath frame pull a wire coat hanger into a circle. This will provide a wreath equivalent a 25cm (10in) base.

Entrance (just inside the porch)

A flower arrangement at the entrance table is one of the most effective designs in a church. It will be seen by everyone entering and enjoyed from every angle. The arrangement will be viewed first from the front, but the sides and back should always be taken into account, as people will see it again on their way out.

This arrangement could be a simple gathering of roses in a bowl or spring flowers in an attractive vase filled with chicken wire. If something more elaborate is called for the method on the following pages show you how to create a structured design.

left Square wire frames have been mossed and covered in short snippets of plant material. Lengths of beautiful ribbon have been incorporated into the design, repeating the vertical movement which is such an important part of the rhythmic appeal of the composition.

Church: Greek Orthodox Church, Nashville, TN
Photographer: Lee Thompson

above Set on a table against a pillar, this elegant design creates a bright entrance in a dark position.

Church: Paisley Abbey
Arranger: Margaret Neil
Photographer: Bob Brown

Step by step

All round entrance arrangement

You will need
- waterproof container. If your container is porous, line it first with thick plastic such as a piece of black binliner. If you are using a plastic container, which you want to hide, it should be reasonably shallow. If the container is more decorative it can be taller.
- floral foam
- florists' tape
- outline foliage – this could be, *Danae racemosa* (hard ruscus), *Eucalyptus cinerea*, *Gaultheria* (salal), *Ligustrum* (privet) – the choice is very wide.
- smooth textured leaves such as ivy, *Bergenia*, *Heuchera*, *Pelargonium* from the garden or *Galax* from the florist
- line flowers such as mini *Gladiolus*, larkspur, *Liatris*, or any flower in bud
- round flowers such as *Gerbera* (either the mini varieties or larger ones according to the situation), open roses, chrysanthemums
- sprays of flowers and foliage such as *Alstroemeria*, spray *Chrysanthemum*, *Gypsophila*, *Hypericum*, *Pittosporum*, *Viburnum tinus*

Method

1 Soak the foam for about 50 seconds. Place the foam in the dish and secure well using a frog and fix or florists' tape. The foam must rise well above the rim of the container. A very general guide is that the foam should rise one-fifth to a quarter the height of the container above the rim.

2 Place a stem of foliage in the top centre of the foam. Only insert a small amount of stem so that it is secure but not deep in the foam. Leave enough space around the foam to add water easily.

3 Place stems in position about halfway up the exposed sides of the foam and angled slightly downwards over the rim of the container. These should all be the same length. Angle them so that they appear to originate from an imaginary point at the core of the foam. This is very important. Sometimes it is difficult to know how many stems to use – a rough guideline is to use sufficient stems so that the first leaves on the stem emerging from the foam almost touch the ones to which they are adjacent.

4 Place an odd number of stems of the same length out of the top of the foam around the central stem. Again these should all be approximately the same length. Avoid placing these directly above the material that you have already inserted. Place these stems in between those already in position.

5 At this stage it is important that these stems stay within the overall form created by the height of your first stem and the width of your second placements. Check that all stems appear to come from the core of the foam.

6 Next add your smooth textured round leaves. Avoid a frilly effect by inserting stems so that the leaves lie at different angles. Use smaller leaves at the top and larger ones lower down to give good visual balance. The objective is to reinforce the outline created not to systematically cover the foam. The stems should not therefore be cut too short. At this point, you will still be able to see a small amount of foam but there should be a strong framework of foliage.

7 Add line flowers almost to the limits of the design and throughout. Your first placement should reinforce the main stem and be straight upright. If it is angled away from this central vertical position it will be difficult to achieve a well-balanced design. At this point pick up your design and look at it at eye level. Check that some stems are angled downwards over the rim of the container.

8 Place the round focal flowers at intervals throughout your arrangement. It helps if the round flowers vary in size to some extent. If they do, position the smaller flowers higher in the design and the larger flowers more centrally. Again, do not cut the stems too short.

9 Add spray material and any other round flowers to complete. Keep within the framework established by the foliage. If the spray material is light and airy it can extend beyond the outline without upsetting the balance.

10 Ensure that your container always has a reservoir of water.

Tip
It is always easier to disguise a green plastic container than a white one.

right An all round arrangement on the entrance table which has been arranged to be enjoyed at all angles.

Church: St. Paul's Church, Knightsbridge
Arranger: Judith Blacklock
Photographer: Louisa Scott

The font

This part of the chapter concerns the decoration of a traditional font sited near the entrance of the church.

Only with the agreement of the clergy and church authorities can the inside of the font be decorated for special occasions. Some fonts have covers, ranging from the very elaborate carved style to simple wooden ones. An elaborate cover should be removed and stored safely.

The rim of the font

A garland can be created to go around the top of the font for a flower festival but for a Christening it is important to make a horseshoe effect so that access is unrestricted and the minister's hand can reach the water. The following methods are useful for creating a ring of plant material. Be sure that no wet foam lies directly on stone, marble or wood as this will leave permanent damage.

above The Baptismal font is decorated with summer flowers for a flower festival.

Church: Grace Episcopal Church, Charleston, SC
Arrangers: Members of Grace Flower Guild
Photographer: Wally Breidis

Method 1

Make a ring of rolled up chicken wire. Cover the ring with moss, using mossing pins or long hairpins of wire to make it secure. If it is easier, make the ring in several sections. Curve the ring of chicken wire around the top of the font indenting it where you wish to position small jam jars, glass yoghurt pots or similar. Add small bunches of seasonal garden flowers to the mini vases.

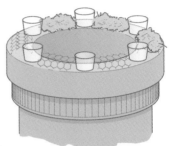

Method 2

Take a template of the top of the font where you wish the flowers to lie and get a metal worker to create metal containers to fit the shape. Make sure the containers are not too deep.

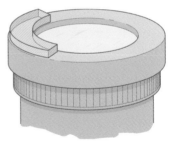

Method 3
The instructions for this design would be the same for decorating the pulpit (see page 209).

right A font filled with flowers for a flower festival. The strength of the stone font provides the perfect foil for the mass of early summer flowers of *Hydrangea*, stocks, tulips, *Danae racemosa* (soft ruscus) and *Matthiola* (stocks) in pinks, blues and greens. The old stone font, original to the colonial church in Georgetown, sits in the narthex of the building.

Church: St. John's Episcopal Church, Georgetown, DC
Arrangers: Stephen McLeod and Laura Scanlon
Photographer: Mark Finkensteadt

Step by step

Font arrangement

You will need
- approximately five low shallow trays (the number will depend on the circumference of the font) or foam wrapped in cling film. Trays such as these are available from DIY stores, craft stores and garden centres. Alternatively use supermarket disposable food trays but do make sure they are sufficiently strong and deep to take a reservoir of water.
- floral foam
- florists' tape
- mix of foliage such as *Eucalyptus*, *Buxus* (box), myrtle, *Hedera* (ivy) or other dense short foliage
- selection of spray and round flowers. One type of flower used must have a round form, such as an open rose, carnation or large headed spray chrysanthemums.

Method

1 If you are using plastic trays fill two thirds of each tray with foam. This will leave sufficient space for a reservoir of water. If you wish to keep the arrangement low, cut each brick of foam lengthways.

2 Place florists' tape over the foam to secure it in the centre of the tray.

3 Cover the foam loosely with foliage, angling some of the leaves over the rims of the containers. Take longer stems out of the ends of the foam so that the stems in each tray meet to give a continuous circle of plant material.

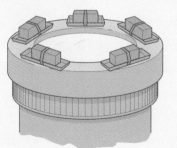

4 Add your flowers ensuring that you also have flowers at the lower edges. You could add trails of ivy to trail down over the font.

above A circle of flowers around the font in specially manufactured metal containers. The flowers include *Alchemilla mollis* (lady's mantle), *Lathyrus* (sweet peas), *Matthiola* (stocks) and roses.

Church: St. Paul's Church, Knightsbridge
Photographer: Judith Blacklock

Inside the font

An arrangement inside the font is not always practical but for major displays – say at Christmas or Easter – the space can be used to great effect. Place a bucket upside down in the opening and place a bowl on the bucket filled with foam. Alternatively a circle of wood may be used on the lid and flowers arranged in a large bowl (for example a washing up bowl) on top. Do check with the clergy before deciding to arrange flowers within the font.

below An original and creative way to decorate a font for a flower festival.

Church: Paisley Abbey
Arranger: Jane Gordon
Photographer: Bob Brown

The base of the font

Avoid arranging flowers at the foot of the font unless for a flower festival as the flowers could prove an obstruction. In addition, they would be hidden by the people gathered around the font.

right Bundled cut willow sprayed gold with *Hippeastrum* (amaryllis) threaded through creates height. At the base the pots of *Hippeastrum* were covered in black plastic and moss and secured in place with raffia. *Aspidistra* leaves, curved and pinned to each of the *Hippeastrum* stems add distinction.

Church: St. Michael and All Angels, Barnes
Arrangers: Jeanette Bell
Photographer: Mike Pannett

8 The Nave

In traditional churches, the area between the entrance and the area known as the choir, chancel or quire is the nave. This is where the pews or chairs are placed and the congregation sits. The pulpit and lectern are usually facing the pews, one on either side, at the entrance to the choir. Formerly, the 'high altar' always used to be at the far end of the choir in the area called the sanctuary. Recent reforms have often resulted in the placing of the altar centrally at the point where the nave and the choir meet. This must be taken into account in the placing of flower arrangements.

Pews

The upright ends of pews are traditionally decorated for weddings, sometimes for special services and at Easter and Christmas. If economical use of flowers is desired, designs can be created on every other pew, starting with the ones opposite each other closest to the altar. This restrained use of flowers often looks better than decorating every pew end. With a good covering of foliage you can create effective designs with only a few flowers on a small budget.

following pages Hanging arrangement on every pew end, each in memoriam.
Church: St. Illtyd's Church, Llantwit Major
Arranger: Members of the St. Illtyd's Flower Guild
Photographer: Pam Lewis

left A pew-end showcasing the floral offerings of autumn. Touches of autumn include bronze and burgundy chrysanthemums, wheat, *Eucalyptus* and autumn leaves with a touch of bittersweet. A piece of foam was strapped to a pre-made wreath. The bronze chrysanthemums serve as the focal point for which all the other flowers radiate.
Church: St. Philip's Cathedral, Atlanta, GA
Arranger: Laura Iarocci
Photographer: George Westinghouse

The shape of the pew end determines how the design will be suspended.

The usual mechanic is a container with a handle, bearing a hole for hanging, called a spray tray (see page 24). It is also referred to as a 'pew end'. You could also use an OASIS® Florette cage with a handle (see page 21) but I usually use the former – it is less expensive and serves the purpose well. OASIS® Le Clip can also be used for the decoration of pew ends with a straight top (see page 22).

If the aisle is wide it is possible to create a design on the floor at the foot of the pew.

below Colourful carnations and spray chrysanthemums arranged on the ledge between the pews in narrow containers to give a rainbow of colour.
Church: Confederacy Church of Richmond, VA
Photographer: Judith Blacklock

opposite

top left A pew-end arrangement artfully designed to give the appearance of freshly cut flowers. Rose stems are placed in the bottom of the foam, contained within a plastic bag with a surround of chicken wire, to give the appearance of a bouquet.
Church: Grace Episcopal Church, Charleston, SC
Arranger: Grace Church Flower Guild
Photographer: Wally Breidis

top right Pew-end at the base of the pew using dried and glycerined plant material.
Church: Douai Abbey, Reading
Arrangers: Debbie Braeger and Ninon Linnell
Photographer: Allen Rout

bottom left A lazy 'S' design using the curving stems of *Molucella laevis* (bells of Ireland) to create a pew-end.
Church: Grace Episcopal Church, Charleston, SC
Arrangers: Grace Church Flower Guild
Photographer: Wally Breidis

bottom right A length of white ribbon gives a visual link between the simple pew-end design of three roses and the painted wood pew-ends.
Photographer: Lee Thompson

Tip

Pew ends are seen more from the side than the front so ensure that your designs also have interest and flowers on both sides.

above Foam spheres covered with carnations
are suspended from tall metal stands.

Photographer: Svetlana Atasheva/iStockphoto.com

right A stunning pew end design on a distinguished
metal stand.

Church: The Cathedral of St. Philip, Atlanta, GA
Arrangers: Morgan Ellington, Darrin Ellis May and Pattye Munro
Photographer: George Westinghouse

Step by step

Pew end design

The pew end designs should be ideally arranged *in situ* to ensure that the design is well balanced and attractive from all sides. They can however be arranged in advance and then attached to the pew on the day. Pew end designs such as this can double as table arrangements and be taken to the reception after the wedding service. This step-by-step, described below, uses trays without a cage. If you are using the caged version the technique of arranging the flowers is exactly the same.

You will need
- spray tray with handle or a caged pew end (Florette)
- floral foam
- florists' tape
- line foliage
- round flowers
- spray flowers
- filler foliage

Method

1 Cut the foam to fit the tray tightly. The foam should rise approximately twice as high out of the container as the container is deep. When inserting the flowers, *in situ*, you might find you get a flood of water on the church floor. To avoid this either cover the foam with cling-film or wet the foam 24 hours in advance and hang it up to drip outside.

2 Strap the foam firmly in place with floral tape. Avoid taking the tape across the centre as this is where you will want to place a central stem.

3 Place a stem centrally to create depth. This should not be too long for if the aisle is narrow there will be no space through which to walk.

4 Place a stem in the side of the foam so that it lies over the handle. It should be slightly longer than the handle. Place another stem in the other end of the foam to create the length you want to choose. A good guide is to have this one and a half times the length of the stem over the handle.

5 Add two further stems out of each long side so that the outline has an oval form.

6 Place further stems out of the top of the foam, radiating each stem from the core of the foam. Add further stems to give a good covering of plant material.

7 Add a second foliage if you so wish. Be sure at some point to include a smooth texture.

8 Add your flowers.

9 If the pew end does not already have a hook or nail (some churches do), suspend the pew end arrangement by threading ribbon through the hanging hole and tie it around the side of the pew or use a wire hook. If the top of the pew is straight, you could bend a length of wire through the hole in the spray tray and hook it over the centre of the pew end. The method will depend on the shape of the pew.

Aisle

Many churches have only one central aisle. Others may have a central block of seating and two side aisles. Bigger churches may have side aisles leading to special small chapels such as Lady Chapels, War Memorial Chapels, and chantry chapels. The placement of decorations in the aisle or aisles should take this into account.

Tip

Aspidistra leaves are ideal for giving decorative interest to the sides of hassocks and for concealing the foam. Simply remove the stem, and the rigid part of the midrib of the leaf, and wrap around securing with decorative pins.

Floral hassocks

Floral hassocks are totally impractical but lovely to look at so can only be used if the church is not going to be used for services while the decorations are in place. They are easy to create from a brick of foam cut in two lengthways and joined together with hairpins of wire. Attach bin liner to the bottom to prevent water leakage or arrange in a flat container of the size to take the brick of foam.

below Colourful tapestries of flowers create floral hassocks for a flower festival.

Church: North Shore Methodist Church, Blackpool
Arranger: Barbara Hurst
Photographer: Barbara Hurst

Floral carpets

Floral carpets have become a feature of flower festivals in recent years. They attract many visitors to a church and are a style of decoration that can be arranged by volunteers who are not expert flower arrangers. Long-lasting chrysanthemums with their strong, round form and spray carnations with their bright colours are ideal.

Good organisation and timing are essential to success. Someone should be available to give help with pattern planning, such as a fabric designer.

The following methods are examples of how floral carpets can be made.

Method 1

- It is essential to have containers that are waterproof. Plastic seed trays or trays without holes are suitable. These can be filled with foam which should be first covered in thin plastic film. This will hold in the moisture. An alternative mechanic is OASIS® Designer Foam. This is a large (but rather expensive) piece of thin foam with a polystyrene base which can be cut or sawn into smaller pieces.

- Assemble the trays or foam pieces together on the floor.

- Cover the foam with sprigs of short strong foliage such as yew or box.

- Following the pattern, previously designed, add flowers using a sharp implement or skewer to make holes through the plastic film if necessary.

- Ribbon, strips of *Aspidistra*, *Phormium* or other foliage can be used around the edge to hide the seed boxes or the base of the Designer Foam.

Method 2

- Plan the pattern on graph paper, basing it on a square module or unit size so that when all the separate units, filled with flowers, are placed together the tapestry is formed.

- Give each volunteer a paper on which the pattern is drawn for a particular unit and a piece of foam with the base wrapped in thick plastic film or an alternative 'Designer Foam'. Each unit should be numbered according to the overall plan so that quick, accurate assembly is ensured later. The colours should be marked and possibly the type of plant material.

- At an appointed time the units are delivered to the church and assembled on a sheet of strong plastic sheet to protect the floor.

- Conceal the sides of the foam or trays with foliage.

right A magnificent floral carpet is created annually in ChristChurch Cathedral, New Zealand. Thick plastic sheeting is laid in the central aisle of the cathedral and custom-made aluminium trays are set on trestle tables. The trays are filled with foam and lightly covered with *Sphagnum* moss. The design is then marked on to the foam and the basing of the design begins. Many volunteers support the head designer to get all the foliage, flowers and materials to create a 23 metre carpet in just over a day. The trestles are then removed and the carpet displayed to the public for five to ten days.

Church: ChristChurch Cathedral, Christchurch
Head designer: Jan Leaper and design students from Academy NZ under the guidance of Anne Elwell
Photographer: www.floraldesignmagazine.com

Pillars and columns

Strong and vertical, pillars and columns create a stately avenue, leading the eye down through the nave from the door to the altar. They also present some of the most challenging surfaces on which to arrange flowers. Negotiating curved surfaces and great heights, with nothing from which to hang your arrangements, makes pillar and column designs a difficult but rewarding exercise.

When is a pillar a column or vice versa? A column has a round cross section – think of ancient Greece. It may be fluted. Octagonal pillars can be thought of as columns. A pillar can have any cross section – usually square or rectangular.

left The vertical movement of the *Anthurium* is in complete harmony with its placement at the base of the pillar.

Church: Temple Church, London
Arrangers: Ealing Flower Club
Photographer: Lyndon Parker

right In this inventive design, the backing covered with decorative mesh has become part of the design. A baseboard 60cm (2ft) x 7.5cm (3in) was painted matt black. Three pairs of copper nails were hammered from the back equally spaced to support three placements of foam. Gold mesh was wrapped round the baseboard and stapled at the back. A wire loop was made for hanging. Three pieces of foam were cut to the width of the board and about 5cm (2in) deep and wrapped in Clingfilm. This was impaled on the copper nails and secured with florists' tape. Looped *Phormium* at the top created a bow and bay, *Skimmia japonica* 'Rubella', gold cones, red carnations and sprays of holly berries and leaves were arranged so as not to obscure the gold mesh. The final touch was the *Phormium* tails.

Church: East Bergolt Church, near Ipswich
Arrangers: Eileen Akehurst and Jan Holden
Photographer: Jan Holden

left A hanging representing sundials of various shapes and sizes using fabric and preserved plant material – a standing birch twig sundial decorated with sundials of various heights using miscanthus, oranges, poppy seed heads, twisted willow, skeletonized leaves, beads and sisal.

Church: Lincoln Cathedral
Arrangers: Gainsborough and District Flower Club
Photographer: Dick Makin

right For reasons of health and safety no access was allowed to water flowers on the pillars so the arrangers at The Cathedral Church of St. Peter and St. Paul, Sheffield created these designs with artificial flowers and foliage. The mechanics are an oblong of plywood, slightly larger than a block of dry floral foam, with two holes drilled at the top of the board for a hanging cord. The foam was fixed with spray glue and taped for extra security. The finished arrangements were surprisingly light in weight and are hung (by the verger with authority to climb a ladder) from nails already in the pillars.

Church: The Cathedral Church of St. Peter and St. Paul, Sheffield
Arrangers: Helen Drury, Jose Hutton, Julia Legg, Sue Smith, Glyn Spencer, Catherine Vickers, Betty Wain
Photographer: Oliver Gordon

Points for consideration

- Pillar decorations can be used either to lengthen or shorten a church depending on the desired effect. Placing designs on alternate pillars draws the eye in a zigzag movement, thus lengthening the apparent distance to the altar.

- Arrangements placed at the top of the pillar will appear to lower the ceiling, which might be best avoided if it is already rather low. They do however serve the purpose of drawing the eye upward to the heavens.

- Opinions differ as to whether it is acceptable for a pedestal arrangement placed at the base of a pillar to exceed its width. Personally I do not object to a pedestal being wider than the pillar but care must be taken not to over-extend it.

- Do not place a pedestal too close to the pillar. If a pedestal does not have plant material extending out of the back, it will not be physically well balanced and a knock from a member of the congregation may well send it reeling.

Pillars differ from church to church and each presents the flower arranger with a different challenge. There are three separate elements to a pillar or column, collectively known as the 'order' – the capital, the shaft and the base.

above The ladder was created from bamboo canes sticks cut to size to fit the pillar in the church. They were first secured with twine. This proved insufficiently strong so it was reinforced with green insulating tape from a hardware store. Strong reel wire was taken around the top of the pillar (around the lip) with a length hanging down from which the ladder was suspended. A similar support was created at the bottom to make doubly sure the ladder was secure. Orchid tubes were filled with water and two were placed on each strut wire, secured with florists' wire. Lilies and ivy were arranged in the tubes.

Church: Emmanuel Church, Stoughton, Guildford
Arranger: Linda Covey
Photographer: Adam Fox

above A band of flowers and foliage at the top of the pillar is easily created by suspending five spray trays at intervals around the pillar.

Church: Grace Episcopal Church, Charleston, SC
Arranger: Judith Blacklock
Photographer: Judith Blacklock

The capital

The capital is the element at the top of the column, and may be plain, scrolled, intricately carved, or indeed absent entirely. The ridge between the capital and the shaft (if such exists) is very useful for suspending mechanics.

The following methods show how the capital can be decorated.

Method 1

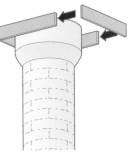

Nail, screw or bind three equal lengths of wood or cane together to form three sides of a square. Place this around the top of the capital and then add a fourth piece in place to complete the square. Nails can be driven into the wood and pew-ends hung from them. For a more contemporary look, lengths of ribbon or fishing line can be used to attach objects and flowers.

Method 2

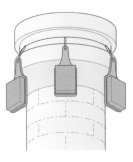

Take a length of strong fishing line or reel wire around the top of the ridge. Take further lengths of wire and thread each through the hole in the spray tray, containing foam, and hang them at intervals so that they lie flat against the wire around the pillar.

Fishing line is extremely strong but you may wish to pass two or three lengths through the spray tray to be absolutely certain it is sufficiently strong to support the weight of the plant material. For everyone's safety it is essential that there is no danger of the line snapping.

Angle foliage out of the foam so that a circle of plant material is created around the column and the trays are hidden. Then add long-lasting flowers to give interest.

This circle of plant material can also be created easily around a square pillar.

right Specially made iron bands support an arrangement on the pillar.

Church: Chelmsford Cathedral
Arrangers: Arrangers from Central Baptist Church, Chelmsford
Photographer: David Lloyd

left A bamboo frame was made from four stout lengths of bamboo to form a rectangle and a grid of lighter bamboo was bound within. Two spray trays were bound onto the frame for the flowers and foliage. The bird was created from a frame of chicken wire over dry foam. Space was left for the neck. The head was made from clay and two sticks were inserted into the clay before it dried. The sticks were then pushed into the dry foam. Small feathers in different shades of green and blue were purchased from a craft shop. These were inserted into the dry foam at an angle, starting at the neck with the smallest feathers. The breast was composed of the fluffiest feathers. The tail was made of long peacock feathers. An 'eye' was cut from another feather.

Church: All Saints' Church, Banstead
Arranger: Jan Warren
Photographer: Mike Pannett

The shaft

Garlands look wonderful wound around the shaft of the pillars, especially at Christmas. Making them can be a good group activity.

Method 1

This is a quick and easy way to create a garland and the result is great.

1   Purchase long stems of *Danae racemosa* (soft ruscus). These can also be grown in the church garden relatively easily.

2   Take two stems and entwine them together, overlapping their stems and tips. They will naturally entangle.

3   Secure at intervals with wire or paper covered wire.

4   Continue in this way to create a garland of the desired length.

5   Take wire around the capital, above the ridge, and attach one tip of the garland. Wind round the shaft and attach the other tip to a circle of wire around the base.

6   To decorate cover orchid tubes with green or brown stem tape, spray with adhesive and cover with leaves or bind sisal around the tubes with decorative wire. Insert heads or stems of *Cymbidium* orchids, white daisy *Chrysanthemum* or Singapore orchids (*Dendrobium*), for long-lasting effect.

Method 2

Use a garland of foam covered with green plastic netting from a specialist supplier. These garlands are manufactured by Smithers-Oasis. Suspend as for Method 1.

Method 3

Slit open a large plastic black bin liner so that it forms a long sheet. Bundle this together to form a long strip. Wire a length of foliage onto one end and bind in so that the foliage extends beyond the plastic. Add in more pieces of foliage, angling equal amounts to each side and the central portion. Add more strips of bag to create a longer garland.

The base

The base is the area between the shaft and the floor and may be raised or flat. If it is raised, then you are provided with a small ledge on which to place flowers. Otherwise you could place a low design around the circumference of the column on the floor. Alternatively place a pedestal at the base to complement the pillar in its proportions.

right A pillar decorated with a luxurious garland of flowers and foliage for a wedding.

Church: St Mary's Church, West Worlington, Devon
Arranger: Rosemarie Webber
Photographer: Terry Brown

9 All around the Church

Walls, floor plaques and memorials, window ledges, ceilings, grids, niches and alcoves, shrines and statues are areas of the church which can be decorated according to the occasion and their location in the church.

Walls

A large expanse of bare wall offers a wonderful opportunity to create large and striking arrangements. Remember to be sensitive to the colour and texture of the wall. The biggest problem will be finding fixing points or nails in the fabric. If no fixing points are available, and nails are not permitted, then freestanding decoration is all that is possible.

Banners

Banners can be fixed to wall brackets, or the structure of the church, to create a wonderful display inexpensively. The task of making the banners can take time but is most enjoyable.

- Sisal fabric is easily made by laying finely teased out fibres on a cellophane sheet painted with PVA glue, overlaying with another sheet of cellophane and leaving to dry thoroughly under pressure (such as a board and weight). The cellophane is peeled away to reveal the compressed fibres. It can be made in varying densities to suit the purpose for which it is required.

- Ribbon banners can be created by hanging lengths of gorgeous ribbon over a projected wall bracket or over the top of cage suspended on a wire from a wall bracket. Long-lasting flowers can be tucked into the ribbon fabric. Wires supporting tubes containing water and flowers can also be suspended from the wall bracket or cage.

left Against the stone niches in the oldest part of Salisbury Cathedral are delicate structures enhanced with ribbons and Vanda orchids. They are hung from bars that are part of the structure of the church. Lightweight square frames were hung from the bars. Organza ribbons of varying widths and lengths were then attached by staple guns to the frame. The *Vanda* orchids were in individual tubes on bullion wire wrapped in sisal.

Church: Salisbury Cathedral
Arrangers: Members of Christ Church, Worton, St. Peter's, Portesham and St. Laurence, Hilmarton
Photographer: Ash Mills

Plaques

These should not to be confused with 'Floor plaques and memorials'. This is also a term for a suspended design where the background, which could be of slate, fabric, metal or wood, is an integral part of the design.

Swags

A swag is a suspended design with no mechanics or container showing.

above A green background, framed with wood supports a sinuous design of *Anthurium*, *Aspidistra*, bloom *Chrysanthmum*, *Cymbidium* orchid, *Hypericum* and *Rosa* 'Aqua'. Note how the swirl of pink ribbon and the pearl-headed pins links the design and adds rhythm.

Arrangers: Tutbury Flower Club
Photographer: Judith Blacklock

above Swags created with spray trays can be hung on a nail in any part of the church. Ribbon or wire can be threaded through the hole in the handle and tied around pillars, pew ends or any other structure.

Church: St. Paul's Church, Knightsbridge
Arranger: Judith Blacklock
Photographer: Judith Blacklock

Floor plaques and memorials

Most churches have plaques and memorials remembering the previous incumbents, the deceased, benefactors and victims of war. When decorating it is important not to obscure the wording on the memorial. If a person is to be especially remembered a surround of foliage and flowers, or foliage alone, can create a very special effect.

Floor plaque

To surround a floor plaque either of the following two methods can be used.

Method 1

Fill low narrow plastic trays (you may be able to find these as packaging at the supermarket) with wet foam and lay them end to end. The trays need to be as narrow as possible as the addition of flowers and foliage will give a much wider effect. Cut a corner off the foam in each container so that water can be added with a watering can with a long spout. Cut the same corner in each tray so you know where to pour.

> ## Tip
>
> If you have standard plastic trays into which a brick of foam fits perfectly then cut the tray in half lengthways with scissors, slot one inside the other and glue in place. As the plastic is flexible this is very easy to do. The tray will now take half a brick of foam cut lengthways. This will create a narrower, longer support that is suitable for this purpose.

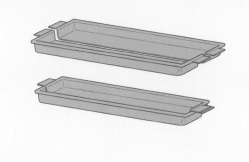

Method 2

Make a tube of plastic film filled with foam. Take a length of thin plastic film and cut into strips about 30cm (12in) wide and any length. Fold over the entire length. Join the edges by taking a cool iron over the join. Place a tea towel over the edge of the plastic before you iron. Be careful with the iron's temperature. If it is too hot, the plastic will burn. You may have to employ trial and error to find the right setting for your iron.

Slot the soaked rectangles of foam down the tube. If the strip is to be straight, push the foam close together. If it is to be curved, then leave spaces between the foam. You can knot the plastic between the pieces of foam to stop them sliding together. The rectangles need to be able to slide down the tube easily so make sure they are narrower than the sealed strip.

> ## Tip
>
> Never let the iron be in direct contact with the plastic or you will have a very difficult time cleaning your iron.

As the garland described in Method 2 is flexible it can be used to decorate many other parts of the church.

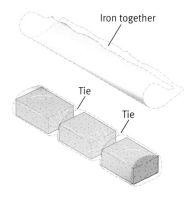

This Window was Erected
BY ANNIE MONCRIEFFE RUNDLE, AND
GEORGE EDWARD RUNDLE,
IN AFFECTIONATE REMEMBRANCE OF THEIR SISTER
ELIZA MARIA
WIFE OF THOMAS E. BEAUMONT,
AND WIDOW OF GEORGE WOSTENHOLM
OF KENWOOD PARK SHEFFIELD.
BORN DECEMBER 11TH 1840, DIED DECEMBER 6TH 1886.
MARK 14. 8. "She hath done what she could".

above Artificial flowers and foliage were used in this garland as fresh flowers would not have lasted for the length of the festival. It also meant that they could be prepared in advance. Lengths of rope, with loops at each end, were covered with green tape (to disguise the rope) before the flowers and foliage were wired on individually or in groups. The garlands were then hung from nails already in the walls.

Church: Cathedral Church of St. Peter and St. Paul, Sheffield
Arrangers: Hazel Drake, Kathleen France, Trish Nield, Sue Smith, Glyn Spencer, Catherine Vickers, Betty Wain
Photographer: Oliver Gordon

top right At the west end of the nave in Westminster Abbey is the grave of the Unknown Warrior which is decorated with poppies.

Church: Westminster Abbey
Photographer: Toby Smith

bottom right The Chapel of St. Edmund and St. Thomas. Flowers are arranged the length of the tomb of the Long Family.

Church: Salisbury Cathedral
Arrangers: Melksham Flower Club
Photographer: Ash Mills

For both methods

Cover the foam with long-lasting foliage so that you can only see the foam if you look hard. Use a mixture of different textures such as *Buxus* (box), *Cupressus, Laurus* (bay), mature *Ligustrum* (privet) or *Myrtus* (myrtle). If the area to be covered is large, increase the size of the leaves you are using. If it is difficult to get the stems through the plastic, use a sharp, pointed implement such as a bradawl or cocktail stick to make a hole.

Tips

- If the stems are pushed in on a slant the mechanics are soon covered.
- Use woody rather than soft stems.
- Do not work systemically around the mechanics but balance the design as you go by placing one type of foliage at intervals throughout the design and then adding a second in the same manner.

Tombs

With permission flowers may be placed on a tomb for
a special occasion.

left Hanging spray trays
contain a joyous mix of
flowers to decorate The
Arundel Tomb.

Church: Chichester Cathedral
Arranger: Val Leggate
Photographer: Christina Bennett

above This wonderful arrangement of summer plant material
near St. Richard's Shrine was grown by Val Leggate and the
gardeners of the Aldingbourne Trust at one of Chichester's
spectacular flower festivals. The flowers were arranged in large
deep containers containing foam and chicken wire.

Church: Chichester Cathedral
Arrangers: Denise Foster and Di Cawley
Photographer: Christina Bennett

Window ledges

Flat window ledges provide the perfect location for flower arrangements as they are easily seen and get in nobody's way! Many churches however have sloping window ledges but with the right purpose-built mechanics they will be just as easy to use.

Flat window ledges

Flat window ledges are a popular choice for flower arrangements in churches. If an arrangement is placed on each ledge, then the church will feel full of flowers even if the designs are relatively small. The ledge has the obvious advantage of adding height to an arrangement without the need for a pedestal or a plinth.

There can be a problem with light flooding through the window so you only see the outline of the arrangement. If this is the case, create a strong backing of dark green foliage to showcase your flowers. Alternatively keep your flowers low.

A landscape design is extremely suitable for window ledges. Colour and interest are taken the full length of the window. They are quick and easy to create and look particularly effective with garden flowers.

Tip
If the window is south facing use robust flowers and foliage and keep well watered.

top right A specially made long slim metal stand has been laid on its side. Two shallow rimmed plastic trays have been positioned inside the stand one to each side. Two further trays were placed on top of the stand in the central area. All the mechanics were sprayed purple. *Phormium* leaves were woven through the design together with the hapene, sprayed pink, to help hide the mechanics. Height was created with dried plant material, also sprayed red and apricot and arranged with *Aeonium, Dianthus* (carnations), *Celosia, Gerbera, Gloriosa, Leucospermum* and *Liatris* together with apricot roses.

Church: All Saints Church Banstead
Arranger: Anna Sparks
Photographer: Mike Pannett

bottom right Two landscape designs, one each side of the cross.

Church: The Church of St. Lawrence, Gonalston
Photographer: Xander Casey

below Ten oriental lilies could not look better! Here they are arranged in a landscape design with foliage picked from the garden, ready for a village wedding.

Church: St. Leonard's Church, South Cockerington
Arrangers: Betty and Karen Needham
Photographer: Susan Teanby

Sloping window ledges

Sloping ledges need purpose-built mechanics. This can be a problem and without help new arrangers may think the task impossible. The flower arranger needs the help of the DIY man who may be found in the congregation if an appeal is made.

For this type of mechanic a masonry nail (or nails) is needed in the stonework to tether the shelf and prevent it from sliding down the slope. Do not rely on friction. Most churches will agree to this if the argument is presented fairly and logically by a well-known and respected member of the congregation, showing that the need is essential if flowers are to be in this area.

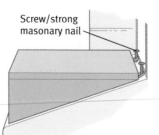

Screw/strong masonry nail

above An inaccessible ledge holds three placements of dried plant material and long-lasting bloom chrysanthemums.

Church: All Saints Church, Banstead
Arrangers: Elaine Coomber, Joan Goswell, Celia Champion
Photographer: Mike Pannett

right Wooden slats were painted white and placed on the sloping windowsill where the flowers were arranged in oblong trays.

Church: All Saints Church, Banstead
Arrangers: Kanella Matthews and Julie Sillence
Photographer: Mike Pannett

The most common way of creating mechanics for a sloping ledge is to construct a shelf out of wood to create a horizontal platform for the arrangements.

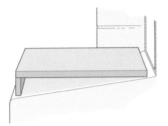

If the angle is gentle, then a rectangle of wood with a lip is sufficient, but if the angle is sharper than 10° then a wedge shaped support is required.

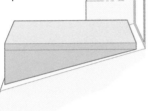

In many churches with sloping window ledges, each window is unique thus necessitating the need for a specific shelf for each window. The angle of the side of the shelf needs to match the angle of the sloping window ledge. The support could bear a longer plank, placed on top, if a longer container is needed to fill the space.

If there is a tiny ledge at the bottom of the slope, perhaps only 2.5cm (1in) high the shelf will lodge against this.

Tip

Once created, the supports should be labelled with the reference to their window (not all windows are identical – especially in churches). They can then be reused as required.

ET VERBVM CARO FACTVM EST

Sometimes there is a protective metal grid on the inside of the window, to which wire can be attached. If this is the case then consider the following:

- A plastic bag containing a piece of foam makes an excellent concealed container and can be used for awkward places such as sloping windowsills. It should be wrapped in chicken wire and wired to the window frame with reel wire. The plastic holds in the water. Avoid placing stems through the bottom of the bag where water gathers as it will drip out through the holes. Do check that the grid is strong and will not be pulled down by the weight of the wet foam.

- If there is a risk of the chicken wire scratching the surface, then place it next to the foam and inside the plastic. Make a hole in the plastic and place reel wire or paper covered wire through it and twist onto the netting. This enables the 'container' to be hung up or wired into a certain position. Cut away surplus plastic after the bag has been tied up tightly. Woody and hard stems will go easily through the plastic holes for softer stems may have to be made with a skewer.

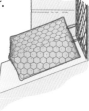

Flower arrangers and florists from outside the church community should check what mechanics are available to decorate the areas concerned but should NEVER presume to place a nail of any description in either wood or stonework. They must simply choose other areas to display flowers and use freestanding mechanics.

Ledge design

This design is suitable for a ledge anywhere in a church but is particularly effective in a window. The outline is a low triangle with flowing plant material that offers a certain elegance. The dimensions given here will create a design between 90–120cm (3–4ft).

Step by step

Ledge design

You will need
- three quarters of a brick of foam
- a low rectangular dish
- outline foliage, ideally with a gentle curve which is often found in *Eucalyptus*, *Danae racemosa* (soft ruscus) or *Hedera* (ivy)
- round leaves with a smooth texture such as x *Fatshedera*, *Galax* or *Hedera* (ivy)
- line flowers such as closed roses
- round flowers such as mini gerbera or open roses or lilies
- spray foliage or flowers

Method

1 Place the soaked foam in the dish and secure well. Place a stem of outline foliage (A) centrally, three quarters of the way back. This will be the height of the finished arrangement so cut it to the length required.
2 Place two stems of the same line material in both long ends of the foam (B and C), from the centre of each side, angled downwards. These pieces can be short or long depending on the overall width of the arrangement.
3 Place two short pieces of outline foliage (D and E) out of the top of the foam so that they radiate from the core of the foam and are equidistant from A, B and C.
4 Your aim now is to create a gentle crescent outline at the front. This is achieved by imagining a curve between B and C and angling foliage out of the front of the foam (F, G and H).
5 Add round leaves to reinforce the entire outline and not just the central area. You should now have a good strong framework. The foam will show but will not be too evident.
6 Place the first flower so that it reinforces the vertical placement of the foliage. Add other flowers through the design, almost to the limit of the foliage outline.

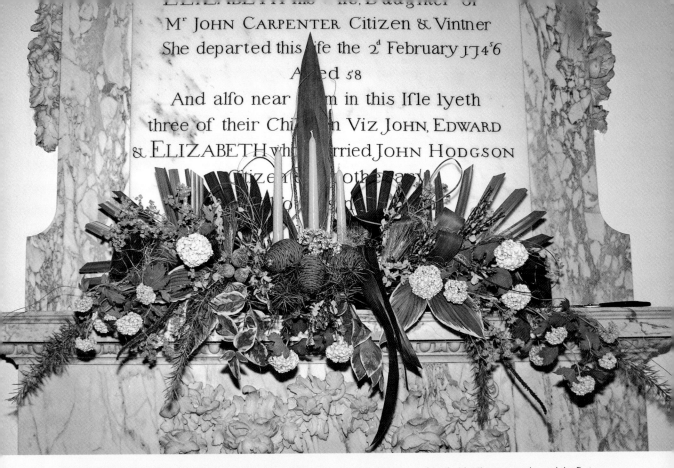

above A bold, stunning design using garden foliage, candles, cones and seedheads, combined with *Viburnum opulus* and the first shoots of *Forsythia*.

Church: All Saints, Banstead
Arranger: Sally Greaves
Photographer: Mike Pannett

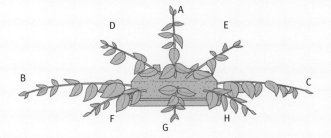

7 Place the round focal flowers at intervals through the arrangement. Avoid a tendency to have an all-round arrangement with two arms attached. The smallest focal flowers should be closer to the edges, the largest in the centre and the others between.

8 Add filler material to complete, including spray flowers or berries. If unsure keep within the framework established by the line material.

9 Ensure that your arrangement always has water in the bottom of your container.

following pages A landscape design along a long ledge, creating a colourful display of bold, summer garden material. A raised rattan edge, in front of the long low hidden containers, raises the design to give space beneath.

Church: Salisbury Cathedral
Arrangers: Sue Beveridge, Sally Dredge and Doreen Till, Bemerton Flower Arrangers
Photographer: Oliver Gordon

Ceilings

Hanging baskets

The easiest form of suspended design is to create a sphere of flowers and foliage in a single hanging basket. If you use two baskets wired together to form a sphere this will weigh a massive amount and it will be difficult to suspend safely. It is always vitally important to use strong chains and an additional safety chain for each hanging basket. You need to think about creating these with someone who can give practical advice. You will also need a tall ladder and someone who is strong to hold the basket while it is being hoisted into place.

Floral curtains

Curtains of flowers were recently seen at a magnificent flower festival at Salisbury Cathedral and are spectacular for special occasions. There is however a lot of work involved in their creation, see page 266.

right For each banner two metal panels were specially commissioned onto which grids were attached. Each of the flower heads was cut and put into a small polythene bag to which water was added and secured with rose wire. These were slotted through the grid so the bags were behind with the orchid heads protruding. Strands of tiny mirror circles were hung between the orchids to give light and sparkle.

Church: St. Dionysius, Market Harborough
Arranger: Lynda Stamp and members of The Flower Club of Market Harborough
Photographer: Tim Simmons

Step by step

Hanging basket

You will need
- hanging basket, approximately 55cm (22in) in diameter
- 2 bricks of foam or a large piece from a block of OASIS® 'Jumbo' foam
- plastic sheeting
- three chains of the appropriate length for hanging, with the means for attaching them to the basket
- flowers and foliage

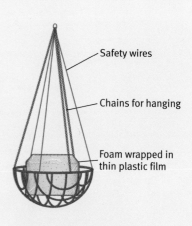

Safety wires

Chains for hanging

Foam wrapped in thin plastic film

Method

1 Soak the bricks, or a piece of OASIS® 'Jumbo' foam, to fill two thirds of the area of the basket and rise one third of its height above the rim. 'Jumbo' or high density foam will take about 10 minutes to be soaked.
2 Wrap the foam in a single layer of thin plastic film and secure with tape. Use as little tape as possible as it will makes the insertion of stems more difficult.
3 Attach chains to the side of the basket. You will also need a second safety chain. Do not even think about hanging an arrangement like this without a safety chain.

4 Place the first stem pointing up from the top and the second pointing down from the bottom, through the struts of the hanging basket. Create a sphere of plant material to the size required to create a strong outline. Only use plant material with strong, woody stems – short lived soft stemmed flowers such as *Iris* would not work in this design.
5 Add your flowers.

Shrines and statues

Before the Reformation in most churches there were statues of various saintly figures, predominantly the Virgin Mary and the infant Jesus. These were usually brightly painted and were objects of devotion during a time when the Mass was said in Latin. Certain branches of the reformed church were hostile to these and many statues were destroyed in England as idolatrous.

Today statues may again be found, particularly in Roman Catholic and High Anglican churches, though not usually in churches of the non-conformist denominations. In churches that still have statues, there may be representations of their patron saints, but the Virgin and Child still predominate.

Tom Sopko of Church of the Advent, Boston has given me the following information on how flowers can be arranged in these areas. Tom suggests that floral decorations of shrines can vary from a few simple flowers in a vase to elaborate decorations on a special feast day. In his parish, they have small brass vases that fit on the corners of the votive candle racks at the shrines of Christ the King and Our Lady and small bouquets are placed there most of the time. On major feasts there will be a larger arrangement beside the shrine.

These arrangements must not obscure or overpower the image and must not obstruct the kneeler or be ignited by the candles. They should be able to be appreciated both by someone kneeling at the shrine and also by others in the main body of the church. If the statue is on a plinth, without votive candles or a kneeler directly in front, a seasonal garland is most effective.

Simple vase arrangements of flowers are suitable at the foot of freestanding statues – to complement and not to overwhelm. Lilies, iris and roses are associated with Our Lady and would consequently be especially suitable.

Customs do vary and it is important to consult the clergy to determine what is suitable.

above Flowers complement the Madonna and Child.

Church: Santuario Nostra Signora del Soccorso, Pietra Ligure, Italy
Arrangers: Carla Barbaglia and her students: J. Gambetta, L. Grasso, R. Marco and M. Volpe
Photographer: Emanuele Zuffo

left The Shrine of Our Lady of Guadalupe, Patroness of the Americas, decorated with roses to honour 'The Mystic Rose'.

Church: The Cathedral of St. Mary of the Assumption, San Francisco, CA
Arrangers: Ramon and Roberto Ponce
Photographer: Jocelyn Knight Photography

left Flowers frame The Shrine of Our Lady of Guadalupe, Patroness of the Americas.

Church: The Cathedral of St. Mary of the Assumption, San Francisco, CA
Arrangers: Ramon and Roberto Ponce
Photographer: Jocelyn Knight Photography

right A wooden figure of Christ with a simple jug of *Alchemilla mollis*, daisies, *Anaphalis triplinervis* 'Summer Snow' (pearl everlasting), cranesbill, *Crocosmia* 'Lucifer' and flowering mint at His feet.

Church: Our Lady of Lourdes Roman Catholic Church, Hungerford
Arranger: Christine Ealding
Photographer: Mike Pannett

below Complementing the shrine in the Chapel of Christ Light of the World is a tall candle stand design. Mikado sticks were inserted in a willow wreath, placed on the top of the stand. Wires were threaded with beads, sequins and petals and suspended. Aluminium wire was twisted around the necks of *Ornithogalum* and the free end inserted in the wreath.

Church: Southwell Minster
Arrangers: Liz Prissick, Val York, Sleaford Flower Lovers Club
Photographer: Toby Smith

right The arrangement in the Chapel of Christ Light of the World reflects the peace and tranquillity in this chapel.

Church: Southwell Minster
Arrangers: Sleaford Flower Lovers Club
Photographer: Toby Smith

Grids

In some churches a division between two areas of the church is created by a metal grid that can be seen from both sides. If you wish to decorate the grid you need to ensure that you have matching mechanics so that they can be put back-to-back and thus be hidden.

right On either side of the Presbytery, dried and preserved plant material, together with fresh long-lasting *Aspidistra* leaves, adorn the mediaeval iron grilles.

Church: Salisbury Cathedral
Arrangers: Members of the Salisbury Floral Arrangement Society
Photographer: Oliver Gordon

Niches, alcoves, nooks and crannies

Niches, alcoves, nooks and crannies are to be found in many old churches. In some churches they held statues of the saints that were removed during the Reformation. These provide excellent positions for flower arrangements. They draw attention to the flowers because they frame them and fewer flowers are necessary because the backs and the sides of the arrangement are not as important. Very often these niches are at eye-level or higher and so display the flowers to everyone's view.

Care must be taken to consult with the church authorities about the use of some niches, as they may in fact be places for the reserved sacrament or holy water.

In some older churches, you will find a see-through niche. This is the place in a pillar that permits a worshipper, standing behind, to see through to the choir and the altar. In the middle ages, lepers were obliged to use these see-through niches. In a flower festival this is the ideal point for arrangement. A cohesive pair of designs needs to be installed back to back or a background inserted to show two arrangements to perfection. If one design is placed centrally in the niche then it is imperative that it is a design in the round.

right The layered design in this outside niche used a wood frame with horizontal slats to hold an assortment of robust plant material chosen for its form, colour, texture and ability to last outdoors.

Arrangers: Ashover Flower Arrangers Group
Photographer: Judith Blacklock

left Three niches provide the location for three stylish designs using carnations and bloom chrysanthemums. The arrangements were created in three long trays. The arches were commercially produced canes with twisted palm decoration. It was difficult to get them into an arch shape but this was achieved by wiring a strut across, about one third of the way up, to hold the canes apart. They were then angled outwards when putting the ends in foam so that the pressure forced them into shape.

Church: Cathedral Church of St. Peter and St. Paul, Sheffield
Arranger: Ros Kelson
Photographer: Judith Blacklock

10 The Choir

In churches with a traditional layout the singers and clergy are seated in the area known as the choir (chancel or quire). This may be distinguished by entry to it through a formal rood screen, or just a notional border between the nave and the choir. In simpler churches, or those of other denominations, the singers are sometimes seated facing the congregation, sometimes at the front of side-aisles and sometimes at the back of the church. Account has to be taken of the seating for the singers in designing a festival or providing arrangements for special occasions.

Usually, the pulpit and the lectern are at the junction of the choir and the nave. The preacher and readers face the congregation. Both pulpit and lectern present opportunities for decoration for special events and flower festivals. In mediaeval churches, the pulpit was usually placed on the north side at the east end of the nave. Most of the Mass would be conducted in the chancel before the altar. The Reformation churches often put the pulpit in the centre of the east end of the nave. The first part of the service was conducted here and the communicants moved into the chancel for the consecration and communion hence 'draw near with faith' in the exhortation to confession in the Book of Common Prayer. With restored emphasis on the Eucharist from the middle of the 19th century, the pulpit was returned to its mediaeval position and a lectern for the lessons was put on the opposite side. This has been the usual plan, but there are many instances where the pulpit is on the south side and the lectern on the north.

left Flower designs behind the stalls in Sheffield Cathedral's Chapel of the Holy Spirit repeat the colours of the flowers decorating the lectern (see pages 214, 215).
Church: Cathedral Church of St. Peter and St. Paul, Sheffield
Arrangers: Hazel Drake, Jose Hutton, Hilary Robinson and Val White
Photographer: Oliver Gordon

following pages The design is staged in front of the Bishop's Throne or Cathedra for the present Bishop of Salisbury to express his pastoral duties and love of music. The bun moss at the base of the stands gives good visual weight and thus helps provide stability to the design.
Church: Salisbury Cathedral
Arrangers: Angie Miles, Penny Cooper and Clare Antone, St. Mary's, Shrewton and Salisbury Floral Arrangement Society
Photographer: Oliver Gordon

Choir stalls

Any decorations on the choir stalls must be well out of the way of the choristers entering and leaving as they may be accidentally knocked to the floor. Of course, if you are sure that choristers will not be present then you may decorate the area as you wish.

If the choir stalls are at right angles to the altar, one of the best ways to decorate them is to range a line of landscape arrangements on the floor in front of them to lead the eye to the altar. Landscape designs are also known as parallel or continental designs but as the overall form now tends to be less rigidly parallel – partly due to the inclusion of less uniform garden plant material – I will be referring to them throughout this book as 'landscape'. You could use plastic trays with floral foam inside, placed end to end. Turn to chapter 13 'Other Mechanics' for a method of creating an inexpensive, easy-to-make container suitable for a large landscape design.

Tip
For large landscape designs you could use window boxes as containers.

left A landscape design in front of the choir stalls in the Chapel of the Holy Spirit.

Church: Cathedral Church of St. Peter and St. Paul, Sheffield
Arrangers: Hazel Drake, José Hutton, Hilary Robinson, Joy Smith, Val Smith and Glyn Spencer
Photographer: Judith Blacklock

Step by step

Landscape design

You will need

- low rectangular dish – it should be relatively narrow in relation to its length. Special containers can be made for large areas.
- foam to fit inside the container.
- line plant material such as *Delphinium*, *Eremurus*, *Gladiolus*, larkspur or *Liatris*. You will need at least three types of linear material. You could also consider smooth and interesting stems such as bamboo stripped of its leaves, *Cornus* (dogwood) and *Salix* (willow).
- flowers and foliage chosen for their form and texture to cover the foam loosely. *Hydrangea*, in season, when it is strong, covers large areas quickly and effectively. Leaves such as *Bergenia*, *Galax, Hosta* or *Hedera* (ivy) are ideal for layering. You will probably need more material than you originally thought to cover your foam.
- flat moss, reindeer moss, *Tillandsia* (Spanish moss), hydrangeas or sisal all of which can be used to cover the base inexpensively.
- fruit, vegetables and/or pebbles will give inexpensive colour, form and texture.

Method

1 Soak your foam and place in the container. Slice off a corner at the rear to allow easy watering. The foam should rise sufficiently above the rim of the container so that you are able to layer the ends and sides of the design.

2 Create your vertical placements. For a container approximately 25cm (10in) long, three verticals look effective. The central placement of the three verticals is often the shortest. The verticals can be bound with raffia, bunched at the same height if their stems are interesting, or simply graduated down in length. Many stems, however, will have its own point of origin and will not radiate from a central core, although minor radiation does frequently exist to give a less rigid design.

3 You will now need to cover your foam with plant material. This is kept short and is used in blocks of contrasting form, texture and colour. This is often referred to as 'ground work'. It is vital that your plant material appears to flow over the rim of the container, particularly at the front and sides of the design. Try and find a green or black container as white containers are too dominant against the green of the foliage.

4 Paths can be created through the central two thirds of the design with plant material meandering through from front to rear.

right A fine example of how ancient choir stalls, such as those in Sheffield Cathedral, can be embellished but not overwhelmed with simple flowers and foliage.

Church: Cathedral Church of St. Peter and St. Paul, Sheffield
Arrangers: Elsie Burnside, Kathleen France, Pat Leach and Kaye Stobbs
Photographer: Judith Blacklock

5 Stones, moss and pebbles, as well as fruit and vegetables can be added to the design to give greater interest and cut down on cost. Fruit and vegetables should be mounted on cocktail or barbecue sticks or Cowee sticks to avoid slipping out of place due to their weight and pegged into the heart of the design.

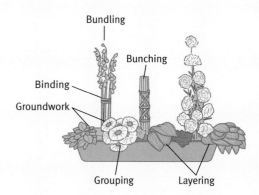

Bundling

Bunching

Binding

Groundwork

Grouping

Layering

Organs, pianos, harmoniums and other keyboard instruments

Free standing instruments are easy to decorate. A triangular or landscape design across the top would be ideal. An organ is more difficult. You could place a design on the seat in front of the organ (in the event, of course, that the organ is not being used). What is vital is that there is plastic or cloths under any arrangement close to a musical instrument and that watering is done with extreme care.

right In front of the organ pipes, this interpretative design provides the rhythm of music with bamboo pipes, a swirl of notes and the clever choice of plant material. The bamboo 'pipes' are slotted onto stands which are screwed into baseboards.

Church: Cathedral Church of St. Peter and St. Paul, Sheffield
Arranger: Glyn Spencer
Photographer: Oliver Gordon

above In an African church a harmonium doubles as an altar with flowers from the roadside placed humbly at its foot. The photo was taken without ceremony by Marion Gough who helps run a charity 'Orphans in the Wild' that helps and supports children orphaned by AIDS and to help improve living standards in an environmentally sustainable manner. www.wildorphans.org

Church: Kibao Church, Mulfindi
Photographer: Marion Gough

left In a niche next to the organ this design created for a flower festival uses bamboo in imitation of the pipes.

Church: Southwell Minster
Arrangers: Pauline Foster
Photographer: Judith Blacklock

right Pedestal stands of varying height stand at the base of the pulpit. Note the clever use of *Dracaena sanderiana* (lucky bamboo) hanging vertically to take interest down.

Church: Paisley Abbey
Arranger: Maureen Mitchell
Photographer: Bob Brown

The pulpit

On many pulpits it is possible to create a ring of flowers around the top. Here care must be taken that the flowers and foliage flow outwards and do not restrict the movement in the pulpit itself. The method is the same as for the font (see page 144). It might be a good idea to check that the preacher has no objections and does not suffer from hay fever, especially during the summer months.

Reformation churches often had a three-decker pulpit, with the preaching part at the top, the reading desk for the lessons and prayers in the middle and a lower place for the clerk to make the responses. This was a popular form in England in the 18th century and can be seen in many illustrations. A pedestal design at the base of the pulpit would be appropriate but make sure that it does not impede access to the stairs. Sometimes there are shallow indentions in the pulpit which would allow arrangements of flowers for a festival but it is safer to use dried or artificial plant material which do not need water.

below A sweeping design beneath the pulpit moving round into the aisle of the South Nave. This design enhances but does not detract from the carvings on the pulpit by G.F Bodley (1896). Glass bathroom bricks at the bottom, to give height, were topped with black rectangular foam trays. *Fatsia* and *Hosta* leaves at the base cover the mechanics together with looped *Phormium* leaves. Yellow *Achillea, Gladiolus, Gerbera*, cream roses and lilies are arranged with vertical and crossed *Phormium* leaves, sisal and green apples.

Church: Southwell Minster
Arrangers: Irene James and Jane May, Roundhill Flower and Garden Club
Photographer: Toby Smith

right A fine example of how a pulpit can be decorated to great effect with a moderate budget. Notice how a gap has been left at the centre so that the preacher can have easy access.

Church: Fairford Church, Hungerford
Arranger: Mary Cover
Photographer: Richard Greenly

The rood screen

The rood screen is found in older churches and cathedrals. It is the barrier or gate between the clergy and choir (who in the Middle Ages would have been monks) and the congregation (who, in the Middle Ages would not have actively participated in the service, and were unlikely to even get a seat). A large crucifix often surmounted the screen. Modern worship is more inclusive, and it would be quite surprising to find a church built in the last 100 years with a significant rood screen. That said, where they survive, they are things of beauty and once again lend themselves to tasteful decoration.

Sometimes flowers can be placed in front of, or even on top of a rood screen, where they catch the eye very attractively. Arrangements are usually high and ladders will be needed to gain access. This is a time when artificial plant material can be used. In any event, be sure to choose plant material that is robust and does not need copious amounts of water.

above Decorated rood screen.

Church: The Priory Church of St. Mary and St. Michael, Cartmel
Arrangers: Members of the Church Flower Guild
Photographer: Judith Blacklock

left The baskets wobbled so the inventive designers created a framework of plaited *Rubus* to keep them steady. Inside two giant plastic plant pot bases were placed, one upturned to give about 15cm (6 in) of extra height. The only foliage used within the baskets was *Rubus tricolor* to soften the rim of the baskets. The structures of the two designs were made from bunches of dried wheat, dock and grasses, mostly picked from the fields. *Helianthus* (sunflowers) plucked of their petals, *Buddleja*, *Crocosmia*, *Eustoma* (lisianthus), *Gladiolus*, *Hypericum*, *Ornithogalum* (chincherinchees) and poppy seedheads were added.

Church: Southwell Minster
Arrangers: Wendy Freenan and Gwen White, Dover Beck Flower Club
Photographer: Toby Smith

above A rood screen decorated for a wedding.

Church: St. John's Parish Church, Baildon, West Yorkshire
Arranger: Madeleine Sheen and Lesley St. Ruth
Photographer: Madeleine Sheen

The lectern

Lecterns can be difficult, but are guaranteed to get attention from the congregation. Some are extremely ornate, others have intricate brass work and others have an asymmetric shape.

Some lecterns have interesting columns on which the desk for the Bible is mounted. An arrangement at the base, or a garland round the column, can be an attractive complement at festival times or for example on Bible Sunday.

A simple arrangement at the base of the lectern may be the best option. You could get a metal stand made to stand in front of the lectern (below any carving) or use a low pedestal design.

left The outer structure was made from dried *Foeniculum* (fennel) stems. The interior was composed of dried stems of *Ammi major* (or kexey, as it is known in Lincolnshire), joined together with paper-covered wire. *Taraxacum officinale* (dandelion clocks) and *Clematis tangutica* seedheads were sprayed with spray glue to keep them intact. Also used were small bunches of *Gypsophila* sprayed peach with roses and *Ornithogalum arabicum* in tubes. The overall effect was natural, light and airy.

Church: Southwell Minster
Arrangers: Dorothy Cleal-Harding and Anne Culling, Future Concepts
Photographer: Toby Smith

right A simple but effective arrangement of spathes, sprayed gold, and *Lilium longiflorum*.

Church: Paisley Abbey
Arranger: Eileen Murray
Photographer: Bob Brown

following pages In the Chapel of the Holy Spirit designs in spray trays decorate the front and back of the lectern. Spray trays containing foam were covered with cling film, helping to keep water in the foam and reduce drips.

Church: Cathedral Church of St. Peter and St. Paul, Sheffield
Arranger: Glyn Spencer
Photographer: Oliver Gordon

11 The Sanctuary

The sanctuary is the area beyond the altar rail where the altar usually sits. In many large churches and cathedrals however, in accordance with reforms adopted in recent times, the altar has been moved to a central position in the nave or choir.

In the post reformation Anglican Church, the altar was originally set up only for the Eucharist Service and for many centuries no decoration was allowed. The cross and candlesticks would have been carried by the crucifer and acolytes in a procession. The cross would then be placed at the back of the altar and the candlesticks on each side. The design of the candlesticks is usually in harmony with the cross. This worked well when the priest celebrated facing the altar with his back to the congregation. If the priest is celebrating the Eucharist from behind the altar, facing the congregation, as is the custom today, sometimes the candlesticks are placed on the altar to his left side (as he faces the congregation) and the cross to his right, so that the candles theoretically illuminate the service book from which he reads.

Today, flowers may be seen on the altar. Ensure that arrangements, when completed, do not exceed the height of the cross and do not dominate. Consider also the effect of light as the altar may be seen first in daylight and then in artificial light. If the altar is small it is best to arrange a pedestal to one side. Many members of the clergy prefer that the altar be free of flowers in which case pedestal arrangements are always more suitable.

A reredos is the screen behind the altar, and may have small shelves or ledges on which flowers may be placed. In the United States and many other parts of the world, flowers are often placed here rather than on the altar. The retable is the flat horizontal surface behind the altar.

The altar rail between the choir and the high altar particularly lends itself to garlands for flower festivals but cannot be decorated if people are to receive communion at the rail. If however the altar in general use has been placed in a central position in the nave, then it may be possible to decorate the altar rail.

Remember that the aim is to decorate, enhance and embellish the altar but never to overwhelm or distract from its centrality.

left A framework of stems provides support for individual orchid heads in glass tubes.
Church: Alden Beisen
Arrangers: Stef Adriaenssens
Photographer: Judith Blacklock

Altar vases

Many altar vases are copies of ones used centuries ago for perhaps one stem of *Lilium candidum* – the Madonna lily. They look best arranged simply, perhaps using only a few stems. The mechanics are not easy because such altar vases are tall and with a very narrow opening and they will probably have been gifted. As they are commonly of brass, copper or silver the greatest care must be taken in selecting the mechanics so as not to scratch them.

There are several ways of supporting the flowers.

- Fill two thirds of the vase with clean sand or fine gravel. This gives extra weight, which is good for stability. It also means that a pinholder or a crumpled ball of chicken wire can be placed on top. Water should be poured on the sand until there is about 5cm (2in) of clear water on top. Deep sand, without a pinholder, or wire netting, will often support stems if they are not heavy.

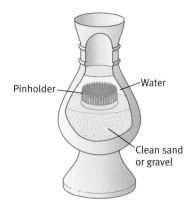

Pinholder — — Water

Clean sand or gravel

- If there is no danger of harming the precious metal, a candle cup may be secured with florists' fix to the top of the vase. A piece of foam (capped with chicken wire if you want extra support) can then be placed in the candle cup.

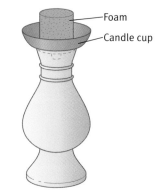

— Foam

— Candle cup

- Cut a stout pole the length of the container plus 1cm ($^1/_2$in). Screw a flat piece of wood onto the top of the pole and place the pole in the altar vase. Arrange the flowers in a low dish taped on to the wooden platform, making sure you hide the pole.

previous pages The water lily painting is reflected in the arrangement in the Airman's Chapel at Southall Minster. The clever use of blue and silver metallic wire gives the effect of rippling water but does not distract from the central message.

Church: Southwell Minster
Arrangers: Stamford Flower Club
Photographer: Toby Smith

right Using the method above, the altar vase is able to provide the perfect container for a large number of flowers skilfully arranged.

Church: St. Paul's Church, Knightsbridge
Arranger: John Chennell
Photographer: Lyndon Parker

- Turn the vase upside down (with permission) and place a container on the base. Secure it well.

- Use a straw circle and strong sticks to support a piece of foam centrally and position a large church candle on the foam. Arrange your flowers around the candle, supported by the straw circle.

- Use large gauge chicken wire about 30cm (12in) wide and 60cm (24in) long, forced into the neck of the vase, to support the flowers. Again, take care that the chicken wire does not scratch valuable vessels.

right A straw ring adds a different dimension to this arrangement of flowers in an altar vase.

Church: St. Paul's Church, Knightsbridge
Arranger: John Chennell
Photographer: Lyndon Parker

above The magnificent painting behind the altar needs little embellishment. *Lilium longiflorum* in altar vases complements the altar painting perfectly.

Church: St. Mary and St. Michael's Church, Great Urswick
Arrranger: Ada Wood
Photographer: Judith Blacklock

following pages
A simple but beautiful design of lilies on the altar.

Church: Southwell Minster
Arranger: Anita Butt
Photographer: Toby Smith

right The orange and pink tones of the *Rosa* 'Cherry Brandy' link with the colour of the pink *Alstroemeria*. Together they provide the perfect complement to the warm tones of the wood panelling behind the altar.

Church: Church of the Advent, Boston
Arranger: Tom Sopko
Photographer: Matt Samolis

right The design had to be big and bright so that it could be seen at the entrance to this magnificent cathedral. The organ pipes in the designs on the steps were made from cardboard rolls that hold fabric. These were covered in corrugated cardboard, fabric or Polyfilla® to produce different textures. The musical notes, uniting the individual designs, were created from manipulated *Phormium tenax* leaves. The flowers on the altar were arranged in a rise and fall effect to depict the multitude of high and low notes that the cathedral organ can produce.

Church: Liverpool Cathedral
Arranger: Muriel Simpson
Photographer: Graham Rodger

below The beauty and clean lines of the contemporary altar of green Westmorland slate, designed by Robert Potter, are undisturbed by the placement of a tapestry of plant material at the base.

Church: Chelmsford Cathedral
Arrangers: Wickham Bishops Flower Club
Photographer: David Lloyd

Designs for the foot of the altar

A good design for the foot of the altar, facing the congregation, is the landscape design. It is only suitable during services if the clergy celebrate from behind the altar or from the north end (a practice still occasionally seen, though now rather rare). This style of design creates a strong impact with minimal plant material. It can also be used on the altar if it is not in service but again care must be taken not to rise above the arms of the cross.

Tip

Keep the flowers in scale with each other. Sunflowers, *Gladiolus* and *Hydrangea* are all good choices for creating a strong, bold landscape design that can be easily seen from a distance.

The colours of the Church

It is the custom of the Church to mark the season and festivals by using specific colours for the vestments and for altar cloths. There are many possible choices but below are the four colours which are commonly used. You will need to take this into account when planning the flowers.

- **White, yellow or gold** is used at times of particular joy and praise. White is the 'official' liturgical colour and the yellow and gold are included as a matter of interpretation. It is the colour for the Christmas and Easter seasons, for great gospel commemorations like the Transfiguration, Trinity Sunday and festivals of the Virgin Mary.

- **Purple** is the colour of repentance, for recognising the frailty of our human nature. It is used during Advent and Lent, often for funerals, although white may be chosen as a sign of praise for the gift of eternal life.

- **Red** commemorates the martyrs who shed their blood and died for their faith. It is also the colour for Pentecost, when the power of the Holy Spirit came in tongues of fire, as well as feasts of apostles and evangelists.

- **Green** is the colour in general use between Trinity Sunday and Advent and in the weeks after Epiphany. It is the colour of nature in the world created and sustained by God, a reminder that the environment, which we too often take for granted, is itself holy. It is a gentle, restful colour which helps us to feel the calm assurance of the love that is all around us. For festivals and Saints' days falling between Trinity Sunday and Advent, the liturgical colour reverts to white (including yellow and gold).

right The colour of the flowers on the reredos is in total harmony with the altar cloth.
Church: St. Illtyd's, Llantwit Major
Arrangers: Glenys Davies, Thelma Holmes and Trixie Randell
Photographer: Pamela Lewis

below "How great is God Almighty, Who has done all things well." This was the theme that inspired Jean Seagrave in this beautiful uplifting arrangement in white, yellow and gold to complement the embroidered altar cloth.
Church: All Saints Church, Banstead
Arranger: Jean Seagrave
Photographer: Mike Pannett

The United States of America

In the United States, there are thousands of different kinds of churches in which the use of flowers differs considerably depending upon the tradition and theology of their worship practices. Church architectural design ranges from simple, austere spaces to more decorated sanctuaries with extensive adornments such as stained glass windows, carved woodwork and marble. Altar arrangements in the larger churches and cathedrals tend to be more elaborate.

On pages 232–239 Laura Iarocci, Chair of the Flower Guild at The Cathedral of St. Philip in Atlanta, Georgia explains how typical designs are created for Festivals and special occasions. She adds that a recent trend among brides is to request festival arrangements for their wedding ceremonies. An additional fee is charged for this as extra flowers and mechanics are required to accomplish these designs.

above Soft, white hydrangeas are placed low around the brim of classic urns. Tall blue and white larkspur were added to create a vertical dimension in the soaring cathedral space. A low box filled with complementary material links the two sides of the arrangemet and gives the illusion of a much larger arrangement.

Church: The Cathedral of St. Philip, Atlanta, GA
Arranger: Josh Borden
Photographer: George Westinghouse

Festival arrangements

Arrangements for high festivals can be spread across the entire retable, the area behind the altar. The mass of flowers used in this festival style of arrangement creates a dramatic impact which accentuates the cross. The arrangements can be designed with the tallest flowers on the outside and the rest of the flowers in descending heights towards the cross. Alternatively, the area behind the cross can have the tallest flowers and the arrangement would descend away from the cross. This style is particularly appropriate at Pentecost when creating the illusion of flames surrounding the cross. Festival arrangements can also create the look of a naturally growing garden. Such a festival arrangement is accomplished by assembling a collection of low dishes across the altar.

following pages A vertical garden was created to celebrate Easter and springtime in Atlanta. Flowers were placed in groups and vertically as they would grow in nature. Double cherry blossoms add height and drama. Flowers were inserted into rectangular boxes with foam or vases. Rocks and lichen covered logs create the sense of flowers springing up in a garden and also help to hide the containers.

Church: The Cathedral of St. Philip, Atlanta, GA
Arrangers: Victoria Denson, Laura Iarocci and Harriet Segars
Photographer: George Westinghouse

Step by step

Festival arrangement

You will need
- collection of low, rectangular, well weighted dishes (preferably ceramic so they do not flip over) each holding one brick of foam with room for watering around the edges.
- low, round plastic dish 30–35cm (12–14in) filled with a denser foam (OASIS® Premium). The depth of the containers should not be greater than the depth of the reredos. The foam should rise well above the rim of the container.
- pots of trailing ivy (optional)
- foliage (greenery) – a variety of seasonally available foliage to gently cover the foam.
- flowers – depending upon the space to be covered use 5–10 stems of four or five varieties of flowers. Include round, focal flowers such as *Helianthus* (sunflowers), *Gerbera*, peonies or roses together with spray flowers such as *Chamelaucium* (wax flower) or x *Solidaster*.

Method

1 Set rectangular boxes across the altar. Place the round plastic dish in the middle, under the cross. The boxes do not need to touch one another.

2 Fill the boxes with foam and tape to secure.

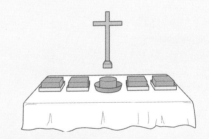

3 If using trailing ivy, place the pots between the containers and cover with moss or stones.

4 Insert the tallest greenery and flowers. Begin at the highest point of the arrangement and use these flowers to create the shape of the design, either ascending towards or descending from the cross.

5 Cover the base of the arrangement with a variety of greenery. Use the foliage, moss or stones to span the gaps between the boxes.

6 Add the focal flowers, concentrating them in the centre of the arrangement.

7 Fill in any gaps with one to three different varieties of flowers.

Tips

- The quantity of boxes needed depends upon the span of space to be covered. Potted ivy, rocks or logs are sometimes tucked into the spread of flowers.

- Heavy glass vases filled with water can be used in between the boxes to hold blooming branches or flowers which survive best in water rather than foam.

- Garden foliage adds a lushness and texture to these arrangements.

Festival columns

The columns of the reredos can be used to add height and colour to a festival design. Column flowers require a significant amount of mechanics so they are typically used for only major festivals. Boxes are placed on the counter between the columns and filled with flowers to create a continuous design of flowers.

The basic mechanics for festival columns are foam bricks attached to the front of a column. Since most churches will not allow nail holes on the face of a reredos, a system to anchor the foam to the back or sides needs to be created. Strips of wood with cup hooks attached can be anchored to the back or side of the columns. Cages filled with foam are then wired to the cup hooks. There are two methods described, one using OASIS® Raquettes and the other OASIS® FLORACAGE® (USA)/Florette (Europe).

Raquettes cover the entire span of a column because they can stack upon one another. The disadvantage of Raquettes is that they come covered in plastic to minimize evaporation and cannot be watered after the initial soaking. However water can be added using chemistry pipettes or syringes. Raquettes are easily penetrated by hard stems although it is difficult to use them with softer stems of flowers such as tulips.

As an alternative, FLORACAGE® (USA)/OASIS® Florette (Europe) can be used. The advantage of the cages is that they can then be watered with a watering can as needed. They can also be lighter in weight because not as much foam is needed. This is also a preferred mechanic if the stems are soft. The downside to the cages is that there are gaps between them that must be covered. The cages are not inexpensive and the used foam can be removed and replaced with fresh and in this way used time and time again.

Step by step

Festival columns

Using OASIS® FLORACAGE® Holder (USA)/ OASIS® Florette (Europe) or equivalent

You will need
- OASIS® FLORACAGE® Holder or OASIS® Florette – these have a strong rigid plastic moulded base and handle. The base holds foam covered by an open plastic cage. They come in three sizes, mini, midi and maxi. Other manufacturers such as Artesia® (USA) provide a similar product.
- strip of wood
- cup hooks
- reel wire

Method

1 Wire the cages to a strip of wood with cup hooks.

2 Place the strip to the front of the column and secure with wire to the wood strip on the back or sides of the column or the reredos. There is no need to use nails.

3 Set rectangular boxes with foam bricks on the retable to cover the span between the columns.

4 Lightly cover the foam on the columns and the table with greenery using a variety of materials. Use greenery to span the gaps between the cages.

5 Add focal flowers spreading up and down the column and across the table.

6 Fill any gaps with additional flowers.

left and following pages Festival columns
Church: The Cathedral of St. Philip, Atlanta, GA
Arrangers: Barbara Beach, Darrin Ellis-May, Victoria Denson, Grace Foster, Leslie Heinz and Laura Iarocci.
Photographer: George Westinghouse

Using a Raquette

You will need
- OASIS® Raquette(s). Determine the length of the floral columns to calculate the number of Raquettes needed.
- thin long strip of wood
- cup hooks
- bark wire or paper covered twine

Method

1 Soak the Raquette(s) in deep water until it (they) rests horizontally on the water.

2 Insert cup hooks at 30cm (12in) intervals down a thin wood strip.

3 Find a discrete spot to nail or screw the strip of wood to the back or sides of the columns of the reredos. The strip can be removed after use. Instead of nailing the wood strip into the reredos, a bungie cord or bark wire can be wrapped around it to secure it to the column. If possible, the wood strip should be anchored at the top, middle and bottom of the column. If the wood strip cannot be attached to the reredos (or there is no reredos), a plastic container, filled with cement, can be used as an anchor. Measure and place the wood strip in this plastic container first at the back.

4 Place one Raquette on the front of the column resting it on the surface of the reredos table. Secure the Raquette by wrapping bark wire or paper covered wire around the Raquette and tying on to the cup hooks. If appropriate stack additional Raquettes on top of the first one, securing each in a similar manner to the strip with hooks.

5 Add focal flowers spreading up and down the column and across the table. Fill any gaps with additional flowers.

On high days and special occasions, arrangers have the opportunity
to really show some imagination and excellence.

For many, the pedestal is an essential arrangement for every Sunday when
flowers are permitted. Sometimes it is the only arrangement in evidence.
To be seen and appreciated it needs to be big, even on a normal Sunday.

Large arrangements require large and structurally sound mechanics.
High festivals of the church provide the opportunity to create something
special, themed to the event being celebrated.

Weddings need careful attention, and can be lavish when accompanied
by a commensurate budget.

Finally, the church is a lovely place to hold a flower festival. Creating one takes
time, organisation and lots of willing helpers but the effort is always worthwhile.

Large Arrangements
and
Special Events

12 Pedestal Designs

The pedestal arrangement is perhaps the most important and popular design in church flower arranging. It is created in churches up and down the country every Sunday outside Lent.

It can be created weekly for Sundays, for festivals, weddings and just about every other occasion. It can be positioned in front of a pillar, at the entrance, in a side chapel or before the font but it is most often seen close to the altar, to accentuate the focal point of the church.

As everyone who has done church flowers knows, stable, effective mechanics are essential to keep flowers safely in position and show them off in a large location. For basic pedestal and plinth designs the mechanics are relatively simple.

Pedestals

A pedestal is the term given to a stand that is tall and relatively slender. It is often made from decorative ironwork but could also be made from wood or another material.

If you use a decorative ironwork stand, it must be strong and able to bear the weight of a large heavy piece of soaked foam and numerous stems. They often have an integral container at the top, but I prefer to insert a plastic bowl inside this container so that it can be easily removed and the pedestal moved to another position.

Plinths

A plinth is a solid structure and consequently more in keeping with the volume of plant material required for a church display. They are reasonably easy to construct. They are often made of plywood on a wooden frame but can be made of stone, fibreglass or cement. They are very stable but those made from heavier materials will be difficult to move around. A plastic bowl, containing foam, is placed on the top of the plinth.

left A pedestal created from three carpet rolls of different heights glued together to create one stand. This has then been placed on an upright wooden post, with a heavy base for stability. The stand was then painted with textured masonry paint. Holes were made in the sides of each tube and bowls wired on. The beautiful flowers and foliage cascade down from the three levels.

Church: Temple Church, London
Arranger: Susan Phillips
Photographer: Lyndon Parker

below A pedestal design on a
decorative ironwork stand.

Church: Cathedral Church of
St. Peter and St. Paul, Sheffield
Arranger: Glyn Spencer
Photographer: Oliver Gordon

right A traditional design in
an urn.

Church: Cathedral Church of
St. Peter and St. Paul, Sheffield
Arranger: Jane Steeples
Photographer: Oliver Gordon

Arranging the plant material

The plant material should be arranged so that it can be viewed from three sides – the front and the two sides. If placed near the altar, it can be seen by those sitting in the nave, choir and in any side pews. It is important that the flowers are arranged three-dimensionally. This is achieved by taking plant material around to the back of the design to create depth. It is vital to have actual and visual stability. Plant material to the rear contributes to both.

In a classic pedestal it is important to build up a strong structure or framework of foliage before attempting to add a single flower.

right 'A Garden for all Seasons' – a magnificent pedestal design using only garden foliage.
Arranger: Mary Robinson
Photographer: Dick Makin

20 tips for creating a successful pedestal design

1 On the first occasion you create a pedestal, take along a friend to give moral and physical support and artistic judgement. Ask him or her to advise, from a distance, as this view is often different from that close up.

2 Be careful using dark blue or purple flowers as they appear to disappear if viewed at a distance or in poor light.

3 If you wish to make a matching pair of arrangements for the altar, divide the flowers and foliage equally before starting to arrange.

4 Keep the area around the pedestal design tidy. It is very difficult to create good design in the middle of a muddle.

5 The most effective pedestals usually use large bold plant material.

6 All the stems should appear to radiate from the core of the foam.

7 Pedestals should be arranged where they will stand. Their weight and sheer size means it is difficult to keep them intact when moved.

8 When creating your first pedestal, plan on up to three hours with a reserve of time in hand. It is amazing how quickly the times goes and if there is a wedding planned at noon, panic will quickly set in!

9 Make your first placement tall and central to give stability.

10 Ensure the overall shape is triangular.

11 The strongest, largest flower should be placed two thirds of the way down from the tallest stem and in the central area.

12 Ensure there is a leaf under the lowest flowers otherwise these flowers may appear to be falling out of the arrangement.

13 Avoid a horizontal line of flowers across the centre of the arrangement.

14 Check that the flowers are in scale – spray carnations only work well in relatively small designs.

15 Use flowers at the sides and to a certain extent at the back to give depth and balance.

16 The pedestal arrangement should be wider at the bottom than the top to give good balance.

17 If you are using white flowers against a white wall ensure that there is a backing of green so that the flowers will be noticed.

18 If you are using lilies for a festival or special occasion, then purchase them at least five days before when they are in bud so that you are assured they are open on the day. There are no tricks to getting them open if they are immature.

19 Ensure that the stamens of lilies are removed before the beginning of the service to that there is no chance of them marking any robes.

20 Good lighting will make every design look better.

above A pedestal design with a lower placement. Both placements are in close contact to give continuity of rhythm.

Church: Chelmsford Cathedral
Arrangers: Chelmsford Cathedral Flower Guild
Photographer: David Lloyd

right A modern pedestal design for a flower festival depicting grandfather and grandmother long case clocks.

Church: Lincoln Cathedral
Arranger: Geraldine Forrest
Photographer: Dick Makin

Seasonal flowers and foliage for pedestal designs

Spring

Outline foliage

alder catkins
Camellia
Corylus (hazel)
Eucalyptus cinerea
Photinia x fraseri 'Red Robin'
Rhododendron
Ribes (flowering currant)
Sorbus (whitebeam)
Tilia (lime)

Bold leaves

Aspidistra
Bergenia
Fatsia japonica

Line flowers

Lilium (in bud)
Syringa (lilac)
Viburnum opulus

Round flowers

Anthurium
Chrysanthemum (bloom)
Gerbera
Hippeastrum
Lilium (open lilies)
Paeonia (peony)

Spray flowers

Acacia (mimosa)
Alstroemeria
Chamelaucium (waxflower)
Cytisus (broom)

Summer

Outline foliage

Camellia
Cotinus (smoke bush)
Fagus (beech)
Philadelphus
Ribes (flowering currant)

Bold leaves

Aspidistra
Bergenia
Hosta

Line flowers

Antirrhinum (snapdragon)
Buddleja
Delphinium
Digitalis (foxglove)
Eremurus (foxtail lily)

Round flowers

Anthurium
Chrysanthemum (bloom)
Gerbera
Helianthus (sunflower)
Hydrangea
Paeonia (peony)

Spray flowers

Alstroemeria
Gypsophila (baby's breath)
Matricaria
Solidago (golden rod)

Autumn

Outline foliage

Cotinus (smoke bush)
Fagus (beech)
Ribes (flowering currant)
Viburnum opulus 'Roseum'
   (guelder rose)

Bold leaves

Aspidistra
Fatsia japonica
Parthenocissus tricuspidata
   (Boston ivy)

Line flowers

Delphinium
Gladiolus
Liatris
Physalis (Chinese lanterns)

Round flowers

Chrysanthemum (bloom)
Dahlia
Gerbera
Helianthus (sunflower)
Hydrangea
Rosa

Spray flowers, fruits and berries

Aster
Chamelaucium (waxflower)
Rosa (rose) hips
Solidago (golden rod)
Sorbus (rowan) berries
Symphoricarpos (snowberry)
   fruits

Winter

Outline foliage

Camellia
Eucalyptus cinerea
Laurus nobilis
Rhododendron
Photinia x fraseri 'Red Robin'
Pseudotsuga (Douglas fir)

Bold leaves

Aspidistra
Bergenia
Fatsia
Hedera helix

Line flowers

Cymbidium orchids
Ilex (holly) berries
   (the deciduous form)
Liatris
Lilium (lily) in bud

Round flowers

Anthurium
Dianthus (carnations)
Hippeastrum (amaryllis) – open
Dianthus (carnations)
Lilium (lily) open

Spray flowers

Chamelaucium (waxflower)
Hypericum (St. John's wort)

right A bold, contemporary pedestal design.
Arranger: Ashover Flower Arrangers Club
Photographer: Judith Blacklock

Step by step

Pedestal arrangement

You will need

A. Mechanics

- pedestal or plinth.
- container to take the foam. I like to use a plastic bowl or pot. Select a green container as these are easier to disguise than white ones. The average pedestal design needs a bowl approximately 20–25 cm (8–10 in) in diameter and about 10 cm (4 in) deep. For a smaller design a dog's large water bowl works well.
- floral foam – OASIS® 'Jumbo', or 'high density foam' as it called in the USA, is strongly recommended. It will support heavier stems and in the UK is available in either one or three units in a box that could also take 20 bricks. I use half of a block that is sold three to a box. If you do not have access to 'Jumbo' foam, use two standard bricks. A large piece of foam, when wet, will stand secure on its own and will need no tape, frog or additional support.
- chicken wire to give additional support. Only use chicken wire if you are using two pieces of standard foam rather than a single piece of stronger foam or if you are creating a very large design. It should not be pulled tight over the foam but should stand slightly proud.
- extension cones (optional).
- if you are preparing a pedestal that will be taller than you are, steps or a box to stand on will be required.

B. Plant material

- outline foliage – lightly branching stems that overall produce a linear form. This will create the initial outline/structure of the arrangement.
- bold, smooth textured leaves.
- line flowers to take colour from the outline edge into the centre of the design. Line flowers can be diverse in form but overall the effect should be linear with flowers coming down at least part of the stem.
- round flowers to give strong focal interest and hold the eye.
- spray flowers to fill in and complete the design.
- additional foliage to give contrast of shape, form and texture – the amount needed will depend on the size of the pedestal design.

Church: St. Paul's Church, Knightsbridge
Arranger: Judith Blacklock
Photographer: Judith Blacklock

Method

1 Soak the foam by placing it in water deeper than the piece you are soaking. You will need access to a large sink or container such as a dustbin – or even the bath – so that the water is deeper than the piece of foam being soaked. OASIS® Jumbo foam takes much longer to sink to its level in water. It is extremely heavy when fully saturated so make sure you can remove the foam easily from where it is being soaked.

2 Place the foam in the container. The foam needs to rise well above the rim (approximately one and a half times the height of the container above the rim). The weight of the foam should be sufficient to keep it in place without the need of additional mechanics, but do add tape if you feel this would make the foam more secure. The piece of foam should be of a size that can be wedged in the container but with space left for water to be easily added.

3 Place the first stem of outline foliage in the foam two thirds of the way back in the centre. This is stem A. It should be angled slightly backwards. Most of the plant material will be coming forward, so to achieve good visual balance placing the first stem angled slightly backwards, rather than upright, gives stability. The height of this stem will establish the finished height of the pedestal.

4 The next two stems you add will create a triangle ABC. Stems B and C should be two-thirds the length of stem A. One should be placed out of each side of the foam, in the central area. The stems should be angled slightly downwards. The angle should not be so sharp that they give the impression of dropping out.

5 Stems D and E are very important. They should be positioned out of the top of the foam so that if an imaginary line was drawn from A to B and A to C, stems D and E would not extend beyond this line. They are approximately half the length of stem A.

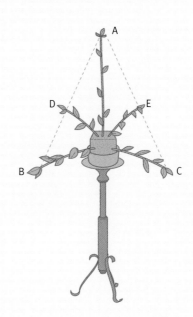

6 F and G are two short stems coming from the front of the foam. These do not extend down to an imaginary line between B and C. They are shorter and with B and C will create a gentle crescent. If these stems are long they will create a design that will appear unbalanced even if it is not!

7 At this point I like to add a stem *behind* stem A to reinforce it (stem H). This will be slightly shorter than stem A. This gives visual and actual balance front to back.

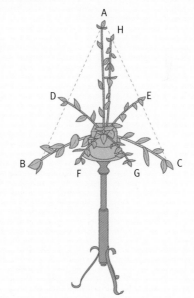

8 There should be no large, bare expanses of foam. If there are then add additional stems of foliage, always angling from the core of the foam.

9 Add bold leaves with a smooth texture. Again, these should be angled from the central core of the foam.

10 At this point you will probably still be able to see the foam but plant material will predominate and you will have to look hard. Do not add flowers until you are satisfied you have a strong foliage outline.

11 Place the first stem of line flowers centrally to reinforce foliage stem A. It should be just short of the tip of the foliage. Take other stems through the design following the shape.

12 Strong, bold flowers with a round form are the next placement. These are placed in the central area, approximately two thirds of the way down from the tallest stem.

13 Fill in with spray flowers and any other flowers or foliage you may have available.

Cones/extension tubes

If you are using cones or extension tubes to give additional height, you need to place these in position after point 2. These can be used individually, with the end pushed into the foam or taped singly or with several around a pole if you wish to arrange a very large pedestal.

If you are using chicken wire, place the stick through this into the foam. Fill every tube with water. If the tubes are high on the stick, you may wish to fill the tubes before placing the stick in the pinholder or foam. Make sure the stick of tubes is secure and it may be necessary to squeeze the wire netting around the stick. It is important to conceal the tubes and sticks with foliage or flowers placed in front of them. For this reason, use as few tubes as possible to provide height to the flowers unless you are creating a tightly massed design.

Tip

It is extremely important to remember that the pedestal arrangement must be balanced from side to side, top to bottom and front to back. Never add a stem that will create greater imbalance than before it is added.

right A glorious pedestal design using different forms and textures, positioned in front of a mellow stone wall.

Church: The Cathedral of St. Philip, Atlanta, GA
Arrangers: Victoria Denson and Laura Iarocci
Photographer: George Westinghouse

Beehive design

A 'beehive' pedestal has its origin in the USA. The mechanics, which are simple, inexpensive and effective, enable the designer to create a cascading design.

You will need a plinth or pedestal with a flat top. A large piece of foam, cut from an OASIS® Jumbo block, is placed in the centre of a large, shallow saucer.

An upturned hanging basket, of a size to fit snugly inside the saucer and over the foam, is then wired in place. If the saucer has a rim, it is easier to wire this to the basket. Plant material can be inserted through the lower part of the wire frame to give a trailing/cascading effect. Height can be created or the design kept low with the emphasis on the downward movement.

left From the palest tints to much deeper tones this pedestal design of roses shows the effect that can be achieved through using one flower with contrasting foliage. The roses used were from top to bottom *Rosa* 'Avalanche', *R.* 'Pink Avalanche', *R.* 'Aqua' and at the bottom *R.* 'Cool Water'. The foliage was mainly grey and included *Brachyglottis*, *Eucalyptus*, *Hosta* 'Blue Wedgewood', *Danae racemosa* and some deep red *Codiaeum* (croton) leaves.

Church: Southwell Minster
Arranger: Shelagh Barnes
Photographer: Toby Smith

above This multi-coloured design contains *Anthurium* 'Nexia', *Chrysanthemum* 'Anastasia', *Dianthus. Lilium*, *Rosa* 'Evergreen' and *Zantedeschia*.

Church: Southwell Minster
Arranger: Ann Bull
Photographer: Toby Smith

13 More Mechanics

This is the chapter that may be of most interest to those of you who are reasonably experienced in arranging flowers for the church but would like to know more.

In order to create large designs, mechanics can be elaborate. It is this technical aspect which particularly worries arrangers. They must not feel inadequate just because they do not know how to suspend a ball of flowers from the ceiling or create a 6m (20ft) arrangement. With the help of this chapter you or a handy friend may be able to construct most of the mechanics described. However a carpenter or metal worker would be able to do the task with ease and the church may well come up with a budget to help you with the cost.

This has been the most difficult chapter in the book for me to write and without the help of inspirational mechanic makers it would just not have come to fruition. You never know there may be someone in the congregation with these skills who is just waiting to be asked to help.

There is room for imagination and resourcefulness when creating mechanics, but you must be sure that what you create can take the weight of the flowers that you use. They should not topple over even if knocked or pushed. Once you have the mechanics you can create your own designs that will have people wondering at your mastery.

Firstly I discuss the mechanics for constructing tall columns of flowers. These may be created anywhere in the church and consequently do not fall under any specific chapter. I then relate captions to photographs with a brief explanation of the mechanics and how the design was put together. These ideas are those created by church flower arrangers and we can all learn from their expertise. If you have any other ideas do get in touch. I would be delighted to add to the next edition of the book.

left Floral curtain of carnations threaded onto fishing wire.
Church: Salisbury Cathedral
Arrangers: Angela Turner and members of 17 churches of the diocese of Salisbury
Photographer: Ash Mills

Columns

The descriptions below are for free standing columns but they can be adapted so that they are attached to the fabric of the church, perhaps with paper covered wire, florists' waterproof ribbon, pipe cleaners or wire covered with sisal so that no damage is caused.

Method A

This structure provides points from which spray trays or other florists' special mechanics can be hung. This structure can be used time and time again. See the step by step instructions on the right.

Method B

Ask the local blacksmith to create a long slender open mechanic of mild steel or decorative ironwork that is 10–15cm (4–6in) wide and as tall as needed.
Reinforce horizontally at regular intervals to give added strength and to give bases on which containers may be placed.
The base of the stand should be on a hinge that can open and shut firmly and be fitted with a locking device.
Alternatively, the metal can be bolted permanently to the base.

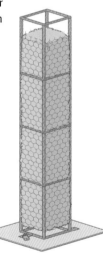

Fill the centre with bricks of wet foam, one on top of the other. Do note that a large volume of water will be displaced from the foam so make sure this design is outdoors or is prepared well in advance. Pin *Sphagnum* moss over the foam so that it is more or less hidden. Cover with 2.5cm (1in) chicken wire to give extra support. Add your flowers.

Step by step

Free-standing column of flowers with hidden structure

You will need

- pole or straight branch of required height perhaps 1.5–3m (5–10ft). The thickness should be at least sufficient to provide stiffness. A square sectioned pole is easiest to use. The idea is that the pole will be totally covered in plant material.
- nails 3–5cm (1–2in) in length
- 4 sturdy shelf brackets or a Christmas tree stand or Metpost® stand/holder
- screws
- spirit level or plumb line
- spray trays, OASIS® FLORACAGES® Holder or OASIS® Florette foam holders
- foliage and flowers

Method

1 Screw the shelf brackets to the base of the pole thus creating feet so that it stands by itself. To provide additional weight and stability, you can screw a square base of 5 or 7 ply to the brackets. Use the spirit level or plumb line to check that the pole is vertical when placed on its feet or base. Adjust if required.

2 Lay the pole horizontally on a bench or table with the feet hanging over the edge. If you can use a vice to hold the pole, so much the better. Otherwise, you may have to get someone to hold while you hammer. If you are using a Christmas tree stand wait until the end of the process to secure the pole, so that it is easier to manoeuvre.

3 Starting 15cm (6in) from the base, hammer in two nails, one on each side. About 1cm ($^3/_8$in) should protrude. Moving up another 25cm (10in), hammer in two more nails at right angles to the first two, again on opposing sides. Move up the pole at 25cm (10in) intervals, hammering in nails on alternate faces.

4 You can now use the nails to hang spray trays containing foam, starting from the bottom. It is often wise to wire the top of the pole to some nearby stable structure (column, screen etc.) as they can get very top heavy.

5 Cover the foam with foliage. Add your flowers. Avoid working systematically from top to bottom or bottom to top but randomly to create good balance.

left Two columns of flowers flank the entrance to Grace Church.

Church: Grace Church, Charleston, SC
Arrangers: Members of the Grace Church Flower Guild
Photographer: Wally Breidis

Method C

This is for a tall free-standing column that is visible. Where a larger cross-sectioned column is required, a solid wooden pole will be too heavy. It consists of a hollow plinth that can be decorated with garlands or other hanging arrangements.

Step by step

Free-standing column of flowers with visible structure

You will need
- 4 identical pieces of 3-ply to form the sides (see directions below)
- 4 identical pieces of square section timber the same length as the board, 2–3cm (1in) square
- square piece of 5-ply, sides equal to the width of the hardboard 3-ply. (This is the top.)
- square piece of 5-ply, at least 2 or 3 times wider than the top. (This is the base.)
- 6 screws 2–2.5cm (1in)
- nails 2–3cm (1in)
- angle brackets or irons
- spirit level or plumb line
- emulsion paint
- spray trays
- foliage and flowers

Method

1 The dimensions will depend on the space to be filled and the ambitions of the arranger. A short column would be around 1.5m (5ft) and would be 10cm (4in) square. A large one would be 3m (10ft) high and would be 20cm (8in) square.

2 Nail each piece of timber flush to the edge of a side.

3 Nail the four sides, now edged with the timber together to form a square column.

4 Add the top, screwing it to the ends of the four pieces of timber. Ensure that the column is square in section.

5 The base can be attached by brackets or angle irons. Alternatively use 4 pieces of 5cm x 5cm (2in x 2in) timber to surround the base of the plinth and then screw each of them into both the base and the column. Either way use a spirit level or plumb line to ensure that the column is vertical.

6 Insert a nail, a screw, or a screwed ring into the centre of the top of the column. This will provide the support for all the material that will hang on and around the column.

7 Paint your column a neutral colour to suit the environment. Stone grey is a good choice.

8 Hang spray trays, swags, or garlands from the ring or screw in the top. Decorate as you wish.

Other ideas from around the world

Extremely tall designs

This design of over 4m (12ft) was one of a pair either side of the magnificent oak doors at Southwell Minster. The bottom mechanic was a ironwork box stand 110cm (43in) high. The second, of the same dimensions, stood on the radiator cover immediately behind. A 1.5m (5ft) pole with two adjustable shelf brackets and a mesh top was fastened to the side of the second stand.

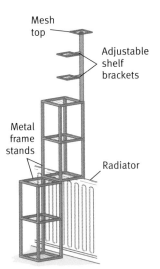

Mesh top

Adjustable shelf brackets

Metal frame stands

Radiator

right

Church: Southwell Minster
Arrangers: South Notts Flower Club
Photographer: Toby Smith

Hanging floral tapestry

This hanging floral tapestry 3m x 2m (10ft x 7ft) was designed to resemble a sunburst, yellow at the centre radiating to oranges and reds at the periphery. The spokes of the rays were fresh cobs of yellow corn. The rays moved from a centre of yellow straw flowers to orange peppers to deeper orange carnations to Chinese lanterns to red peppers, *Gladiolus* and carnations. The light colour borders consisted of green hydrangeas interspersed with loops of cornhusks, the darker border were overlapping *Gaultheria* (salal) leaves.

The materials were fastened to Styrofoam sheets 1.5m x 1m (5ft x 3ft) covered in 1cm ($^1/_2$in) chicken wire. The design was mapped out on the Styrofoam and the appropriate colours were painted so that when the flowers dried and shrivelled the white Styrofoam would not show. The back of each section was reinforced with criss-crossed wooden slats. All the materials were glued or stapled to the sheets. The dove was fashioned from chicken wire for shape, masking tape was used for dimension and then covered with honesty petals. It looked amazing for more than a week.

below

Church: Holy Rosary Church, Toronto
Arrangers: Beth Porter, Dodie Wesley, Garden Club of Toronto members. Design Ralph Neal
Photographer: Bruce Connor

MDF boxes

These boxes were positioned horizontally and vertically around the nave altar of Southwell Minster and filled with flowers for a special festival. The boxes were made of MDF and framed internally with bearers supporting a mesh of fine copper wire to which the plant material was fastened. Inside the box, on the bearers, were foam dishes with some of the plant material inserted in the foam. Other plant material was in orchid tubes and the remainder was plant material that stood well without water.

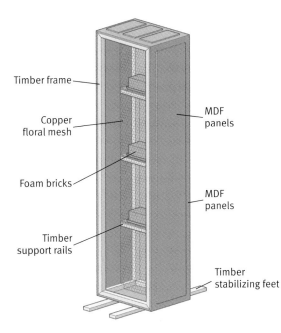

Timber frame

Copper
floral mesh

Foam bricks

Timber
support rails

MDF
panels

MDF
panels

Timber
stabilizing feet

right
Church: Southwell Minster
Arrangers: Diana and Paul Knight and Margaret van Oudheusden
Photographer: Toby Smith

Floral curtains

These glorious floral curtains were created with individual strands of flowers and leaves which had been threaded onto heavy duty fishing line. Each strand was hung individually from cross bars above the crossing about 18m (60ft) high. The plant material used was large laurel leaves and the heads and stems of *Dianthus* (carnation) used separately. The stems were bundled and bound with green raffia. Two or three components were threaded on the wire and then prevented from slipping by a hand made knot (not an easy task but worth the effort). The designer Angela Turner advises that you would need a large open area to create this – cloisters are ideal. Four to five people worked on each strand. Although the lengths of fishing wire were all the same length more plant material was threaded on some of the strands so that the comparative weights would mirror the arch.

The curtain of carnations was quicker to create as carnation heads were simply threaded onto the fishing line. Do make sure that you use a weight of wire that is sufficiently strong that it will not stretch with the weight of the plant material.

Church: Salisbury Cathedral
Arrangers: Angela Turner and members of 17 churches of the diocese of Salisbury
Photographer: Ash Mills (above), Oliver Gordon (right) and Judith Blacklock (below)

Floral carpets

To create their splendid floral carpets – like the one shown opposite – the Garden Club of Toronto uses made to order galvanized metal pans. They are shallow, only 5cm (2in) deep and are painted black. The sides are so inconspicuous that they need no camouflage. The flowers are cut very short and inserted into wet sphagnum moss. The pans are 60cm x 120 cm (2ft x 4ft) and get much too heavy to transport if wet foam is used.

As an alternative brown plastic cafeteria trays are good – they are small, rigid and easy to transport if a thin layer of wet foam is used.

right
Church: Holy Rosary Church, Toronto
Arrangers: Beth Porter, Dodie Wesley, Garden Club of Toronto members.
Design: Ralph Neal
Photographer: Bruce Connor

Hanging baskets

The baskets shown above were made using some round decorative ironwork frames that were specially made for the occasion. These were then filled with foam. The arrangements had to be 3m (10ft) in diameter to make impact. Feathers were lengthened by attaching them to garden canes in a variety of sizes and added to the arrangements of orchids, lilies and *Zantedeschia* (callas). They were suspended with 1cm ($^{1}/_{2}$in) metal link chain.

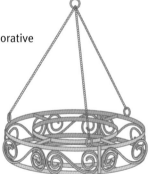

above
Church: Chichester Cathedral
Arrangers: Adine Copeman, Dinny Green, Lorna Marsh and Iona Wheatley
Photographer: Michael Chevis

Hanging shelf

Where there is a horizontal gate, fence or railing, the opportunity exists to hang a support from it. A simple mechanic consists of two identical pieces of timber or plywood about 1cm (¹/₂in) thick at the desired length and approximately 20cm (9in) wide. These are screwed together at right angles. For extra load bearing security, nail a fabric strap at each end, at an angle of 45 degrees to each of the pieces. These two pieces form the back and the shelf of a support.

Add two or three U-shaped metal brackets to the back. The width of the bracket (the bottom of the 'U') should be a little more than the width of the fence, or gate on which the mechanic is to be hung. A spacer of wood will need to be added at the back of the shelf to ensure that the shelf hangs horizontally.

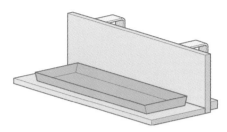

When the shelf is in position and horizontal, tray(s) with foam can be placed on the shelf. It would be wise to fix the trays with florists' fix or some other adhesive. The trays can also be used for a landscape design. Here low plastic trays containing foam were filled with *Anthurium, Dianthus, Gerbera, Gladiolus*, large *Hedera* (ivy) leaves and apples on kebab sticks.

below
Church: Southwell Minster
Arrangers: Newark and District Flower Lovers' Club
Photographer: David Connor

Foliage cones

The basic mechanic for these cones of foliage and apples were two ironwork obelisks from the garden centre placed on plinths of an appropriate size. Foam was cut to shape and fitted inside each obelisk. Moss was pinned to the foam to pad it out where necessary and fill in the gaps. Chicken wire was then used to cover the foam and moss to give additional support. Sprigs of *Skimmia* and variegated *Pittosporum* were used to cover the foam with a band of curled *Aspidistra* at the base. Tape was used to mark a spiral from the top downwards. Bramley apples, impaled on kebab sticks, were then inserted into the line of the spiral. The Bramley apple was found and developed in Southwell in 1809 and has enjoyed success ever since.

right
Church: Southwell Minster
Arranger: Pat Musgrove and members of Mansfield Flower Arrangement Society
Photographer: Judith Blacklock

Decorative urns

Mary Jane Vaughan regularly arranges flowers in Westminster Cathedral, London where the soaring pillars and vast area of this Roman Catholic Cathedral lends itself to tall and stately design. The mechanics for this design are:

- decorative urn on a plinth
- bucket with foam packed inside which fits inside the urn
- a second bucket of the same dimensions with three wooden stakes attached at the sides

The stakes of the second bucket are inserted in the foam of the first so that they create an open column of approximately 1m (40in) between the two.

left

Church: Westminster Cathedral
Arranger: Mary Jane Vaughan
Photographer: Mary Jane Vaughan

Tiered designs

At a flower festival at Salisbury Cathedral a series of tiered designs about 1.8m (6ft) tall with cascading flowers and foliage were arranged using a palette of pastel colours enhanced with the fragrance of freesias. The Sarum 'cake' stand, designed by Roger Hardy, consists of a central tubular stem on a pentagonal base. Sliding onto the tube are a series of steel collars to each of which are welded four arms that, according to their size, support foam rings. The collars are held in place on the stem by a screw which is threaded through the collar and into a hole in the central tube so that they are absolutely secure and there is no risk of them slipping. The rings are held in place on the radial arms by small vertical lugs welded to the arms.

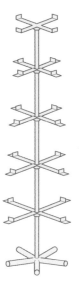

This stand is designed to take 40cm (16in), 37cm (14in), 30cm (12in) and 25cm (10in) rings and a 20cm (8in) posy pad on top. The rings have to be soaked and assembled in sequence starting at the bottom.

right

Church: Salisbury Cathedral
Arrangers: St. John and St. Andrew's, Lower Bemerton.
Photographer: Ash Mills

Large landscape design

For large scale landscape designs custom made containers are probably best but a cheap alternative is the following:

Purchase flat based, plastic guttering with clip on ends, readily available from builders' merchants in varying lengths. This is easily cut to the required length and floral foam blocks can be spaced at intervals to allow for easy watering. If you are using round piping fit the caps of spray paint cans over the ends.

I have used the term 'Landscape' to describe designs with a horizontal emphasis and with some or all of the plant material placed in vertical positions.

right

Church: St. Paul's Church, Knightsbridge
Arranger: John Chennell
Photographer: Lyndon Parker

Contemporary pedestal

Tie a bunch of willow, hazel or coloured cane about 1.5m (5ft) onto a decorative ironwork stand. Fill two square containers with wet foam and place these at a distance from each other, within the twigs. Bring the twigs around them and tie where they meet. Place flowers through the design.

left

Church: St. Mary's Church, Barnes
Arranger: John Chennell
Photographer: Toby Smith

Drainpipe design

Using a Christmas tree stand as a base, you can make a drainpipe design. The square drainpipe can be any length, but for a freestanding design, 1.5m (5ft) is probably the maximum. The top is made from two square pieces of wood. The smaller is sized to fit snugly into the pipe. The larger is approximately 22cm (9in) square. Nail the smaller onto the larger, in the centre. Insert the small square into the top of the pipe. If you want a ledge(s) down the pipe, saw half way through the pipe and slot a board into the cut at an angle.

When arranging the flowers make sure that the design is well balanced. The taller the design the more you must consider stability and security. It is easy to attach the pipe to a church pillar with wire and this will make it more secure. Wider placements at the base will also help to give good physical balance.

right

Church: St. Mary's Church, Barnes
Arranger: John Chennell
Photographer: Toby Smith

Pseudo garland

The angel is sitting on a dark wood pedestal in front of the iron choir screen flanking the entrance gates. Four OASIS® Corso Holders are used for the pseudo garland – two behind the figure, one on top of the pedestal at the feet of the angel and one hanging on the side of the pedestal about one third of the way down. The cages are attached to the screen with plastic cable ties. The one on top of the pedestal is wired on and the one to the side is hanging on a small hook. Black plastic bin liner was used to protect the figure and pedestal from water damage. The plant material used was *Artemesia ludoviciana, Cocculus laurifolius*, seeded *Eucalyptus, Gaultheria* (salal tips) and leather leaf. The flowers were *Alstroemeria*, Asiatic lilies and *Chrysanthemum*.

left

Church: Church of the Advent, Boston, MA
Arranger: Tom Sopko
Photographer: Matt Samolis

Tip

Corso holders are open cages that enable you to insert foam on all sides. At the present time they are only available in the USA. As an alternative you could use an OASIS Dekorette or OASIS Mini Florette. You could wrap half bricks in a small mesh chicken wire but be sure it will not scratch the fabric of the church.

Spiralled topiary

Two conifer spiral trees, 2m (7ft) high, were the foundation of this design. Floral swags were then created by using 3m (10ft) long strips of chicken wire, encasing foam wrapped in cling film. Greenery was inserted whilst these were on the ground. They were then lifted into place and coiled into the spirals of the trees and secured with paper-covered wire. The flowers were added in situ.

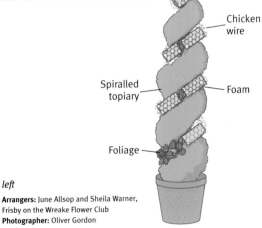

Chicken wire

Spiralled topiary

Foam

Foliage

left

Arrangers: June Allsop and Sheila Warner, Frisby on the Wreake Flower Club
Photographer: Oliver Gordon

Easter cross

To make an Easter cross like this take two pieces of timber. Cut a half lap mid-way on the shorter piece and at the appropriate height on the taller piece. Bolt or screw the two pieces together and place in a Christmas tree stand.

Wrap chicken wire around. Cover the ends of the daffodils in stem tape to keep in the moisture and push through the chicken wire.

left
Church: St. Mary's Church, Windermere

Photographer: Judith Blacklock

Tall moveable designs

The 2.5m (8ft) mechanics for these tall moveable
designs was composed of a slim wooden round pole
about 5–7.5cm (2–3in) in diameter. This was
attached with screws to a square wooden base about
20in square and three quarters of an inch thick. This
was placed in a planter to which four casters had
been placed on the underside. Bricks were placed
over the base, inside the planter to give stability.
Three plywood shelves were attached, in a line, to the
pole and a plinth was screwed to the top.

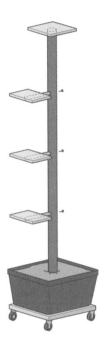

Plastic dishes were placed on each shelf. Slim
triangles of flowers and foliage were arranged on
each shelf and on the plinth to create an overall
vertical feel. The *Gladiolus* in the top placement
enabled a design of over 3.5m (11ft) to be created.

right

Church: Southwell Minster
Arrangers: Newark and District
Flower Lovers' Club
Photographer: Toby Smith

Window design

A metal frame was purpose built to fill the void. Visual impact from a great distance and at an upward angle was needed. The stained glass behind is relatively clear which meant that light might flood through the window. Therefore the design had to be big and bold.

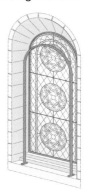

The circles were made of cardboard, padded with wadding. Florist's waterproof ribbon was wrapped around the circles to hold the wadding in place. These were then decorated with dried spathes, sisal, lotus pods, Abaca material (in ribbon widths), wicker spheres, wood shavings, twigs and other plant material. The circles were attached to the frame with plastic electrical ties.

left

Church: Southwark Cathedral
Arrangers: Doreen Stainton and Cleethorpes Flower Club
Photographer: David Connor

Ironwork mechanics

These tall ironwork mechanics were designed by Harold Burns to allow the designs to be constructed in sections (i.e. not working on ladders). They consisted of three interlocking stands 120cm (4ft) x 40cm (16in). The geometric shapes were taken from the floor pattern. They were made from polystyrene from a DIY store and were 240cm x 150cm (8 x 5ft) sheets about 5cm (2in) thick. They were cut with a small handsaw and the edges rubbed down. The backs were painted green and the front cream. Four elements covered each shape – silk paper, pinned leaves, woven leaves and fabric. To attach, holes were made through the polystyrene with a BBQ stick. A plastic straw was threaded through and cut to be flush with the shape. Fishing wire was then threaded through (the straw was necessary otherwise the wire would have cut through the polystyrene). On the top of the stand was a grid and the top shapes were suspended from this with the fishing wire. All the other shapes overlapped and supported each other by the inclusion of small polystyrene shapes between each one to act as a spacer.

right
Church: Southwell Minster
Arrangers: Moira Galloway, Joan Woodhead and Grimsby Flower Lovers Club Members
Photographer: Toby Smith

14 Church Festivals

This chapter considers the many festivals in which church flower arrangers may be involved from time to time. It is divided into three sections:

- The church's year.
- Holy days not directly related to the church year but some or all of which may be celebrated.
- Other occasions which are not 'sacred' but which are important in the life of local communities. It is important to remember that observance of traditions varies very much and the local clergy should be consulted at all times.

The church's year

The calendar for the church year in the Church of England is set out very clearly at the beginning of the book of *Common Worship* (which contains the modern services and largely supersedes the *Book of Common Prayer*). There are comparable calendars and service books in use in most of the other Christian denominations.

left In commemoration of Maundy Thursday, white *Zantedeschia* (arum lilies) are artfully displayed. Placing the flowers to highlight the beauty of the different angles of their asymmetric form increases interest.

Church: Westminster Abbey
Arranger: Sue Slark
Photographer: Toby Smith

Advent

The church's year begins with Advent Sunday, which starts the Advent season, which comprises the four Sundays before Christmas. It is the time of preparation for the coming of Jesus. Advent Sunday may fall on any date between 28th November and 3rd December. This is an ideal time to get involved with your local church Flower Guild as it may need extra help at a busy time.

Historically Advent was a season of penitence and fasting in preparation for the coming of Christ. The four Sundays were originally associated with the themes of Heaven, Hell, Death and Judgment. In modern times, there has been less emphasis on these penitential themes and Hope, Love, Joy and Peace have gradually taken their place.

Decorating the church

Advent wreaths

It is believed that the first Advent wreath in modern times was introduced in the middle of the nineteenth century by a Protestant pastor working in an orphanage in Hamburg, Germany. Though originally a Protestant custom the tradition has spread and is now very familiar in both Protestant and Catholic communities all over Europe and the United States of America.

An Advent wreath is a ring of evergreens with four candles equally spaced around the ring to represent the four Sundays in Advent. The colours will vary locally. One candle is lit on the first Sunday in Advent, the next on the second Sunday and so on. The circle of the ring symbolises eternity. A white central candle representing salvation through the coming of Christ is lit on Christmas morning.

Step by step

Advent wreath

You will need
- foam ring with a plastic or styrofoam base
- four candles to represent the four Sundays of Advent and a larger white one for the centre
- cocktail sticks or medium-heavy stub wires
- florists' tape
- evergreens of choice but suggestions are *Buxus* (box), *Hedera* (ivy), *Myrtus* (myrtle), sprigs of conifer of various colours, *Skimmia*, *Viburnum tinus* (laurustinus)

Method

1 Wet the foam ring by immersing it upside down in deep water at a slight angle for about 50 seconds.

2 Chamfer the inner and outer edges of the foam by cutting off the sharp angles with a knife.

3 Take 4–5 cocktail sticks, or stub wires bent into a hairpin shape, and tightly tape these around the base of each candle. The tops of the sticks or bent wires should rise just above the tape which should be wrapped close to the candle base. You could alternatively use plastic holders designed for candles.

4 Distribute the four candles evenly around the ring and place the fifth candle in the centre. Alternatively this can be added for Christmas morning.

5 Cover your foam with sprigs of evergreen. Either use one type of foliage or a mix, chosen for its form and texture. You should always include one smooth textured leaf in every arrangement of mixed foliage.

above Advent: A traditional Advent ring of evergreens with fir cones bearing three purple and one pink candle. The pink candle represents the Virgin Mary and the three purple candles the time of waiting. Red candles are sometimes used instead of purple.

Church: Southwell Minster
Arrangers: Margaret Ursell and Hillary Brian Nottingham Flower Club
Photographer: Toby Smith

Tip

To ensure your evergreens last well, immerse them in warm water for half an hour before using, and spray with a fine mist of water at regular intervals throughout Advent.

Christmas

After Easter, Christmas is the most important festival in the Christian calendar. At Christmas the Church celebrates the nativity of Jesus on the 25th December – a date agreed upon in the 4th century AD. Feasts celebrating the unconquered sun (immediately after the winter solstice) had ancient roots. The Romans celebrated the pagan Saturnalia near this date with evergreens. The Norsemen also held pagan celebrations on 21st December when shrines were decorated with holly, ivy and bay. For centuries evergreens have been the symbol of life when other plants are dormant. Candles are an ancient symbol of heat and light.

As Professor Raymond Chapman says "Christmas is for many people an occasion for a midwinter holiday, for pleasant indulgence, family gatherings, and a happy time for the children. This is not its true meaning in the Christian faith, but they are good things if we see them as among God's gifts to us. Christmas is not complete unless it includes an act of worship, a thanksgiving for the greatest of all possible presents when Jesus Christ came into the world."

Decorating the church

The liturgical colour for Christmas, as a major festival, is white (including yellow and gold), and arrangements of flowers should follow this. However today most churches have a Christmas tree, white not being the dominant colour.

Nativity scenes

Many churches have a Christmas crib with figures representing the stable, the Holy Family, the shepherds and magi. These are often placed and decorated, (perhaps by children), without the aid of flower arrangers. A simple complementary arrangement may be called for. This may be made of palm-type foliage – suggestive of the Holy Land – or simple flowers such as lilies, or single white spray chrysanthemums to suggest the innocence of the infant Jesus and his mother. Some churches leave the nativity scene in place until the Feast of the Presentation of Christ in the Temple (2nd February), formerly called Candlemas.

The Christmas tree

Trees may be purchased but are often donated. The tree can be decorated with baubles or with natural plant material and suitable lights. It is a task in which the junior church may wish to be involved. Trees tend to be big so it is important that the work is on a reasonably large scale. Some ideas are as follows:

1 Thread *Physalis* (Chinese lanterns) on decorative reel wire. Twist the wire after each addition to the garland to keep each seedhead in position. For a smaller tree use *Hypericum* berries.

2 Dry orange or apple slices slowly in the oven on absorbent paper. Wire two or three together. Twist the wire, create a loop for hanging and twist the ends together to secure.

3 Bind three or four long cinnamon sticks together with wire and cover the wire with raffia. Place a second wire through the binding and create a loop for hanging.

4 Wire pine cones, spray gold and dip in sparkle or sequins. If so desired add a ribbon bow. Alternatively twist thick aluminium wire around the cone leaving a hooked end for hanging.

5 Make gingerbread biscuits in seasonal shapes to hang from the tree. Remember to make a hole for hanging before baking.

6 Grow lavender in the church garden, harvest and dry in the summer. For the tree bind the lavender into generous bundles with twine and over tie with ribbon which can also be used to suspend the dried flowers.

7 Wrap thick aluminium wire closely round an empty orchid tube leaving a hook for hanging. Place a bold flower in the tube.

8 Provide a lightweight star for the top of the tree. It has to be light enough not to bend the topmost stem of the tree. Stars can be bought, but these are often heavy. Try making one from polystyrene or from twigs such as birch or stems such as thin garden bamboo. The stars can be spray-painted and glittered or covered with leaves.

right Long screws are embedded at regular intervals around the arch. These have been used to keep garlands of artificial foliage in place and festive plastic baubles. At other times of the year lengths of foam wrapped in chicken wire are hung on the screws.

Church: St. Paul's Church, Knightsbridge
Photographer: Toby Smith

below A graceful floral garland where the swag effect gently frames and accentuates the cross. To create depth and contrast a lush combination of greenery and red flowers is used including poinsettias, carnations, *Hypericum* and roses. The design is accomplished by hanging two large cages on the reredos, just below the level of the arms of the cross. Chicken wire, shaped into garlands and filled with foam and moss, is attached with wire to the cages. Potted poinsettias are placed in plastic bags and wired into the focal points of the garland. The garland is lightly covered in greenery and then the red flowers are spread throughout.

Church: The Cathedral of St. Philip, Atlanta, GA
Arrangers: Victoria Denson and Laura Iarocci
Photographer: George Westinghouse

above An entrance design for Christmas of kale, *Hydrangea*, *Viburnum dilatatum* berries, *Pinus strobus* (white pine) and bay with a few glass balls wired to the branches to give shiny, smooth texture and a festive atmosphere.

Church: South Freeport Church, Freeport, ME
Arranger: Stephanie Pilk
Photographer: Benedetta Spinelli

Decorating with plants

Plants can be placed in decorative outer containers
and create an appealing display lined up on a window
ledge or around the base of the font. Pot plants can
create a long-lasting display needing little attention
but make sure that any wilting outside leaves are
removed.

Tip

Take care when purchasing poinsettias that you buy
plants that have not stood outside the shop or in a
draught. Poinsettias hate the cold and wind and will not
last if exposed for even the shortest of time.

Poinsettia tree

In Canada and the United States poinsettias are the traditional flower of Christmas and elaborative and impressive displays are created using numerous plants. Here Laura Iarocci explains how to create a poinsettia tree.

"A tree filled with poinsettias and glowing candles creates a warm and inviting welcome during the Christmas season. The poinsettia trees are a particularly effective way to add a huge amount of red in spaces with soaring heights. They are effective if placed in entrances. Parishioners marvel at the trees. Some churches set them up for the entire month of December; while others set them up for Christmas Eve and keep them going for the twelve days of Christmas.

The poinsettia tree is created using a special frame designed by a company in the United States. The frame has a series of circles ascending from a large circle on the bottom to one small one on the top. Rods with smaller circles designed to hold poinsettia pots are clamped on to the circles. The poinsettias are placed in the smaller circles. It may seem easy to accomplish, however care is required to ensure that the overall shape of a tree is maintained and that there are no gaps between the pots. It takes about six hours with six volunteers to set up a 3m (10ft) tree."

Tips

- Frames come in varying heights. Consider purchasing the battery operated candles as well. They have LCD lights which last over 1000 hours. Creative Display Center in the USA at *www.creativedisplaycenter.com* can provide these frames. Although they do not ship to the UK at the moment you may be able to find a metal worker who could create one for you. (See page 406).
- Pre-order poinsettias: the manufacturer will provide recommendations as to the number required for the height. The number varies depending upon the fullness of the poinsettias that you order. A 3m (10ft) tree requires about 200 15cm (6in) potted poinsettias. With pre-ordering, local growers will ensure that the plants delivered are in the proper condition and that you have matching plants. Be sure to order a few extra.
- Order red foil liners for the pots when you order the frame. It helps to fill the gaps between plants. Green liners create dark gaps and the tree does not look as full.

Step by step

Poinsettia tree

You will need
- a specially constructed frame to provide support and structure for tree
- poinsettia plants
- red foil liners
- water saving product

Method

1 Water poinsettias and add a water saving product. Watering the plants on the top half of the taller trees is quite precarious once the tree is set up. We use a product called DriWater which is plastic tubes filled with a gel comprised principally of water. The tubes slowly release water into the plants. The product is expensive, but the plants can survive for the entire twelve days of Christmas without watering. (Creative Display Center also supplies this product).

2 Set up the tree frame. Attach rings around the frame. If using, add candle extensions and candles loaded with batteries.

3 Begin placing plants from the top down. Find an especially beautiful poinsettia with a conical shape for your top plant. Place a candle in the soil in the centre of the pot.

4 Place plants taking care that there are no gaps between the plants and that the plants are facing forward.

5 The pots on the bottom ring of the frame are exposed. You can cover this ring by adding another ring of poinsettias or fabric.

right A tree filled with poinsettias and warm glowing candles create a warm and inviting welcome during the Christmas season.

Church: The Cathedral of St. Philip, Atlanta, GA
Arrangers: Members of the Cathedral of St. Philip's Flower Guild
Photographer: George Westinghouse

After Christmas: Epiphany to Lent

The next festival after Christmas is the Feast of the Epiphany (6th January). Most churches take their Christmas decorations down immediately after this. It is a time when flowers are expensive, and some churches rely on displays of green plants during this season. This is appropriate as the liturgical colour for a Gesima Sunday is green.

Lent

After the forty days of Christmas and Epiphany we have the forty days of Lent, a reflection of the forty days when Jesus fasted and suffered temptation in the wilderness. It begins on Ash Wednesday and finishes with Passiontide during the final two weeks of Lent. It is a time of preparation and penitence, whether as preparation for baptism or recalling our baptism and observing penance for our sins.

In most Churches, flowers are removed during this 40 day period. One ancient variation on this is the Fourth Sunday in Lent, sometimes called Refreshment Sunday or Rose Sunday, when people were permitted to relax the severe Lenten disciplines of fasting. It is the Sunday now known better as Mothering Sunday, when suitable flowers may be permitted according to local tradition.

In the Church of Scotland however, flowers may be displayed throughout Lent. This is also the case in the Methodist Church.

There are some occasions during Lent when plant material is in evidence in the Church:

Mothering Sunday

Suitable arrangements may be placed in church and in addition small posies made for distribution to mothers in the congregation. Children love to be involved in this and could be invited to make the posies in advance of the service.

Palm Sunday

The day commemorates the entry of Jesus into Jerusalem riding on the back of a donkey. The crowds of people, gathered to celebrate the Jewish Passover, waved olive branches and palm fronds which were carried in ancient times as a symbol of victory or triumph and are still used on festival occasions. These were strewn in front of Jesus.

The palm of the scriptures is the date palm *Phoenix dactylifera* with pinnate mid-green leaves up to 2m (7ft) long. It is not indigenous to northern Europe because it requires a temperature never less than 14°C (55°F). Substitutes for palm and olive have therefore been used in ceremonies for centuries. The most common has been willow which is in bud at this time of the year. It is often called 'palm' because of this symbolic association.

When British life was more rural, country-folk cut long stems of willow and box on Palm Saturday, with which houses were decorated – an activity called 'a-palming'. Processions carried branches into the churches to re-enact the story of Palm Sunday. Flowers and willow were also strewn to make a path for the processions.

Decorating the church

There are many plants with the vernacular name of 'palm' but traditionally it is *Salix caprea*, the goat willow – golden with male catkins or 'goslings'. The female catkins are less spectacular and grow on separate bushes.

Sabal minor, commonly called palmetto, grows wild in warmer countries such as Bermuda and the southern states of America. It has a fan shaped leaf which can be trimmed with scissors to a variety of shapes. It dries easily. The leaves are often used by flower arrangers to interpret the sun's rays, triumph, rejoicing, victory or exultation.

right A design for a Gesima Sunday using a wide range of foliage chosen for form, colour and texture. In the bottom arrangement the plant material includes *Dracaena sanderiana* stems, *Strelitzia reginae* leaves, *Phormium* 'Yellow Wave', *Monstera deliciosa*, *Hedera colchica* 'Sulphur Heart', *Dracaena fragrans* 'Massangeana' and *Codiaem* (croton).

In the top design are dyed bamboo stems, *Dracaena sanderiana* stems, *Rubus tricolor* stems (defoliated), *Phormium* 'Sundowner', *Monstera delicosa*, *Strelitzia reginae*, *Hedera colchica* 'Sulphur Heart', braids of *Fascinia fascicularis* and *Chamaerops humilis*.

Church: Southwell Minster
Arranger: Scunthorpe Flower Club
Photographer: Judith Blacklock

Our native willow, dried *Cycas* palm or palmetto leaves can be arranged for Palm Sunday with fresh spring flowers but if Easter is late the willow may be past its best. *Salix* x *sepulcralis* (weeping willow) is beautiful but wilts quickly when cut, making it unsuitable for church arrangements unless it is defoliated.

Tip

House plant foliage of various kinds can be cut and used for Palm Sunday.

Maundy Thursday

This is the traditional name for the Thursday before Easter and is said to be a corruption of 'Mandati, dies Mandati' (the Day of the Commandment), referring to the night of the last supper which was itself a celebration of the Jewish Passover when Jesus commanded his disciples to love one another. In washing the disciples' feet, Christ performed this menial task to teach the lesson of humility.

During the Middle Ages bishops, abbots and noblemen washed the feet of the poor on Maundy Thursday in imitation of Christ's act. English sovereigns washed the feet of as many old men as the sovereign's years of age but all that remains of this ceremony, which began in the reign of Edward III, 1327–1376, is the bestowing of gifts to the poor. Special minted silver coins are distributed by the monarch to a group of specially selected men and women. All those taking part in the ceremony carry posies of flowers which in earlier days were supposed to be a protection against the plague.

left Cycas revoluta (sago palm), Aucuba japonica (spotted laurel), Rhapis excelsa (lady palm), Aspidistra elatior (cast ion plant), Alpinia zerumbet 'Variegata' (variegated shell ginger) and Brassica oleracea (variegated ornamental cabbage) in this design for Palm Sunday.

Church: Grace Episcopal, Charleston, SC
Arranger: Grace Episcopal Flower Guild
Photographer: Wally Breidis

Sometimes Maundy Thursday is called 'Green Thursday', because of the custom of providing penitents, who had made their confessions on Ash Wednesday, with green branches on this day. This indicated that penance had been completed and they were received back into full church membership.

Decorating the church

If any significant decorations are wanted in church on this day, green branches or a group of lilies would be appropriate, but more usually churches are left bare.

Good Friday

All ornaments, altar frontals and other hangings are usually removed and the church is left bare to commemorate the trial, crucifixion and death of Jesus.

Decorating the church

Most churches are left undecorated. If however flowers are wanted, simple white arums or *Lilium longiflorum* would be suitable.

Easter

Easter is the greatest and the most joyous festival of the Christian Church. It commemorates the resurrection of Christ. The date of Easter changes because it is the first Sunday after the first full moon which happens on, or the next after, the spring equinox, 21st March. Therefore it may fall on any date between 21st March and 25th April. This is in the western tradition. (The Orthodox churches have a different way of calculating the date of Easter.) Colloquially the term 'Easter' is applied to the week beginning with Easter Sunday. In the Church year Eastertide extends until the Feast of Pentecost celebrating the coming of the Holy Spirit, which is seven weeks after Easter Sunday.

Easter has been observed continuously since Christianity first came to Britain. The Venerable Bede derives the word 'Easter' from Eostre (Eastre), a pagan goddess whose festival was held at the spring equinox. It is said that the Christian Church took this time when 'the old festival was observed with the gladness of new solemnity'.

The history of the Easter egg is also linked with pre-Christian times when the egg represented fertility and rebirth and so was adopted as part of the Christian festival and came to represent the resurrection. Some believe that the egg is a symbol of the stone blocking Jesus' sepulchre being 'rolled' away. Others see the empty egg with its broken shell as the empty tomb and new life escaping from it. The giving of an Easter egg after the Easter service is not just a gift but one with great significance.

Decorating the church

Easter calls for purity and richness and white and gold are the colours for this special occasion. Easter lilies (*Lilium longiflorum*) are the perfect flower with their strength of form and purity of colour. Do beware that an immature *L. longiflorum* will only mature in its own time and no hairdryer, immersion in a hot bath, standing under bright lights or any other method will encourage this lily to develop before it is ready.

right A mossed cross was hung on the door to welcome parishioners at Easter. *Lilium longiflorum* serve as the focal point with a variety of flowers which complemented those in the Easter décor. The cross was created by attaching moss, with mossing pins, to a foam cross. A large OASIS® Iglu is attached to the middle of the cross to hold the flowers.

Church: St. Philip's, Atlanta
Arranger: Laura Iarocci
Photographer: George Westinghouse

below A spray tray was wired to the cross and the arrangement was created within.

Church: Paisley Abbey
Arranger: Maureen Mitchell
Photographer: Bob Brown

above A simple interpretation of the Crucifixion and the empty tomb. The stone had been rolled back revealing the entrance to the cave where the linen sheet that Jesus had been wrapped in was found on the Sunday morning.

Church: St. Hilary's Church, Llanrhos
Arranger: Phyl Evans
Photographer: Phyl Evans

Lilium longiflorum in altar vases is seen time and again and nothing could be more effective. Altar vases were created for the lily and I sometimes wonder why more elaborate mechanics are not made so that something more stupendous can be held. Flowers in church are an adjunct to the cross and the altar at this time of the year and simplicity is the key to glorification.

Tips

Purchasing and arranging lilies

- Ask your supplier how long he thinks it will take for the flowers to gain full maturity.
- Purchase in bud at least 5 days before Easter Sunday to be sure that the lily is open and in full flower. If you hold the bottom of the stem it should be strong and stay upright.
- Only purchase *L. longiflorum* where the buds are full and showing colour.
- Arrange where the pollen from the stamens will not soil the clergy's vestments. Warn the clergy if there is a chance of this happening. Most people prefer to remove the stamens altogether.

Paschal (Pascoe or Pace) is the Passover, or Easter, hence the word 'paschal' belonging to this time. A paschal candle is sometimes blessed and placed on or near the altar, or close to the font (many baptisms took place at Easter in the early church, and this still happens today). It represents Christ, the true Light of the World. It stands lit in the sanctuary from Easter to Ascension in some traditions, or from Easter to Pentecost in others. It symbolises the promise of Jesus to be with his people until the end of time. Sometimes the paschal candle is set in the midst of a flower arrangement.

For the purpose of this book I visited many churches over the Easter period. I was struck by the amount of love and dedication which was spent by so many people glorifying the church for this special occasion. Budget was an issue but when you have the simple daffodil to give colour and beauty over this period you do not need to think long and hard about how to decorate your church. The inclusion of Easter eggs into arrangements, whether blown, chocolate or jewel encrusted, would be most appropriate.

right Carnations, spray carnations, *Limoniuim* (statice) with *Brachyclottis* syn. *Senecio* arranged around the Paschal candle with the four nails to represent the four wounds of the cross.

Church: All Saints Church, Banstead
Arranger: Doris Taylor
Photographer: Mike Pannett

left Children decorate the church at Easter with evenly spaced containers filled with daffodils around the base of the font. A cross of mustard and cress has been sown to be ready to harvest on Easter Day.

Church: Cartmel Priory
Arrangers: Members of the Church Flower Guild
Photographer: Judith Blacklock

Ascension

Ascension commemorates the departure of Christ to heaven after his post-resurrection appearances to his disciples. It takes place forty days after Easter, a Thursday in our modern calendar. In some churches, the Paschal candle is extinguished to signify Christ leaving the disciples (in others it is kept lit until Pentecost).

Decorating the church

Flowers should be tall and uplifting, and white (yellow or gold) – the liturgical colour for this as for all major festivals. *Eremurus* or *Gladiolus,* would be appropriate, as would white delphiniums, larkspur, *Antirrhinum* and early foxgloves if they are available.

right For this design over 2.7m (9ft) tall and 6m (20ft) across, Alison used seven decorative ironwork pedestal stands of the sort that is commonly found in churches. These were closely placed together but set at different heights. Foam was placed in bowls on each stand. Bamboo canes from the garden gave height, and dried *Grevillea,* sprayed red and orange and reinforced with *Gladiolus* gave the flames. Long plastic sticks, wrapped in red and orange sisal and kept in place with reel wire, were intertwined with long, thin strips of red and orange cellophane to give a shimmer. These were then bent at appropriate angles to represent the flames together with *Leucospermum,* dried and painted *Strelitzia* leaves, *Leucadendron* 'Safari Sunset' and plumed *Celosia* and lilies in various colours. The colour was stronger at the centre to represent the core of the fire.

Church: Paisley Abbey
Arranger: Alison Galbraith
Photographer: Bob Brown

Pentecost

Fifty days after the Resurrection the Holy Spirit came to the disciples, touching each of them with tongues of fire. This is sometimes seen as the 'birthday of the Church'. The Holy Spirit is a gift to the church, to uphold and inspire her forever until the final fulfilment of God's purpose.

Decorating the church

Because of the fire, red is the colour for Pentecost. The choice of florists' flowers is wide and red gladioli, roses, gerberas and carnations would be most apt. From the garden red peonies and rhododendrons might be available depending on when Easter falls.

Trinity Sunday

This is the Sunday after Pentecost, a major festival in the Church's year, but observance varies very much locally. It is kept as a day of thanksgiving for the Holy Communion. After the excitement of Easter and Pentecost many churches do little to mark it. The colour changes after the red of Pentecost back to white (yellow and gold). Trinity Sunday ushers in the long, green season that takes us up to Advent.

Additional sacred festivals including Saints' Days

These are dates in the church year which may be kept specially, depending on local tradition. They do not have the importance of the festivals listed above, but should not be overlooked by those responsible for the church flowers. There are several festivals of the Virgin Mary in this category, some of which are much celebrated locally, especially in churches dedicated to her. Others commemorate ordinary people who have given themselves to God's work or been martyred for their faith. They occur at intervals throughout the year. Many of them celebrate the first apostles, many are patronal festivals, and some are local saints in particular districts (e.g. St. Alban, the first British martyr who gave his name to the town, St. Albans, in Hertfordshire).

Festivals of the Virgin Mary

Larger churches may have lady chapels in side aisles, where it is appropriate to arrange flowers with the Virgin Mary in mind, especially on her festival dates.

The Annunciation – 25th March

This was the subject of many great paintings in which the Angel Gabriel is seen with Mary, often with a lily or other flowers. The festival is kept in many churches but local tradition must be consulted.

As this day usually (though not always) falls in Lent, flowers may not be required. But if they are, or if the church has a painting or statue of the Virgin Mary, a simple arrangement of white lilies would be appropriate.

The Visitation of Mary to Elizabeth – 31st May

Less familiar than the other festivals of the Virgin Mary, it may be noted in some churches, particularly those dedicated to her. Decoration of the church would be similar to that for the Annunciation.

The Feast of the Blessed Virgin Mary – 15 August

This is 'St Mary's Day' which is more widely observed than the other two, especially where it is a patronal festival. Flowers should be arranged in shades of white, yellow and gold, and a special effort made.

National Patron Saints

There are four patron saints of the British Isles, and here are suggestions for how each day may be celebrated with flowers.

St. David's Day – 1st March

St. David, the patron saint of Wales, was Primate of Wales, and died, it is believed, on 1st March 589 AD, or perhaps 601 AD. He is the only Welsh saint to be officially canonized, but very few details of his life are known. His monastery is believed to have been at the site now known as St. David's.

Decorating the church

The two national emblems of Wales, the leek and the daffodil, were known in medieval times (Shakespeare makes much of this in *Henry V*). The date often falls in Lent, but if flowers are required, daffodils are inexpensive, colourful and easily obtainable at this time of year. They are very suitable for the decoration of the church.

St. Patrick's Day – 17th March

There are many legends about the patron saint of Ireland. He lived, it is believed, from about 390–461 AD, and his work was therefore in the fifth century. Some of his writings have survived. Born somewhere between the rivers Clyde and Severn, he travelled to Ireland, where he worked as a missionary, founding churches and forming communities.

below The crossed *Phormium* leaves over a bed of orange tulips and mini shamrock plants interpret the Irish flag to celebrate St. Patrick's Day.

Church: Westminster Abbey
Arranger: Sheila Banks
Photographer: Toby Smith

Decorating the church

Again his feast day falls in Lent, so the local tradition must be consulted. Flowers are usually required, because the size of the shamrock makes it difficult to use in church decoration. Green plants (such as *Oxalis* which look like shamrock but are larger) could be placed in an attractive outer container, and placed in a row along the entrance table. They could be sold off at the end of the service – there would be bound to be takers! Alternatively, small plants could be used in a low bowl, with a few flowers added in the national colours.

above Red and white – the colours of St. George – the patron saint of England. The deeper tones of the *Leucadendron* 'Safari Sunset' and the reddish brown *Hypericum* give depth and contrast of form and texture.

Church: Westminster Abbey
Arranger: Sheila Banks
Photographer: Toby Smith

St. George's Day – 23rd April

St. George, the patron saint of England, is surrounded by legends, many of them concerning conflict with a dragon with much rich detail. Edward III founded the Order of the Garter in his name.

Decorating the church

Sometimes the date coincides with Easter and when this happens Easter flowers will take precedence. However room may be found away from the sanctuary for an arrangement commemorating the patron saint, especially where he is also the patronal saint of the church. The banner of St. George, an upright red cross on a white background, became the flag of England, and the red rose is sometimes regarded as its emblem. Red roses would appear to be an obvious choice for floral decoration, but any red flower could be substituted.

St. Andrew's Day – 30 November

St. Andrew, the fisherman, was one of Jesus' twelve disciples. In early Christian art he is depicted with a normal Latin cross. The 'saltire' was first associated with him in the 10th century and became common in the 14th. He is often depicted with a fishing net. He was adopted as the patron saint of Scotland because of an improbable legend that he had visited Fife and stopped at the place now called St. Andrews. One of the largest abbeys in Europe was later built there.

Decorating the church

The saltire of Scotland, a white diagonal cross on a dark blue background, is taken to symbolise white for purity and blue for the sea (recalling that he was a fisherman). Blue hydrangeas, *Eryngium* (sea holly), cardoons, white chrysanthemums, blue *Delphinium* and perhaps white gladioli would be suitable flowers.

left Blue and white – the colours of St. Andrew – are used in this composition of blue *Delphinium*, white *Dendrobium*, *Matthiola* (stocks), *Dianthus* (carnations) and roses. Note how the *Delphinium* form the cross of St. Andrew.

Church: Paisley Abbey
Arranger: Maureen Mitchell
Photographer: Bob Brown

Other 'lesser' festivals

**The Feast of the Holy Innocents (29 December),
The Feast of the Transfiguration (6 August),
and All Saints Day (1 November).**

The liturgical colour for all of these is white (including yellow and gold).

The Feast of the Holy Innocents, commemorating the slaughter of the young children by order of King Herod, is sometimes observed but falls during the time when Christmas decorations are in place and does not usually call for any special flower arrangements. If desired, a special small arrangement could be placed near the font.

The Feast of the Transfiguration celebrates the story of Christ appearing before the apostles in glory with Elijah and Moses. If it is celebrated locally the vestments and altar furnishings will be changed from the usual green of the Sundays after Trinity to white. Flower arrangers should note this in choosing the appropriate flowers for the occasion.

On All Saints Day those who have died in the faith of Christ are commemorated. Although All Saint's Day is 1 November it may be observed on the Sunday between 30 October and 5 November. Someone who has died in the past year may be particularly remembered, and sometimes the family may like to donate flowers for this occasion. As with many other festivals, local practice varies and should always be considered by those responsible for the church flowers.

The recognised calendar in use in the Church of England also contains a number of festivals which for reasons stated above may be celebrated in accordance with local tradition, and these may also be noted in other denominations, especially where the church is dedicated to a particular saint or martyr. Full lists appear in the *Book of Common Worship* and in comparable service books of the other denominations. Church decorations may take their inspiration from legends or stories about the lives of these saints and martyrs. Remember that red is the liturgical colour for martyrs.

An enthusiastic member of the congregation may enjoy doing a little research. *The Oxford Book of Saints, The Penguin Book of Saints*, and the internet should all provide enough material for rewarding interpretative arrangements. There follows a list of the most significant with their dates:

Joseph of Nazareth	19 March
Mark the Evangelist	25 April
Philip and James, Apostles	1 May
Matthias, Apostle	14 May
Columba, Abbot and Missionary	9 June
Barnabas, Apostle	11 June
Alban, First Martyr in Britain	22 June
John the Baptist (birth of)	24 June
Peter (and sometimes Paul), Apostles	29 June
Thomas, Apostle (or 21 December)	3 July
Mary Magdalene	22 July
James, Apostle	25 July
Bartholomew, Apostle	24 August
Holy Cross Day	14 September
Ninian, Apostle of the Picts	16 September
Matthew, Apostle and Evangelist	21 September
Michael and All Angels	29 September
Luke the Evangelist	18 October
Simon and Jude, Apostles	28 October
Martin of Tours	11 November
Margaret of Scotland	16 November
Stephen, First Martyr	26 December
John, Apostle and Evangelist	27 December

Other occasions which may be celebrated as festivals

Harvest/Thanksgiving

Harvest is not a festival in the Church's liturgical calendar, but for centuries has been widely accepted as a time to decorate the church in thanks to God for all his blessings. Gifts of flowers, tinned and packaged food are gathered in the church and taken to those in need. The church service is one of joy and appreciation with special music and hymns to celebrate the bountiful harvest and the end of the growing season.

The present day service has developed from ancient times. Before Christ there were rituals concerned with the renewal of life. Early man thought that by cutting the crop he might have killed the Spirit of Fertility and that a ceremony was necessary to ensure the renewal of growth the following season.

The church's interest in harvest customs led to greeting the harvest with a peal of bells and later to the blessing of produce in the church. The Reformation discouraged this but in 1843 the Vicar of Morwenstow invited parishioners to receive the Sacrament in the bread made from new corn and the modern tradition of harvest thanksgiving was begun.

In Canada, Thanksgiving takes place on the second Monday of October and in the USA, where it commemorates the first harvest of the Pilgrim Fathers, on the fourth Thursday of November.

Decorating the church

This is one of the most wonderful times of the year to be involved with decorating the church. Autumn is the time of abundance and fruit and vegetables can play a wonderful part in creating designs full of form and texture. People are generous in their giving but perhaps one of the hardest tasks is to provide a display that is cohesive and bold. It is a good idea to ask the congregation to provide their floral gifts from their gardens two or three days prior to the Harvest

service. This means that the organiser will have sufficient time to purchase flowers to complement those given.

With an abundance of donations careful thought must be given to create a satisfying arrangement. It is best to group fruit and vegetables together in the centre of an arrangement with the outer area being covered with foliage and finished off with flowers. Should space be limited consider a series of small arrangements involving fruit, vegetables and flowers in a coordinated repeated pattern and colour scheme along windowsills or ledges.

Where space permits, more innovative designs can be introduced. The many textures and colours of seasonal fruit and vegetables combined with foliage lend themselves well to layered or grouped designs. Pyramids or cones of small fruits and vegetables like tomatoes, crab apples, or Brussels sprouts, supported by larger items, can make for a striking design.

Dominant colours at this time are red, bronze, orange and yellow. A simple way to increase the impact of any design at this time of year is to introduce a harmonising colour. Consider shiny purple aubergines to balance the golden sheaf of corn.

The gifts given in Church at the Harvest service need to be handled with care and appreciation, whatever the offering. This is especially true when they are going to be distributed to the needy afterwards. In order not to conflict with the main display, it is a good idea to have servers receiving the gifts and placing them in designated areas away from the main displays.

left A design for Thanksgiving of purple artichokes with pepperberries, *Laurus nobilis* (bay), *Pinus strobus* (white pine), olive branches and painted poppy seed heads.
Church: South Freeport Church, Freeport, ME
Arranger: Stephanie Pilk
Photographer: Benedetta Spinelli

Wesley Day – 2nd March (Canada), 24th May (United Kingdom)

The evangelists and founders of the Methodist Church, the Wesley brothers, travelled hundreds of thousands of miles preaching.

Decorating the church

A simple arrangement of wild plant material could symbolize the many travels through country lanes to preach. (But note restrictions on cutting wild material – see page 50.)

Every hymn which the Wesley brothers, John and Charles, wrote was packed full of biblical references and a profound understanding of theology. Charles' son Samuel, and his grandson Samuel Sebastian, added great music to the words of these hymns. Methodists are famed for their hymn-singing tradition and creating designs to interpret some of the Wesleys' best known work would be most appropriate for this special day.

Commonwealth Day – 10th March

Commonwealth Day is the annual celebration of the Commonwealth of Nations held on the second Monday in March, and marked by a multi-faith service in Westminster Abbey. It is normally attended by Queen Elizabeth II as Head of the Commonwealth, with the Commonwealth Secretary-General and Commonwealth High Commissioners in London. The Queen delivers an address to the Commonwealth which is broadcast throughout the world.

While it has a certain official status, Commonwealth Day is not a public holiday in most Commonwealth countries and there is little public awareness of it.

Decorating the church

It would be appropriate to have flowers or foliage to represent one of the countries of the Commonwealth for example *Phormium* (New Zealand flax) for New Zealand or *Acer* (maple) for Canada, *Eucalyptus* for Australia, *Protea, Strelitzia* and *Gerbera* blooms for South Africa.

above Thanksgiving is celebrated outside the Confederate Chapel in Richmond, Virginia

Church: The Confederate Chapel, Richmond, VA
Photographer: Judith Blacklock

previous pages
Thanksgiving

Church: The Cathedral of St. Philip, Atlanta, GA
Arrangers: Victoria Denson and Laura Iarocci
Photographer: George Westinghouse

right This magnificent pedestal arrangement in front of a painting of Richard II represents Antigua for Commonwealth Day

Church: Westminster Abbey
Arrangers: Mary Law
Photographer: Lyndon Parker

Local days for celebration

Some communities have events like 'Sea Sunday' (especially where there are fishermen or lifeboat men). Local traditions will dictate which require special flowers and the general principles for festivals set out above can be adapted to make the most of these.

Remembrance Sunday

This is now celebrated on the Sunday nearest to 11th November. The date was chosen because on the eleventh hour of the eleventh day of the eleventh month the Great War came to an end in 1918. It now is the occasion when people also remember those who have died in all the wars since 1918. It is especially poignant during a time when men and women are still losing their lives in the armed forces serving their country. It happens to be the feast day of the soldier-saint, Martin of Tours.

Decorating the church

This is an opportunity to vary or augment the usual flower arrangements. If the church has a war memorial an arrangement, or perhaps a garland, may be placed to draw the eye to its position. Red flowers are appropriate, with symbolic foliage like rosemary for remembrance. Artificial 'Haig' poppies can be purchased in various sizes and used instead of, or in association with fresh flowers. Accessories like barbed wire, small white crosses, military accoutrements and campaign medals can be used with discretion to reinforce the effectiveness of the arrangements.

right Red roses with a tangle of wild clematis vine recalls the battlefields of World War I.
Church: Salisbury Cathedral
Arranger: Jennie Liddiard, Caroline Land, Wendy Wallis and Lowenna Hardbottle, Marlborough Flower Club
Photographer: Ash Mills

below Remembrance poppies
Church: Cathedral Church of St. Peter and St. Paul, Sheffield
Arranger: Sue Smith
Photographer: Judith Blacklock

left The lilac swathe through this arrangement contains the names of all those who lost their lives in the Falklands conflict on ovals of card.

Church: The Falkland Islands Memorial Chapel, Pangbourne College, Reading
Arranger: Diane Gill, sponsored by Diana Batt in memory of her husband Cdr Gordon W.J. Batt, DSC, RN who died in the conflict.
Photographer: Don Somner

right A memorial to those who have died for their country.

Church: Southwell Minster
Arrangers: Jessica Ramsey and Maggie Wright, Enderby Flower and Garden Club
Photographer: Toby Smith

15 Weddings

Weddings are an important part of church life and are occasions where flowers play a vital role. Remember that emotions will be running high so your task must be handled with tact and diplomacy. Needless to say it is important that the flowers look their absolute best.

There are few brides who do not want flowers at their wedding. Flowers provide the perfect backdrop to the bridal party and provide the congregation with a beautiful setting to enjoy before the ceremony begins.

Many of the designs in this book can be adapted for a wedding – it is mostly a case of knowing which flowers will suit the required colour scheme. This chapter includes a list of seasonal flowers available in terms of colour as well as a list of recommended roses.

If you are in charge of the church flowers there is a choice of options:

- Do you allow the bride to bring in her own, unknown floral designer? Do you insist that the bride uses the church's flower arrangers?

- Do you allow the designs to be removed from the church after the service so that the bride can economise and take the flowers to the reception? If so, will other flowers need to be arranged for the Sunday? This is a particular concern if the wedding is late in the day on the Saturday.

above A floral arch decorates the lychgate.

Church: St Michael and All Angels, Lambourn
Arranger: Ms Travis Clark
Photographer: Richard Greenly

left The aisle is lined with handtied bouquets of *Hydrangea* and *Viburnum opulus* 'Roseum' with trails of variegated ivy flowing down the metal stands which are linked with white rope.

Church: St. George's Church, Karykis, Athens
Arranger: Robert Koene
Photographer: Fotis Karapiperis

Outside florists

Bringing in an outside floral designer, can occasionally cause difficulties. To forestall any potential problems there are certain guidelines that the church should lay down. Anyone working with flowers is usually more than reasonable and happy to follow any special requests.

Points to consider

Will the designer:

- Work in a neat and tidy way?
- Work around people and take second place if there is a service at the time when they wish to arrange the flowers if necessary?
- Have respect for reserved parking?
- Co-operate in making arrangements for the disposal of flowers after the wedding?
- Bring mechanics, containers, pedestals etc? If not, will the florist be appreciative of using the church's equipment, and perhaps be prepared to make a donation?
- Undertake not to insert nails into the fabric of the church without the express, explicit agreement of the church authorities?

More than one bride

When there is more than one wedding service on a specific day, it would be perfect if the brides agreed on colour and content. Alas, this is rarely so. This is where the Flower Guild leader has to set out in detail what has to happen and by what time. The first step is to get together the parties concerned.

above Flowers for a summer wedding delightfully arranged on a ledge.
Church: St. Peter's Church, Inkberrow
Arranger: Carol Tooth
Photographer: Chrissie Harten

right A foam ring was placed around the base of each candlestick and filled with flowers to match the others in the church.
Church: Saint-Gummaruschurch, Emblem, Belgium
Arranger: Stef Adriaenssens
Photographer: Stef Adrianenssens

following pages Ammi majus, *Gypsophila* 'Million Stars', *Rosa* 'Avalance', *R.* 'Viviane', *Syringa* (lilac), *Triticum*, *Viburnum opulus* 'Roseum' and *Zantedeschia* fill the church.
Church: Saint-Gummaruschurch, Emblem, Belgium
Arranger: Stef Adriaenssens
Photographer: Stef Adrianenssens

Church flower arrangers

Some churches now insist that the Flower Guild create all the flowers for all weddings in the church. It is, however, easier to insist on this when you have a popular, photogenic church in which everyone wants to get married! Considerable money can be made for the church by this means.

As many arrangers can feel embarrassed negotiating prices it is best to have a fixed list of charges. If a fixed price is made for wedding flowers it is a good idea to make a different lower charge for regular members of the congregation. Deciding who falls into this bracket however can be difficult.

Flower price fluctuations

The price of flowers varies according to location and season. It is probably best to take note of charges from the local florist and charge accordingly but only if the arrangers are experienced and competent. Supplements can be raised for times of the year when flower prices are high. Although demand may only be great in one country or continent, the influence on cost now spreads across the world. Some of the dates when demand is huge and prices are consequently high are:

- Valentine's Day (14th February)
- Mothering Sunday (4th Sunday in Lent)
- International Women's Day (8th March)
- Easter
- St. Jordi, Spain (23rd April)
- Administrative Professional's Day USA (Wednesday of the last week of April)
- Mother's Day USA (2nd Sunday of May)
- Christmas (25th December)

left Elegant floor arrangements take the place of pew hangings. The aisle is sufficiently wide to allow this without impeding access.
Church: All Saints' Church, Cheltenham
Photographer: Xander Casey

Colour

The bride usually wants the church flowers to match the colours of the bridal party. If the bride has met with a florist and selected flowers for the bridal party and the reception, find out which ones have been chosen and try to incorporate them in the church designs as well.

Some notes on the use of seasonal flowers and colours follow over the next few pages.

below Paul wanted to create a completely romantic look for the church, spacing flowers in three layers, the entrance, transept and altar. The use of perspective gives a wonderful feeling of depth. For the larger urns boards are placed across the urn. A purpose made metal 'fountain' is then placed on top which is filled with chicken wire. To create greater height extension tubes are used that are attached to bamboo canes.

Church: The Parish Church of Woodstock
Arranger: Paul Thomas
Photographer: Paul Thomas

right Iron stands were covered with flat moss and covered with *Galax* leaves and bound with waterproof florists' tape. Giant 'Carmen' roses, create from the red petals of *Rosa* 'Red Naomi' were placed centrally. Balls of *Dianthus* (carnations) in red and lime green lie at the feet of the stands, together with rose petals, to line the aisle.

Church: St. George's Church, Karykis, Athens
Arranger: Robert Koene
Photographer: Fotis Karapiperis

White and cream

White and cream flowers are always suitable but are expensive at Easter and before International Women's Day.

Spring

Convallaria majalis
  (lily-of-the-valley)
Freesia
Hyacinthus (hyacinth)
Narcissus
Ranunculus (turban flower)
Tulipa (tulip)

above

Photographer: imagestock/
iStockphoto.com

Summer

Agapanthus (African lily)
Chamelaucium (waxflower)
Lathyrus (sweet pea)
Matthiola (stocks)
Paeonia (peony)
Rosa 'Vendela'
Lilium (lily)
Zantedeschia (calla lily)

Autumn

Dahlia
Hydrangea
Gladiolus
Nerine

Winter

Anemone
Hippeastrum (amaryllis)
Symphoricarpos
  (snowberry)

left Steel grass was glued onto candles 150 cm (7 ft) high. White *Zantedeschia* (calla lilies) were fixed to the candles with small nails. Trails of *Asparagus asparagoides myrtiofolius* (smilax) give softness and movement around the vertical stems of the callas.

Church: Church of Santorini Profitilias, Imerovigli, Greece
Arranger: Robert Koene
Photographer: Fotis Karapiperis

Blue

Blue and purple flowers are widely available during the summer months but are harder to obtain the rest of the year. They are recessive colours so take care when using them in designs to be viewed at a distance. It is safer to avoid these colours altogether in a dark church.

Spring

Centaurea
Hyacinthus
Iris
Muscari

Summer

Allium
Brodiaea
Delphinium
Eustoma (lisianthus)
Gentiana
Scabiosa (scabious)
Triteleia

Autumn

Echinops (globe thistle)
Hydrangea
Limonium (statice/
  sea lavender)

Winter

Anemone
Eryngium (sea holly)
Rosa 'Cool Water'

above
Photographer: anzeletti/iStockphoto.com

Pink

Pink is a favourite colour with brides and bridesmaids all year round. Pink, perhaps combined with cream or white, complements grey, stone walls and slate floors. Pink flowers are expensive before Mothers' Day.

Spring	Summer	Autumn	Winter
Freesia	*Antirrhinum* (snapdragon)	*Anthurium*	*Hippeastrum* (amaryllis*)*
Helleborus (hellebore*)*	*Lathyrus* (sweet pea)	*Echinacea*	*Phlox*
Hyacinthus (hyacinth)	*Matthiola* (stock)	*Gladiolus*	*Protea*
Tulipa (tulip*)*	*Paeonia* (peony)	*Nerine*	
	Zantedeschia (calla lily)		

above

Photographer: Elena Elisseeva/iStockphoto.com

Red

Red flowers are lovely for winter but as December 25th gets closer flowers become more expensive. Avoid, at all cost, the two weeks prior to Valentine's Day and for 10 days afterwards. Bridal bouquets of one type of red flower such as red roses look good but for larger designs, such as pedestals, use tints and shades of red. To give strong impact you could include shocking pink or orange.

Spring	Summer	Autumn	Winter
Ranunculus	mini *Gerbera*	*Amaranthus*	*Anemone*
Rosa	*Lathyrus*	*Callistephus*	*Anigozanthos*
Tulipa	*Papaver* (poppy)	*Celosia*	(kangaroo paw)
		Dahlia	*Euphorbia*
			Hippeastrum

above

Photographer: © Robert Veres/Fotolia

Ilex berries

Yellow

Yellow flowers are wonderful in a church with poor lighting or with an ornate interior.
If the church has an ornate interior, yellow can complement rather than be overwhelmed.

Spring	Summer	Autumn	Winter
Freesia	*Centaurea*	*Chrysanthemum*	*Anigozanthos* (kangaroo paw)
Forsythia	*Eremurus*	*Helenium*	
Narcissus	*Genista* (broom)	*Rudbeckia*	*Euphorbia*
Ranunculus	*Helianthus*	*Solidago*	*Rosa* 'Sphinx'

above

Photographer: Barbara Sauder/iStockphoto.com

Orange and peach

Orange is the colour of autumn and flowers at this time of year are wonderful when teamed with berries and fruits. If the church is full of strong colour, or has brickwork, the matching strength of orange flowers harmonises well.

Peach complements churches with wood, York stone floors and brass ornamentation. Peach flowers are wonderful combined with cream.

Spring	Summer	Autumn	Winter
Hyacinthus	Asclepias	Crocosmia	Gerbera
Ranunculus	Alstroemeria	Lilium (Asiatic variety)	Hippeastrum
Tulipa	Rosa	Rudbeckia	Hypericum
	Sandersonia		

above

Photographer: Peta Curnow/iStockphoto.com

Favourite roses

There are so many varieties of rose available that it is hard to know which to choose. Colour is not the only variable by any means – consider size, shape, and length of stem and how long the rose will last when making your choice. The varieties offered by growers are sometimes are replaced by others with different names so try to see an illustrated catalogue to make sure you get the rose you want. Many commercial growers have online catalogues that show many different roses and lilies, grouped by colour, but computer screens can distort the exact colour values.

below A wedding ceremony in the open air. A few beautiful roses tied at intervals to the end chairs give a glorious summer effect in Durham, NC.
Photographer: Lee Thompson

Cream and white

R. 'Akito' – pure white, well formed, long-lasting rose with medium head.

R. 'Blizzard' – white in bud but opens with a creamy centre.

R. 'Avalanche' – large white rose with guard petals tinged with green.

R. 'Tibet' – large big-headed white rose.

R. 'Maroussia' – very large white rose with touch of green on guard petals, flat head, long-lasting.

R. 'Vendela' – long-lasting cream rose with medium to large head and regular form.

Green

R. 'Florence Green' – lime green with frilly petals, the dark sepals can give the appearance of being damaged.

R. 'Amandine' – lime green rose with a round head.

R. 'Jade' – pale green rose with limited number of petals.

R. 'Limbo' – dark green with frilly edges.

Red

R. 'Black Baccara' – a dark red rose with good form and a long life, very velvety.

R. 'El Toro' – tomato red rose, reliable with undulating petals.

R. 'Exstase' – a very dark red rose with a wonderful fragrance and a rather tight form. It is usually only available during the summer months.

R. 'First Red' – an ordinary red rose but reliable with a slightly pointed form.

R. 'Grand Prix' – reliable long-lasting rose. Flat, multi-petalled and deservedly popular.

R. 'Passion' – very similar to 'Grand Prix' but a slightly brighter red.

R. 'Red Naomi' – a bright red rose when open. It is reliable and long-lasting with a slight fragrance.

R. 'Torero' – tomato red rose with crinkly petals (similar in form to 'El Toro' but darker in colour).

Yellow

R. 'Ilios' – creamy yellow, large head dependable rose.

R. 'Yellow Sphinx' – long-lasting, dependable, daffodil-yellow coloured rose with curvaceous petals.

R. 'Gold Strike' – good strong yellow rose with long, large head.

Orange and peach

R. 'Cherry Brandy' – a deservedly popular large orange rose with pink outer petals.

R. 'Milva' – reliable rose similar to 'Naranga' but with fewer thorns.

R. 'Naranga' – beautiful bright orange rose but the large number of thorns makes it difficult to handle.

R. 'Peach Avalanche' – heavenly peach colour.

R. 'Radio' – long-lasting with a gentle colour somewhere between orange and yellow.

Pink

R. 'Aqua' – popular, reliable rose with a strong pink colour.

R. 'Heaven' – a soft sugar pink rose, medium head.

R. 'Poison' – a beautiful, long-lasting, strong, fuchsia-pink rose with good form.

R. 'Sweet Avalanche' – sugar pink large headed rose.

R. 'Toscanini' – salmon pink rose with a deeper colour to the outer petals.

Blue/blue-pink

R. 'Cool Water' – a deep mauve blue.

R. 'Ocean-Song' – also known as R. 'Boyfriend' – a lavender coloured rose used in many wedding arrangements.

R. 'Cool Water'

R. 'Radio'

R. 'Aqua'

R. 'Sweet Avalanche'

R. 'Red Naomi'

R. 'Ilios'

R. 'Torero'

R. 'Vendela'

R. 'Cherry Brandy'

R. 'Ocean-Song'

R. 'Heaven'

R. 'Grand Prix'

Other considerations

Position

Large arrangements should always be positioned carefully so that they do not get in the way of the clergy and the bridal party. A pedestal near the altar always works well. If pew ends are requested, avoid decorating every pew end as this can give an over-decorated look. The same applies if every window ledge is bursting with flowers. Flowers should draw the eye towards the place where the bride and groom take their vows – a wedding is not a flower festival.

below Two pedestal designs, one each side of the altar.
Church: St. George's Church, Hanover Square, London
Photographer: Xander Casey

Height of arrangements

It is important to place the flowers so that they can be seen above the heads of the standing congregation. Pedestals and shelves may be used and the top of the rood screen (if it has a ledge) is a good place if easy access is available. Swags and tall topiary could also be considered.

right Freestanding pew ends can be easily transported to the wedding reception.
Church: St. Anthony's Church, Clontarf, Dublin, Ireland.
Arranger: The French Touch
Photographer: Mark Nixon, The Portrait Studio

Bridal flowers

Intricate wiring techniques should be left to the florist but for the flower arranger wishing to create something for a friend or relation getting married a handtied bouquet of massed flowers is simple and delightful. It is best created the day of the wedding but if the weather is not outstandingly hot it can be made the day before and kept in a cool place.

previous pages Flowers for a wedding in Dallas, Texas.
Church: Park Cities Presbyterian Church, Dallas, TX
Arranger: Rusty Glenn
Photographer: AO Photography

right and far right
Church: St. Paul's Church, Knightsbridge
Arranger: Judith Blacklock
Photographer: Judith Blacklock

Step by step

Massed rose bouquet

You will need
- 17–20 medium–large roses – if creating this for the first time I would purchase a few more and use any left over for extra buttonholes.
- about 15 large leaves such as *Galax* or *Hedera* (ivy)
- light–medium-gauge stub wire
- stem tape (Parafilm® or Stemtex®)
- ribbon
- pearl-headed pins

Method

1   Cut the stems of the leaves short, about 1 cm ($^1/_2$ in) in length. Using the stub wire make a small stitch through the back of the leaf about two thirds of the way down. Bring the two ends of the wire together and wrap one end around the other and the leaf stem three times. Cover the stem and wire with stem tape. Place the wired leaves on the side.

2   Arrange the roses in your hand so that their stems are parallel and their heads form a gentle dome shape. Make sure that the bunch is even from all sides. Secure the bunch tightly with tape or twine about 3 cm (1 in) down from the top of the stems.

3   Use the wired leaves to make a frill around the edge of the bouquet and bend them downwards slightly so that they frame the roses. Tape again in the same place.

4   To wrap the stem with ribbon, start at the top of the stems. Wrap the ribbon around the stems, overlapping half of the previous layer. Continue for about 7.5cm (3in) down the stems. Stop and continue wrapping the ribbon back up the stem to the middle. Tuck the selvedge under and pin in place.

5   Cut the stems at a length to suit the bride.

Tip

To keep the bouquet fresh it can be sprayed gently with water, wrapped loosely in tissue paper, placed in a plastic bag into which air has been blown and placed in the lower part of a refrigerator overnight.

right A similar idea, can be created for the bridesmaid, perhaps with *Freesia*.

Arranger: Anna Greaves (Redding)
Photographer: Joanna Gallagher

Outdoor weddings

An outdoor wedding ceremony is a perfect setting for a couple who loves nature or wants to celebrate at a special location. They are particularly popular in the USA but the inclement weather in the UK means that they are more difficult to arrange.

Outdoor weddings can take place by the sea, by the lake or even at a golf course. When planning, a focal point should be created for the service, such as an arch or a screen covered in flowers and foliage. Elements native to the location can be incorporated such as shells and palms for a beach wedding or intertwining branches, vines and leaves for a woodlands venue. Provision should always be made for rainy, windy or hot weather.

right The open view. A glorious vista for an out of doors wedding in Durham, NC.

Photographer: Lee Thompson

far right Free-standing metal containers, filled with flowers, line the aisle.

Photographer: Lee Thompson

16 Flower Festivals

This chapter is in three parts. The first deals with general matters, and duties of the principal people organising a festival. The second deals in a more detailed way with particular aspects and what people need to do. The third gives suggestions for designing the festival including themes, colour schemes and music all of which are important for presenting an inspiring festival.

General matters and duties of the principal organisers

Why hold a flower festival?

Why hold a flower festival? There are many reasons that justify the hard work, long hours and commitment that are involved. Firstly flower festivals are inspiring, uplifting occasions. Many people work together happily towards a single purpose and give unselfishly of their time and energy. There are jobs for everyone and this helps people to make friends, welcomes strangers and stimulates a community spirit which helps create a united and thriving church.

A flower festival attracts visitors to the church who would not otherwise have come and this does nothing but good. Additionally, money may be raised that can contribute towards or pay for something that is desperately needed such as repairs to the church, central heating, a new organ or a set of hymn books or for a charity or special project external to the church.

left Plants of bright summer flowers fill the bicycle's wicker baskets to give a warm welcome to a flower festival.
Church: St. Mary the Virgin, Mortlake
Arranger: Penny Cowell
Photographer: Judith Blacklock

The planning

Festivals have to begin somewhere. Once the idea has germinated, the people responsible for initiating the idea have to put it to the church authorities and clergy, and get approval in principle for the project, with an early decision on dates and duration of the festival. Depending on the size of the festival, planning should probably start eighteen months to two years in advance and the organisers meet regularly over the 12 months prior to the festival.

Behind any successful and happy event lies careful planning. Time and thought spent in preparation are always worthwhile and the festival will run smoothly as a result. Most people like to know exactly what, when and how they are to contribute to the event and then no one becomes upset and everyone gives of their best.

It is essential that from the beginning there is a happy relationship between the clergy and other church officials, the Flower Guild and other flower arrangers. If any difficulties arise in the running of a festival it is usually because some problem has not been discussed from everyone's point of view. The proposal and the plan may come from flower arrangers who are not members of the church. They must have the support of the clergy and fully involve the Flower Guild. It is members of the church Flower Guild who create arrangements year in and year out and they must be fully included and respected at all times.

Check legislation on Health and Safety, in particular with regard to the use of stepladders.

The committee and officers

After the project has been accepted in principle, a chairman should be selected to head a committee tasked with the organisation of the festival. Ideally the chairman of the Festival should be both a flower club member and a member of the church's Flower Guild. The person who put forward the idea of a festival may automatically fall into this role. This person may also be the Festival Designer.

If a separate designer is to be brought in, he or she should be chosen by agreement between the chairman and the church authorities at the earliest possible stage, and consulted throughout the planning process.

Include someone with experience of publicity/marketing/media on the committee right from the start. They need to be involved in deciding on the title and focus of the festival, the planning and distribution of publicity from flyers and posters, advertising on appropriate websites, through to the design of the brochure, as well as contact with the media.

right A charming and original way to get the children involved and visitors interested! Flower paintings, created by the local school have been laminated and tied to the railings by parents and staff.
Church: St. Mary the Virgin, Mortlake
Artists: Pupils of St. Mary Magdalen's Catholic Primary School
Photographer: Judith Blacklock

Representatives from participating groups should be included on the committee as well as those with the specialist skills needed. It is helpful to define the areas of responsibility at the beginning and then to appoint a committee member to look after each. Everyone on the committee should have a job which they can get their teeth into. The number depends on the size and scope of the event. If clear terms of reference are drawn up for each committee member, overlaps and omissions can be avoided.

Areas of responsibility can be subdivided if the festival is very large, or for a smaller festival several of the positions can be combined.

Chairman

Being the chairman is a huge responsibility. The chairman needs to find the strengths in each member of the team so that jobs can be allocated to the best advantage. The chairman should be prepared to take overall responsibility for:

- chairmanship of meetings
- the general organisation – being aware of everything
- constant liaison with the church authorities

- co-ordination of the groups of workers and their duties
- keeping his/her deputy or vice-chairman fully informed
- helping, supporting, advising and seeing that there is always a happy atmosphere

Secretary

This is a vital job calling for someone with administrative experience and a painstaking eye to detail. Access to email is very important.

The work should include:

- keeping written records (a help with future events)
- circulation of agendas and minutes of meetings in co-operation with the chairman
- general correspondence
- keeping everyone on track, timetabling, arranging meetings and appointments
- sending out invitations and letters of thanks (usually signed by the chairman) after the festival

Treasurer

This is a position for someone with experience and confidence with book keeping and keeping records. He or she needs to be someone who is good at persuading people to part with their money (unless there is someone else with responsibility for fund raising through sponsorship, advertising and organising events). The work should include:

- opening a festival account
- arranging a quiet place and times for counting the money
- arranging for an audit of the accounts
- arranging insurance (checking with the church which may already have good insurance or at least a good insurer)
- drawing up a budget of expenditure and income
- keeping a cash book and float of petty cash
- paying bills and obtaining and keeping receipts
- providing collection boxes at the festival if required and supervising the banking or the secure housing of the proceeds. The church which may well have a safe for storage of money and valuables may give help with this.
- providing a financial report after the festival

Festival Designer(s)

Trust and companionship which is built up between church, designer and committee is special. The designer must aim for a happy and contented atmosphere between him or her and the flower arrangers, and also be on hand during staging and dismantling. It is essential to soothe any fears and resolve problems. Ideally the designer must enjoy speaking with the public, be able to explain how things were done, listen to comments and give them an insight into the world of flower arranging and artistic design.

For a large church or cathedral two or more designers may be necessary.

Duties and responsibilities of the festival designer include:

- The artistic planning including the theme, the positions, colours, shapes of the arrangements with suggestions for types of flower and foliage.
- Listening to the views of the festival committee and co-operation at all times with the church authorities.
- Briefing flower arrangers, including visits to the church to show people where they are to work and emails/letters confirming details and staging times.
- Organising exhibits such as church treasures, fabrics, vestments, plate. The church authorities may be delighted to co-operate in this sort of venture.

- The provision of working tables and spaces, storage and water facilities.
- The organisation and purchasing of flowers. Many organisers prefer to give the responsibility and work of ordering and preparing the flowers to each individual participant. It is often considered best to let individual arrangers work to a budget and to bring their flowers to the festival ready prepared. To cut down on cost and waste, any left over flowers can be put in a bucket with the name and number and keep for replacement if necessary. The logistics of having all the flowers and foliage prepared in the same area would prove very difficult for a large festival.
- Conditioning of plant material received from sources other than from individual flower arrangers.
- The use of the church flower containers, in consultation with the Flower Guild.
- Viewing, staging and dismantling times for the arrangers.
- Arranging for the protection of furnishings and floors and the movement of furniture (with the church authorities' permission).
- The use of nails and screws (only with permission).
- The employing of a carpenter and electrician if necessary (through the church authorities).
- The provision of stepladders.
- Arranging for the mechanics to be constructed.
- Organising the installation of any extra lighting. This may seem expensive but is essential.

previous pages
The Farming Year – designs depicting the changing seasons.
Church: Lincoln Cathedral
Arrangers: Market Rasen Flower Club
Photographer: Dick Makin

right Behind this stunning arch of pink *Eustoma* (lisianthus) is a purpose built structure created to fit into a specific arch. It was made with hollow steel tubing 1.5cm in diameter. The weight of the mechanic is such that there is outward pressure on each side. This means that it holds itself in place against the church fabric without pins or cables. To create the framework for the flowers, small constructions were made with short sections of a branch nailed together. These were then wired together with 0.9mm steel wire leaving sufficient space between for glass tubes to be wired. The *Eustoma* was then placed in the tubes.
Church: Church of Alden Biesen, Bilzen, Belgium
Designer: Stef Adriaenssens
Photographer: Stef Adriaenssens

Points for consideration at an early stage

The committee should, at an early meeting, consider the following:

- The basis of finance and arrangements for making a sensible budget. The availability and cost of flowers needs to be taken into account. Agree a deadline by which the event will be cancelled if insufficient money has been raised. If you do not have the money, do not go ahead!

- The theme and title, and arrangements for seeking approval of all those involved in the festival, especially the clergy. It is important that the festival flowers convey a message and are not merely decorative.

- Identification of the key dates of what needs to happen when. Also the times of opening, staging and dismantling and length of the festival taking into account:
  - the availability and cost of flowers
  - how long the flowers will last – will the venue be heated? Will this affect the flowers?
  - relevant holiday periods
  - counter attractions in the neighbourhood
  - possible travel problems (e.g. in winter)

- Special services – the flower arrangers might enjoy a service of praise when their work is completed. The church may also wish to have special services during the festival and these normally attract a large congregation. Consideration needs to be given to how normal services will impact on the festival (both during arranging and the festival itself) and whether any special arrangements will need to be made. Cathedrals tend to have short services (10 minutes) regularly. Arrangers need to be aware of this. Services may be conducted in the various chapels and it is helpful for the arrangers to know when 'their' chapel will be used.

- Liaising with the clergy in order to be able to respect their wishes about matters such as the position of flower arrangements in the church, especially for those on the altar/communion table, the font and the pulpit. The clergy needs to provide sufficient time for setting up and dismantling. This always seems to take longer than the time budgeted!

- How to provide care and protection for the fabric of the building and its furnishings.

- If flower clubs are to be involved, and if more than one flower club is to take part, the various responsibilities should be determined. The flower club(s) may be responsible for the whole festival or only for one area in the church.

- If there is to be an official opening, preview reception or special service, where will this be held and who should be invited? Decide who will be paying or whether it will be all ticket sales. Appoint someone to organise, particularly if selling tickets.

Publicity

A vital part of the festival as a well-thought out campaign makes all the difference to the number of people who visit. Ideally it should be in the hands of someone who has had experience in the media or who is persistent and confident whilst remaining polite and tactful.

Printing

The church may have special facilities for printing leaflets, posters, flyers, tickets etc. If it does not, sponsorship can be sought from a friendly neighbourhood printer.

left A sculpture by Philip Jackson complemented with flowers.
Church: Chichester Cathedral
Arrangers: Barbara Garnell and Jan Haughton
Photographer: Michael Chevis

Catering

A church group, flower club(s), or a professional organisation may undertake this. The facilities and scope of refreshments must be agreed, and attention paid to prevailing health and safety regulations. For more details see section on 'Catering Manager'.

Help from organisations attached to the church

Help could come from organisations such as the Bell ringers, Organist, Mothers' Union, Young Wives, Sunday School, Youth Groups, Scouts, Cubs, Guides and Brownies. They will often provide enthusiastic support for different aspects of the festival. In particular, they can provide invaluable help with catering, stewarding and car parking.

General facilities

The provision of good general facilities such as catering facilities, cloakrooms, car parking, working areas and storerooms should be as good as possible.

Unexpected events

Provision for unexpected events, particularly funerals should be made. Weddings and baptisms may also have to be considered but are not usually so unexpected.

Where and how flowers and sundries will be obtained

This should be considered in consultation with the Festival Designer.

Particular aspects and responsibilities

Finance

A simple budget of expenditure and income will be needed. This should include:

Expenditure

- general expenses such as postage, telephone, stationery
- flowers and mechanics
- catering
- travel – a reasonable rate should be agreed in advance – the church often has a mileage rate, which could be appropriate
- good lighting is essential. See if an electrician would be willing to sponsor additional lighting as this is expensive. A contribution towards the extra electricity used should be considered.
- publicity and advertising
- printing
- paid help
- car parking
- contingencies

Income

- gifts and advance donations
- advance fund-raising events
- brochure sales
- catering
- sponsorship

right Lighting is essential at most flower festivals to show off the work of the designers.
Church: Chichester Cathedral
Arranger: Barbara Garnell and Jan Haughton
Photographer: Michael Chevis

Fund-raising, sponsorship and advertising

The person organising fund-raising and sponsorship needs to have similar characteristics to the person in charge of publicity, or it could be the same person. It is important to have money in hand before the festival to pay for most or all of the expenses because unforeseen events such as bad weather or illness among vital people can result in a failure of expected income.

Money in hand can be achieved by:

- A loan from the church authorities, but this may not be available, especially if the festival is to raise money for the church.
- Running special events such as coffee mornings, bring and buy stalls, plant sales.
- An audio-visual evening, a raffle or tombola.
- Sponsorship – local businesses can be asked to give sponsorship and often will, in return for acknowledgment of help in the brochure.
- Selling advertising space in the brochure. For information on putting together a brochure see page 362.

Publicity

The range of publicity depends on local conditions but may include all or any of the following:

- The distribution of flyers and posters. This could be an ideal way to include the Guides and Scouts
- Writing of press releases and provision of digital photographs
- Advertising/promotion on websites such as local events listings, tourist board and library databases, venue and diocesan websites
- Television, radio and newspaper coverage
- Magazine coverage, including 'The Flower Arranger' together with parish magazines and other church publications
- Banners and car stickers, if appropriate
- Press preview arrangements, if any
- Photography for a DVD or for future publicity
- Publicity to other organisations such as other churches, Women's Institutes, Townswomen's' Guilds, Flower Clubs

- Shop window displays
- Advertisements (paid)
- Road signs (AA or RAC)
- Local roadside and verge notices
- Lists of people to be specially invited to a preview and/or dedication service, to be agreed with clergy, chairman and committee
- Photographs for a calendar or postcards
- Preview reception/ official opening
- Collection of press cuttings for future publicity
- Photographs of arrangers' work as a gift to the arrangers

above A decorated board outside the church spreads the word.

Church: Church of St. Mary the Virgin, Mortlake
Arranger: Clare Cowlin
Photographer: Judith Blacklock

Press release

A press release should be double-spaced, simple and quick to read. It can be sent as an email or by post and should include:

- A 'headline' title, to attract attention.
- The title of the festival if different from the headline.
- The venue.
- Days and times of opening.
- Parking and refreshment facilities.
- Special features of the festival.
- Financial aim.
- Flower Club name(s) if they are involved.
- A name, email and telephone number for further information.
- Admission charge if permitted.

Flyers and posters

These should include the same information but condensed and well spaced for rapid reading. If possible someone with experience of graphic design should be asked to help with the layout of these. A good printer will be happy to make helpful suggestions.

right This magnificent sculpture of plant material certainly tells the public that something special is happening!

Church: Sint-Salvatorskathedraal, Bruges
Photographer: Judith Blacklock

Printing Officer

Duties include:

- Printing of all advertising material such as flyers, posters, and car stickers.
- Devising, collating and printing of the brochure (see below).
- Provision of stewards' badges.
- Printing of title cards for flower arrangements (in conjunction with the artistic designer).
- Printing of the direction cards, such as 'exit' (in conjunction with the committee member in charge of stewarding).
- Printing of tickets for any special services, recitals, previews, etc.

Brochure

The brochure needs thought and planning. It will be taken home by visitors and re-read and therefore it seems important that it should include more than factual information. It could include:

- A message from the minister
- Introduction by the Area Chairman (if flower clubs are involved) or perhaps a local celebrity.
- A history of the church
- A plan of the church
- Articles of local interest
- A list of the arrangements, numbered in order of viewing (to correspond with a number on the arrangement and on the plan)
- Names of the arrangers or the club/group responsible for the arrangement
- Appropriate texts
- Details of the themes interpreted
- List of sponsors
- Photography and drawings

Other information to include is the name of the church, flower club, committee, dates and time of festival, church service times, how the money made will be used, organisations that have given help, the thanks of the chairman and advertisers.

The cover should be attractive to encourage sales. Printing such a booklet can be expensive and the total cost should be gone into carefully, as it is important that the printing costs do not exceed the profits made in selling the brochure. A careful balance of content, type of paper, size and so on must be considered. The person putting the brochure together could also be the person bringing in the advertisements.

below Floral hassocks are impractical but for flower festivals they are most decorative placed on steps, ledges or on the pews. Here the bases are large pieces of foam cut to an appropriate size and covered with overlapping leaves, secured with decorative pins.

Church: Grace Episcopal Church, Chalreston, SC
Arranger: Judith Blacklock
Photographer: Judith Blacklock

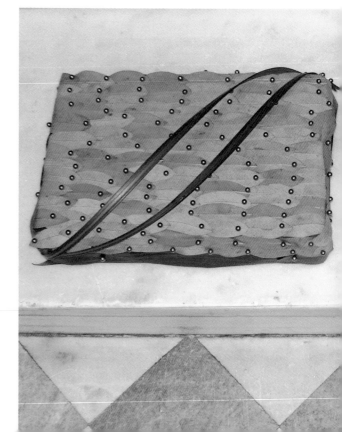

Catering Manager

This position would suit someone with experience in catering or a good home cook who enjoys baking and has friends who could help! This is one of the areas where members of the church organisations may be delighted to be involved. The duties include:

- Deciding the extent of catering for the public and helpers, such as:
  - light lunches
  - snacks
  - tea, coffee and biscuits
  - afternoon tea
  - hot soup
- The charges to the public.
- Provision of a board showing meal prices.
- Ordering and preparation of food.
- Refreshment helpers' rota.
- Collection of tablecloths, cutlery, china, napkins.
- Provision of tables and chairs for serving food and for guests.
- The table flowers.
- Meals for special guests.
- Washing up arrangements.
- Disposal of surplus food.

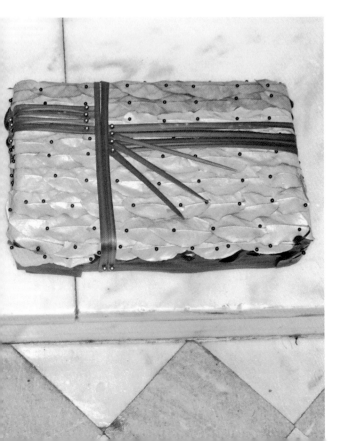

Chief Steward

The qualities required are that the chief steward should be organised, methodical and quick thinking! The duties include:

- Organisation of the viewing route, including doors to be kept shut or open, provision of ropes and stands.
- Placement of direction signs.
- Selling of brochures, photographs, CDs and DVDs.
- Compiling a stewards' rota.
- Car parking arrangements and attendants' rota if appropriate.
- Police notification if appropriate.
- Provision of first aid facilities (the Red Cross or the St John's Ambulance Brigade may be able to attend the festival) and simple first aid equipment at staging time and throughout the festival. Check on use with Health and Safety Regulations.
- Assistance to arrangers when unloading.
- Arrangement of cloakroom and toilet facilities, including soap and towels.
- Provision of extra buckets for flowers, some dustsheets for rubbish.
- Provision of large plastic bags or boxes for rubbish and the disposal of rubbish. Check on local arrangements for recycling.
- Provision of cleaning materials, including brushes and pan, mop and bucket, cloths and dusters.
- Provision of heating if necessary.
- Topping up of flower arrangement containers with water throughout the festival and the replacement of flowers.
- Seeing that the public does not handle flower arrangements and accessories.
- Arranging for photography with the publicity committee member.
- Answering questions from the general public.
- Keeping an eye on the moneyboxes and security of any valuable objects on display.
- Arranging car badges for the committee and helpers in large festivals in crowded cities, and the staggering of the arrival of cars.
- Welcoming visitors.

Suggestions for designing the festival

A church flower festival needs considerable thought with regard to design. It should not be an overdone flower show that exchanges the marquee or hall for the church. Nothing looks worse than an over-decorated effect, with flowers hiding the fabric and furnishings of the church itself. The object of the overall design should be to draw attention to the church's own beauty and not to hide or detract from it in any way. It is therefore essential to plan the position of the arrangements very carefully remembering that restraint and dignity are essential.

The use of only the most dignified and appropriate accessories is desirable. Why hang yards of coloured fabric over mellow stone walls that provide the most beautiful background for flowers? Bases too should be used with discretion as the natural stonework or weathered wood of the church is often more attractive than anything else. Uniform ranks of pedestals or large triangles on every windowsill are not always the best/most beautiful way of showing flowers.

Consider using dried, preserved and silk materials for eking out the budget and for use in places which are inaccessible for watering. They can also be prepared in advance.

Sometimes one type of plant material such as a bowl of one variety of rose with foliage, or a mass of gladioli in one colour, is more striking and meaningful than a mixed flower arrangement. A variety of shapes and sizes can be selected for the arrangements, always being sure that the shape suits the position for which it is intended in the church. Full use can be made of any special features so that attention is drawn to them by means of arrangements.

below The font of Nabrassina stone has eight sides to reflect the seven days of material creation and the 'eighth day' of the new creation when those baptised rise to new life in Christ Jesus. Eight vibrant landscape designs, in pinks and blues, reflect the joy and happiness which children bring into the world. The designs complement perfectly the cruciform shape of the font.

Church: Brentwood Cathedral
Arrangers: Maureen Bailey and Shirley Perkins
Photographer: Phillip Lawrence

Here are some ideas of where to start when planning a festival.

- Obtain a scale plan of the church.
- Walk around the church looking for suitable places to position the arrangements.
- Mark in any of the special features that may affect the positioning of the arrangements.
- Mark on the plan the position of the intended arrangements. In a cathedral or large church these may be divided into groups with a designer for each section.
- Colour coding using small different coloured circles for each group involved is helpful.

Every flower arranger taking part should see the setting for the arrangement and discuss the design with the festival designer. When personal viewing is impossible, because of long distance travel, then a sketch or photograph of the position should be sent.

Decide where special lighting may be needed. Extra lighting, carefully positioned especially in dark places, may greatly increase the impact of a flower arrangement and enhance the interpretation of a theme. Remember that flowers do not show when seen against a light such as in front of a window.

Every flower arranger should receive a letter containing the following:

- The theme of the festival and historical notes on the church.
- The theme of the arrangement.
- Suggestions for accessories, if they are to be used.
- The general idea of the shape, colouring and size of the arrangement.
- The allowance for flowers (a ceiling must be given).
- If the flowers are to be purchased by individuals or if there will be central buying.
- The dates and times for viewing the church beforehand, for staging and for dismantling.
- Where appropriate, information on the Flower Guild and how to join.

right Arranging flowers to complement the Bishop's cope worn on Trinity Sunday. Here the colours and the asymmetrical design are the perfect complement to the robe.
Church: Cathedral Church of St. Peter and St. Paul, Sheffield
Arrangers: Margaret Peers, Pat Peers and Eileen Thomas, Sheffield Cathedral Flower Guild
Photographer: Oliver Gordon

Working with colour

In a small church an overall colour harmony can often be best. One colour used in variety can be very effective. A deep shade may be used for one end of the church, gradually lightening to the other end. In a large church or cathedral colour schemes can be compartmentalized, such as in the nave, the choir or a side chapel.

Green is neglected although much used by our ancestors. It is delightful seen against stone walls and columns, especially in garlands without flowers, or with flowers added in one colour. Growing plants are always lovely and may be massed in groups. There are many greens and textures to give variety and interest. The plants may be borrowed or, given enough time, specially grown for the festival.

The colours of stone, wood, carpets, curtains, cushions, faded coats of arms, glass and silver, rows of hymn books, vestments, the altar frontal in use at the time of the festival, should all be considered when the flower colours are chosen.

Flower arrangements that are adjacent to each other should be in gentle harmony, with a gradual change to make it appear more restful. The time of year also affects the choice as some colours seem more suitable in different seasons, such as oranges and reds when it is cold or in the autumn, yellow in the spring.

Stained glass windows are generally colourful and it is rewarding to link flower arrangements with their colours, but it can be a mistake to pick out every colour in the flower arrangement. The choice of only one or two of the colours for the flowers can be more effective.

When themes are interpreted thought should be given to the colour which has associations for people both in life generally and also as used by the church. In different communities across the world colour has different resonances. For example, in the western world black is associated with sickness and death, solemnity and negation, whereas in China the colour associated with death and mourning is white. Most societies associate red with war, power, hate, but it has also associations with love. Green for many means the resurgence of new life in the spring, and blue with heavenly things.

Complementing the magnificence of festal copes is a popular theme at flower festivals. Here the Dean's festal cope at Salisbury Cathedral is featured. The colour of the flowers – from dark purple to pink – lead the eye to the cope.

Church: Salisbury Cathedral
Arranger: All Saints Church, Harnham
Photographer: Oliver Gordon

The most commonly found scheme for liturgical colour in the church (altar frontal and vestments) is based on white (which is taken to include gold and yellow), green, red, and blue (which includes purple). Sometimes there are variations, and the local clergy must always be consulted about the practice in any particular church or on any particular Sunday. However, the following are the most generally accepted uses of each of the four colours.

White (including gold and yellow)

Major church feasts and festivals: Christmas, Epiphany, Easter, Ascension, Trinity Sunday, the Transfiguration, the two principal Feasts of the Virgin Mary (the Presentation of Christ in the Temple – Candlemas – and the Annunciation), Holy Innocents, All Saints, Apostles and other saints who are not martyrs.

Green

The Sundays between the Feast of the Epiphany and the commencement of Lent (blue is occasionally used for these but this is rare) and the Sundays from the first after the Feast of Holy Trinity until the second Sunday before Advent.

Red

Pentecost, Remembrance Sunday, the last Sunday before Advent (if it is kept as the Feast of Christ the King), martyrs.

Blue including purple

Seasons of penitence and preparation, i.e. Advent and Lent (though in most churches Lent is kept without flowers).

Feasts take precedence over the general colour prevailing in Lent or the Sundays after Trinity and the colour changes to white.

following pages A stunning installation of 21 decorative ironwork obelisks fills this transept, topped with spheres of *Gypsophila*. They are hung with *Gerbera* and Capiz shell held in glass tubes by aluminium wire.

Church: Salisbury Cathedral
Arrangers: Members from 21 churches in the diocese of Salisbury
Photographer: Oliver Gordon

above Trailing clouds of God's Glory in Redemption was executed by Malcolm Benson who suffers from Motor Neurone Disease. He struggled for four hours, mostly on his knees, to produce a design which complemented the simplicity of the altar made from Nabrassina stone from Pisa. Three arrangements of pure arum lilies and white roses were grouped at the foot of the cross – symbol of the price Jesus paid for our Redemption. The gold of the cross was picked up in the golden lilies and signified the Kingship of Christ.

Church: Brentford Cathedral
Arranger: Malcolm Benson
Photographer: Phillip Lawrence

left This design on the altar represents the Last Supper. White flowers were chosen for purity. Other plant material used was *Anthurium* 'Acropolis', *Zantedeschia*, the pure white *Rosa* 'Akito', and carnations. Grapes represent the wine and wheat the bread.

Church: Whiteabbey Presbyterian Church
Arranger: James Burnside
Photographer: Janet Wilson

right One of four designs depicting the seasons. This one is Summer interpreting 'Summer Trees' by Belinda Lyon.

Church: Lincoln Cathedral
Arranger: Grimsby Flower Lovers' Club
Photographer: Dick Makin

Themes

Some of the flower arrangements should be more than simply decorative so that the designs can become a means of communication, and can help a visitor to the church to absorb a deeper knowledge of Christian teachings. There are many ideas for interpretation and the minister of the church will have suggestions and be able to give guidance.

The designer must do some homework on possible themes to give ideas to the arrangers. They can then follow these up with more detailed research. Gimmickry and inartistic accessories should be avoided and the designer should suggest suitable ways of interpreting themes to those who have not used flowers in this manner. If possible the most experienced flower arrangers should be used for this aspect of the festival. The less experienced will be happy to help with garlands and large-scale arrangements under the guidance of more advanced flower arrangers.

left A design interpreting the Synod of Whitby. Fundamental differences over dress, forms of service and the observance of Easter in the calendar caused strife between Celtic and Roman Christians. To resolve the differences, King Oswy of Northumbria convened the Synod of Whitby in 663. Cedd, who could speak Irish and understood Latin, acted as an interpreter. He voted with the Celts, but the Roman bishops won the arguments.
Church: Chelmsford Cathedral
Arranger: Terri Potter
Photographer: David Lloyd

right For a winter flower festival this shepherd and sheep would create a delightful entrance for both young and old. The sheep were made by attaching hoops of willow round and over metal frames consisting of a backbone and four legs with a small spur to attach the head. Wire netting was used to shape the heads and was covered in hessian and natural Finland moss.
Arrangers: Jane Burns, Christine Kent and ladies from the Ambleside, Cartmel and Holme and District Flower Club
Photographer: Judith Blacklock

SCRIBITE SCIENTES

above
A collage depicting the shield
of The Worshipful Company of
Scriveners of London
Church: Lincoln Cathedral
Arrangers: North Hykeham & District
Flower Club
Photographer: Dick Makin

right
Stepping through Time –
The Romans
Church: Lincoln Cathedral
Arrangers: Gainsborough & District
Flower Club
Photographer: Dick Makin

The Calendar of the Church

This makes an excellent theme and title. Included can be all or any of the seasons of the Christian year. The church's own patronal festival may be marked with special services.

Days of Special Significance

There are many days which have special significance in the life of the church. The clergy will always know what is local practice and of course should be consulted at all times. They will advise on appropriate texts and colours.

Sermon on the Mount with ten main themes:

- The poor
- The sorrowful
- The gentle
- The righteous
- The merciful
- The pure
- The peacemakers
- The persecuted
- The salt of the earth
- The light of the world

The life of the Blessed Virgin Mary

- The Nativity of the Virgin Mary
- The Presentation of Christ in the Temple, otherwise known as the Purification of the Virgin Mary
- The Visitation
- The Annunciation
- The Immaculate Conception
- The Birth of Jesus
- The Epiphany
- The Marriage at Cana
- The Crucifixion

Ecclesiastical Concepts

The scope for choice of themes here is infinite but the following are a few suggestions:

'All things bright and beautiful', the Benedicite, the parables and the Psalms. Texts from the Bible such as:

- 'I am the light of the world', John 8.12
- 'I am the good shepherd', John 10.11
- 'Lo I am with you even unto the end of the world', Matthew 28.20
- 'Suffer little children to come unto me', Luke 18.16
- 'This is my body. This is my blood', Matthew 26.26 (for the sacrament)
- 'Go ye unto the world and preach the gospel to every creature'. Mark 16. 15
- 'Consider the lilies', Luke 12. 27
- 'Man shall not live by bread alone', Luke 4.4
- 'Peace, be still', Mark 4.39
- 'If any man will come after me let him deny himself and take up his cross and follow me'. Matthew 16.24 (depicting monastery life)
- 'He that believeth and is baptised shall be saved', Mark 10.16
- 'Greater love hath no man' John 15.13

right and following pages Three of the twelve Stations of the Cross represented in flowers to complement the sculptures by Jonathan Clarke at Southwell Minster.

right Station 3 – Jesus falls for the first time.
Church: Southwell Minster
Arranger: Di Smith
Photographer: Toby Smith

left Station 8 – Jesus speaks to the women of Jerusalem. Jesus turned to the women and said "Daughters of Jerusalem do not weep for me, but weep for yourselves and for your children"
Note the teardrop crystals incorporated into the design to represent the tears.

Church: Southwell Minster
Arranger: Maggie Connor
Photographer: Toby Smith

right Station 11 – Jesus is crucified.
Two pieces of driftwood are screwed together to make the cross. A screw eye at the back enables paper-covered wire to be looped round the base of the sculpture to give added support. The cross was created from barbed wire and the trailing *Amaranthus* glued to the back of the cross.

Church: Southwell Minster
Arranger: Anne Harcombe
Photographer: Toby Smith

Patron Saints

Some patron saints make interesting interpretations in flowers:

St. Agnes (21 January)	Betrothed couples, gardeners and maidens
St. Ambrose (7 December)	Beekeepers and domestic animals
St. Andrew (30 November)	Scotland
St. Augustine (28 August)	Theologians
St. Barbara (4 December)	Builders and firework makers
St. Benedict (21 March)	Coppersmiths and schoolboys
St. Bernard of Clairvaux (20 August)	Beekeepers
St. Boniface (5 June)	Brewers and tailors
St. Catherine (25 November)	Philosophers and spinsters
St. Cecilia (22 November)	Musicians
St. Christopher (25 July)	Sailors and travellers
St. Cornelius (16 September)	Cattle and domestic animals
St. Cuthbert (20 March)	Shepherds and seafarers
St. David (1 March)	Wales
St. Dorothy (6 February)	Brides and gardeners
St. Dunstan (19 May)	Blacksmiths, goldsmiths and the blind
St. Eligius (1 December)	Smiths and metal workers
St. Elizabeth of Hungary (19 November)	Bakers and beggars
St. Francis (4 October)	Animals
St. Gabriel, Archangel (24 March)	Postmen
St. George (23 April)	England, cavalrymen, chivalry and soldiers
St. Giles (1 September)	Beggars, blacksmiths and cripples
St. Gregory the Great (12 March)	Musicians
St. Jerome (30 September)	Students
St. John the Evangelist (27 September)	Booksellers, painters, printers and publishers
St. Joseph (19 March)	Carpenters, engineers and the family
St. Jude (28 October)	The desperate
St. Lawrence (10 August)	Cooks, cutters, armouries and schoolboys
St. Luke (18 October)	Doctors, goldsmiths and sculptors
St. Margaret (20 July)	Women (especially maidens), nurses and peasants
St .Mark (25 April)	Venice, glaziers and notaries
St. Martin of Tours (11 November)	Beggars, innkeepers and tailors
St. Matthew (21 September)	Bankers and tax collectors
St. Michael, Archangel (29 September)	Artists and soldiers
St. Nicholas (6 December)	Children and captives
St. Patrick (17 March)	Ireland
St. Paul (30 June)	Musicians
St. Peter (29 June)	Bakers, butchers and clockmakers
St. Raphael, Archangel (24 October)	Guardian angels
St. Sebastian (20 January)	Armourers, ironmongers and potters
St. Theresa of Avila (15 October)	Those in need of grace
St. Thomas (21 December)	Architects, carpenters and geometricians
St. Ursula (21 October)	Maidens, drapers and teachers
St. Zita (27 April)	Domestic servants

top left
St. Agatha, Patron Saint of Bell Ringers

Church: St. Illtyd's Church, Llantwit Major
Arranger: Wendy Mayle and Marion Price
Photographer: Judith Blacklock

top right
St. Thomas the Apostle, Patron Saint of India and Theologians

Church: St. Illtyd's Church, Llantwit Major
Arranger: Trixie Randell
Photographer: Judith Blacklock

bottom left
St. Justa, Patron Saint of Potters

Church: Holy Trinity Church, Marcross
Arranger: Caitlin Davies
Photographer: Judith Blacklock

bottom right
St. James, Patron Saint of Hat makers

Church: St. James' Church, Wick
Arranger: The Yoga Club
Photographer: Judith Blacklock

Music

Music can play an important part in a festival. The church people responsible for music will often welcome an opportunity to participate, and should be consulted at an early stage of planning. Here there is room for the involvement of local groups of instrumentalists and choirs. If there is an organist, occasional short recitals during opening times may be arranged. The wealth of good church music is enormous, ranging from major orchestral and choral works to little motets calling for only a few voices. It may be possible to put on special concerts during the period of the festival, ranging from a performance of an appropriate oratorio linked to the theme of the festival. For example, a church celebrating aspects of the life of Jesus could perform parts of the Christmas Oratorio, the Messiah, or one of the Passions of Bach. St. Nicholas could be linked with Benjamin Britten's work of that name. Purcell's Ode on St. Cecilia's Day is always enjoyed. In a different mode, there is a wide choice of moving music among negro spirituals, and there are musical riches in the work of composers such as Charles Wesley, Vaughan Williams and Herbert Howells, to name but a few.

Themes can also interpret the life of the town, the history of the church and the life of people buried or remembered. The event can be combined with a major festival, such as a saint's day, Easter, Pentecost, Harvest, Christmas, Mothering Sunday, Remembrance Sunday, or local festivals such as the tulip festivals in the fen country or Plough Sunday.

Poetry

Tributes may be made to ecclesiastical craftsmen, to writers, musicians and famous men and women. Works of art – paintings, carvings, sculpture – can be borrowed from local people, galleries, universities and museums to combine with flowers. Thomas Campbell wrote of daisies and buttercups, Alfred Tennyson of roses and lilies, Wordsworth (famously) of daffodils, William Blake of wild flowers, Milton of 'herbs, fruit and flowers glistening with dew', Longfellow of 'tremulous leaves with soft silver lining'.

right The monks greeted guests arriving for a festival of flowers. The monks were sculpted by the gloved hands of strong women of the Garden Club of Toronto. The wire used was not chicken wire but a much stronger diamond metal lath found at a local building supply outlet. (It is used as a plaster base and also as reinforcement for the base coat in ceramic tile work.) They were sturdy enough to be simply pegged into the ground with wires.

Church: Grace Church on-the-Hill, Toronto
Arrangers: Members of the Garden Club of Toronto
Photographer: Peg Spence

right This simple but evocative design on a window ledge is composed of mini *Gerbera*, bloom *Chrysanthemum* and *Anthurium*. The accessories of the hymnbook and violin are placed sympathetically to tell the tale but do not overwhelm the design. There is the added bonus of a lovely garden outside with red foliage reflecting the colour of the flowers.

Church: Chelmsford Cathedral
Arrangers: Chelmsford Cathedral Flower Guild
Photographer: David Lloyd

right Trading in goods from all corners of the world is part of Liverpool's maritime history. The flowers used are *Anthurium 'Choco'*, *Carthamus*, *Gerbera*, lilies and *Strelitzia* (birds of paradise).

Church: Liverpool Cathedral
Arranger: Sheila Edge
Photographer: Graham Rodger

above St. Mary's Mortlake stands close to the finish of the boat race and this design could depict nothing else! Dark blue *Delphinium* and *Iris* are to one side and light blue to the other. The water is depicted by green and brown foliage with steel grass in loops to represent the waves along the front.

Church: St. Mary the Virgin, Mortlake
Arranger: Jean Mitelman
Photographer: Judith Blacklock

17 Tips from the Experts

In the course of researching and writing this book I have been in contact with floral designers from all over the world, each with their own individual style of design but all sharing the common interest of arranging in places of worship. Some of them were kind enough to share their expertise and their tips for arranging in Church make very interesting reading.

Hillary Brian
National Chairman, Church of England Flower Arrangers' Association

- Consult the minister as to his wishes about church flowers. He is the head of flowers in church and will naturally have this own idea on what he likes and where he likes them placed. (He may leave this entirely up to the person in charge of flowers but it is courtesy to ask.)

- Consider the architecture of the church – the stained glass, carvings, fabrics and statues. Sit for a while and get the feeling for the church and take note where flowers could be placed, being ever mindful of the movement of clergy, choir and congregation.

- Decide on the shape of the arrangements, taking into consideration the position where flowers will be positioned.

- Church flower arranging is different from any other for one must think big. Remember the arrangements must be seen from the back of the church. Choose the flowers wisely so that they are suitable for the size of the arrangement. For large pedestals include some bold flowers that show up well.

- Choose colours to suit the church, the festival for which one is decorating or the particular liturgical colour of the day is this is what the minister likes. Tone flowers to the stained glass when necessary.

- Mechanics are probably the dullest and hardest of a flower arranger's work but it most important that they are done well so that flowers are secure and no accidents occur.

left A wedding candle (always a set of two) for a Greek Orthodox wedding are called 'Lambada' and symbolises the union of the bride and groom. Kabab sticks have been gently hammered into the side of the candle and a section of caged garland (an OASIS® product) hung over the protrusions and decorated.

Church: Pikermi, Greece
Arranger: Robert Koene
Photographer: Fotis Karapiperis

Bob Brown
Paisley Abbey, Scotland (on photography)

- Purchase a 'best buy' digital camera of minimum 3 – 8 million pixels and with a direct viewfinder (those with only an LCD screen are not ideal), an inbuilt flash and a good zoom/close-up lens. View the listings at the back of any up-to-date digital photo magazine for information.

- If your camera can record RAW as well as JPEG images then use it – particularly for high key subtle tones such as *Lathyrus* (sweet peas).
  - JPEG – smallest compressed amount of digital data for a reasonable picture
  - RAW – much more data allowing much greater variations of tone and detail

- Always frame your picture generously – you can always trim more precisely at processing stage. If the data is not there in the first place you can never rectify this.

- A tripod or monopod can be a boon to steady your camera.

- Natural light is best and a simple light reflector can be improvised with a large white handkerchief or sheet of paper to bounce the light back onto the shadow side.

- If you have to use flash then soften it by draping a white tissue over the flash or using white reflectors about the subject.

- Once you have your images, always download and label the ORIGINAL files and save them (preferably in top quality TIFF format) on either a CD or external hard drive.

- There is no one who can process your images with the diligence and refinement that you can by doing it yourself using Adobe Photoshop or Corel Draw.

- Join a Camera Club and use their facilities and backup.

- For the man whose wife is into flower arranging, photography is the only reliable way to sustain the marriage!

above

Church: Paisley Abbey
Arranger: Maureen Mitchell
Photographer: Bob Brown

Harold Burns
(on good stable mechanics)

- Ask yourself and your team what needs to be achieved.

- Decide where the finished design is going to be placed.

- Find out what space you have to work in (height, width and depth). Allow for the material span – large sticking out stems such as palms and ferns – when determining the size of the mechanics.

- Work out how large the mechanics need to be. Do you expect it to be part of the design?

- Do a rough sketch what you would like to achieve. Next, make a sketch to scale and try to be as informative as possible.

- Decide on the material to be used for the mechanics. Is it going to be flexible, rigid, heavy? Must it be transportable – will it fit into the car?

- Find out if the design can be watered. If not then use plant material that will last the duration of the event or preserved material.

above Colourful flowers were chosen to stand out against the dark wooden background. Bowls of flowers decorated the altar rail. Ribbon was taken over the foam and tied securely to the rails to keep the bowls balanced and in position.

Church: Temple Church, London
Arranger: Sheila Adby, Sylvia Barrett, Christine Milburn, Susan Sparham, Jenny Southey, Orpington Floral Art Society.
Photographer: Lyndon Parker

Brenda Hall
Scottish Episcopal Church of St Michael and All Angels, Elie, Fife, Scotland

- Collaborate at all times with the clergy. When the local priest or minister is very relaxed about the flowers in church there is usually only gratitude to the flower arrangers for their devoted and reliable work. Difficulties can arise if the clergy are extremely strict about liturgical colour, for example, because occasionally a saint or martyr may be commemorated and the appropriate liturgical colour may change. So good relationships are very important.

- Avoid the nightmare of a collapsed arrangement. Remember that plant material may continue to grow after being arranged and the physical balance of the arrangement may be affected. This is a particular problem with pedestals where the increase in weight of the forward-facing flowers may cause the whole to tip forward. Put a heavy pinholder or stone into a polythene bag, and tie it securely to the back of the pedestal before arranging the flowers. It should hang a little below the level of the container where it will act as a counterweight and will not be seen once the plant material is in place.

- A pot-et-fleur can be invaluable in providing something pleasant to look at in seasons when flowers are very expensive or when arrangers are few or unskilled. Depending on the size of the available space, a pot-et-fleur can be placed on a plinth in the sanctuary, or on a step well away from traffic, or on a table in the porch or entrance to the church. It is particularly valuable in the season between Epiphany and Ash Wednesday.

- When the liturgical colour is red, although it is an advancing colour, it can look very flat especially in large or dark churches. Increase the impact of the arrangement by using a few shocking pink or orange flowers. The red ones should be larger and more predominant, of course, but the visual effect is much more dramatic. An alternative is the use of lime green flowers and foliage –*Alchemilla mollis* and *Choisya ternata* 'Sundance' are both invaluable.

left

Church: Westminster Abbey
Arranger: Sheila Banks
Photographer: Toby Smith

- Try to dispel the notion that flower arranging for churches is solely for the ladies of the congregation. Some men will respond if encouraged, and if they do not actually wish to arrange flowers they may be willing to help in other ways, such as by looking after plants in containers (see below) or making and maintaining mechanics.

- People who are reluctant to arrange flowers may be brought gradually in to the guild by being invited to take responsibility for keeping the space allocated to flower arrangers' equipment (which may vary from a cardboard box, a shelf, to a whole room); they can be asked to arrange supplies of foam, tape, and containers.

- Share your ideas and get useful advice from the Church of England Flower Arrangers' Association, Registered Charity No. 5134372, website: www.cefaa.org.uk. Put their prayer up in the flower room (shelf or box!), say it together when the flower arrangers meet together, and include it in festival brochures:

Lord, the creator of all things of beauty, grant to those who serve you with their Gifts of floral art a sense of your majesty, and a desire to heighten the worship of the Holy Church by the dedicated use of their gifts. This we ask in the name of Him who with the Father is the Creator and Sustainer of all good things, Jesus Christ our Lord. Amen

Laura Iarocci
Chair, The Cathedral of St. Philip Flower Guild, Atlanta, USA

- Condition your flowers ahead of time – conditioning flowers is critical for church flower arranging and should be part of the weekly arranging schedule. Freshly cutting flowers and allowing them an evening to have a good drink of water and nutrients will ensure that the flowers will open properly and last longer. Arrangers should come in the day before (or two days if using roses or lilies) they plan to arrange.

- Monochromatic colours – many liturgical flowers are set far back from the congregation. To give big impact, try using flowers of the same colour. Our altar frontal has a yellow stripe so arrangements using all yellow flowers generate a "wow" response from parishioners. Our favourite combination is yellow *Eremurus*, 'Teddy Bear' sunflowers with the yellow centre and *Solidago* mixed with green *Aucuba*.

- Use garden materials. Garden greenery creates interesting textures and adds a richness to church flower arrangements. It makes designs look distinctively different from floral shop creations. Church gardens should be designed with evergreen plants that can be used as line greens and filler in arrangements. Using garden greens will also reduce the overall cost of an arrangement.

- Use rectangular boxes. Look for rectangular boxes which can hold one block of foam plus a little room for water. The boxes need to be low enough that at least an inch of the foam is exposed for cascading flowers and greenery. Boxes are a very versatile way to create interesting shapes and spread an arrangement over a large space. Arrangers can use one pair or more than one pair for larger spaces. We sometimes use a combination of ceramic boxes and recycled black dishes from food containers.

- Branches – curly willow or flowering branches soften arrangements and add a bit of whimsy to the design. I particularly like the effect that curly willow creates of growing towards heaven. One bunch of curly willow or flowering branches will last a long time. We start by using the branches in their longest form, gradually cutting off interesting pieces and using them in different arrangements. In the southern United States, we can root curly willow in water and plant it in the garden.

following pages A design using three tall cylindrical vases showcasing the offerings of autumn, enlivened with orchids.
Church: The Cathedral of St. Philip, Atlanta, GA
Arranger: Victoria Denson, Darren Ellis-May, Laura Iarocci and Kat Ottley
Photographer: George Westinghouse

Julia Legg, Sue Smith, Glyn Spencer and Caroline Vickers
Sheffield Floral Club, England

- If you cannot raise sufficient money by fund raising and sponsorship to cover the cost of flowers, do not go ahead!

- Have an identifiable reason for holding a festival such as a special anniversary celebration.

- Decide how long the festival should run bearing in mind how long the flowers will last in the venue and stewarding resources. Our Festival lasted five days which was rather ambitious.

- Involve the Cathedral or Church Flower Guild from the beginning, including representation on the planning committee.

- Start planning the project eighteen months to two years in advance. Decide on end result and start point, key activities and deadlines, then create a time line.

- Decide on a theme which will give focus but allow for a variety of interpretation by different arrangers and enhance the venue.

- Try to get support from city departments promoting tourism. Ask for support, particularly in promoting the event from NAFAS and church networks, any charity for which you are raising funds, local libraries, council and tourism offices, not forgetting any local events listings on the internet.

- Identify a budget and agree a date by which to decide whether it is feasible to go ahead (see first point above.)

- Plan for a preview, either a reception for a small number of people (sponsors and the local 'great and good'), or a ticketed preview if funds still need to be raised.

- Have a visitors' book and invite comments.

- Invite volunteer arrangers, but also appoint team leaders and ask people individually.

right Coal was an integral part of Sheffield's industrial development and has been found in the heart of the city. In this design in St. Katharine's Chapel the heat and intensity of the coal industry as depicted in these stunning designs.

Church: Cathedral Church of St. Peter and St. Paul, Sheffield
Arranger: Gill Harris, Baslow Flower Circle
Photographer: Oliver Gordon

- Allocate a specific sum of money for each arranging team and let them order and obtain their own flowers.

- Arrange photographer(s), particularly if planning follow up publications such as a calendar.

- Decide whether to keep separate totals for different income streams such as coffee, sale of programmes, donations.

- Organise rotas for serving refreshments and stewarding.

The Reverend William McMillan
The First Presbyterian (NS) Church, Dunmurry, Northern Ireland

- A flower festival staged in a Place of Worship is not a flower show. The flowers should interpret the message proclaimed in the cathedral, church, meetinghouse or sanctuary.

- There should be an explanation in the program of how the arrangements were planned so that they can be seen to interpret the proclamation of the gospel, the liturgy and/or the ritual practised there.

- Be very sensitive to the ethos and doctrine of the congregation in which you are working. For example, before considering making use of the baptismal font or placing flowers that could conceal a Cross on the Altar, enquire if it is permitted. If you intend to introduce candles or any statuary or images, (such as masks) enquire if this would be acceptable.

- Take into account the architectural style of the church. Modern designs generally look better in a contemporary building and not in a traditional one. There can be exceptions to this, of course.

- Flower arrangements in a place of worship should not be introduced to fill space but to express faith, belief, trust etc. The Majesty and Creative power of God; the life, death and resurrection of Jesus; eternal life; prayer and other themes can be expressed in a unique and challenging way by "the Church Flower Festival".

- When flowers are used to complement the Christian Gospel in particular, or religious faith in general, they can be as effective as any preacher or evangelist...or, at least, I have found it so.

left Foliage from the garden showing wonderful variety in texture, form and colour in a classic triangular design.
Church: The First Presbyterian (NS) Church, Dunmurry, Northern Ireland
Arranger: The Reverend William McMillan
Photographer: Lyndon Parker

right The mechanics for this splendid altar design were four OASIS® Table Decos. The trays are so handy as they can be made up and brought to the church if time is short.
Church: St. Mary's Church, Innishannon. Co. Cork, Ireland
Arranger: Mary O'Keefe
Photographer: Mary O'Keefe

Mary O'Keefe
Church of the Holy Spirit, Cork, Ireland

- If using lilies in arrangements, try and have these in place the day before the wedding and the church will be filled with the scent for the ceremony.

- If using candles in church make sure they are arranged in suitable containers or arrangements, to avoid candle wax being spilt. If wax is spilt, put some brown wrapping paper on the wax and using a hot iron on the paper it will melt the wax and be absorbed into the paper.

- To use candles in arrangements, make holes in the end of the candle with a hot metal skewer (heated over a gas ring) and then insert a kebab stick which will stay in place when the wax dries. The candles can then be inserted into foam quite easily.

- When watering completed arrangements use a pot plant watering can with a long spout and this enables the water to get into the centre of the arrangements without any spills.

- When tying bows to pew ends, use decorative elastic as a better grip can be achieved. Small bunches of *Gypsophila*, or other small bunches of flowers, can then be inserted between the bow and the pew.

- Some churches may have pedestal stands that are not in good condition, so for weddings drape these with some tulle to match the colour of the bride's veil.

Linda Roeckelein
Washington National Cathedral, Washington DC, USA

- When planning a service, check to be sure participants are not allergic to the flowers being used.

- When gathering greens and flowers in the garden or along the roadside, always have a bucket of water at your side. On the spot, remove lower leaves and cut stems on a diagonal before standing them in water.

- When arranging, to avoid 'front falling disasters,' be sure your foam is positioned front to back rather than side to side in the container. The weight of your foam will help balance your front-facing plant material.

- When working on a matched pair, cut stems for both at the same time. Do not do one arrangement and then try to match the second to the first.

- Never use sticky tape on decorative wood, stone, or metal. It can leave an unsightly residue which is hard to remove (silver plate is never the same).

- Always save floral cages for reuse. Simply snap open and replace foam.

- In your toolbox, be sure to have pipe cleaners, bind wire, bark wire, and green-waxed twine and Band-Aids. A tape measure is also useful.

- Save Chinese carryout containers. They make good liners for baskets or vases or can be used directly on the altar as containers.

- Always be sure arrangements are watered to the top.

- Respect the material you are working with so that you can have a joyous time creating.

Veronica Scott
St. Paul's Church, Knightsbridge

- Many churches have 'coffin stools', used traditionally to support the coffin at a funeral. When dismantling dead flowers in church turn one upside down, with the feet uppermost, and place a black plastic bag between the legs. This makes it very much easier to chop the dead flowers and foliage. Do not overfill. Take the bag out and it will then stand on its own as you continue to fill.

- Church flower arranging can be very rewarding. It is important to get all the regulars in the congregation involved even if they say they cannot arrange flowers. Anyone who is not confident can come along and help a more experienced arranger, thereby learning as they go.

- There is no need to have a grand arrangement in church every Sunday. It is nice to have something simple every now and again.

- When arranging the flowers do not fill the bowl with water to the top as once you add your flowers the stems will raise the level of the water and then overflow. Top up at the end.

- Make sure somebody waters during the week. At the end of the week save any good flowers for use the following week.

- If you have only a few special flowers do not place them sparsely as they will be lost. Put them all close together to make a feature.

- It is not a good idea to lay one brick of foam horizontally on top of another. The water will not seep into the top brick.

Sue Slark
Flower Co-ordinator, Westminster Abbey

- Use a Jumbo block or part cut to size rather than several smaller blocks that will separate when you insert tall stems.

- Always use a large bowl and leave room around the foam to enable you to water easily.

- Top up with water half way through, when you can still see the level and again at the end. It may not get watered again!

- Push the stems well into the foam to keep them in position as the pedestal may be moved.

- Use tall strong leaves such as *Phormium* to give height and large leaves such as *Fatsia* or *Monstera,* towards the centre of the design to bring it all together.

- Some variegated foliage will help to lighten the design.

- Choose flowers that will give a good impact of colour and different shapes and textures to make the design more interesting such as hydrangea, carnations with rough texture and lilies and roses that are smooth.

left

Church: Washington National Cathedral
Arranger: Linda Roeckelein and Tina Roeckelein (Candelabra),
Kevin Aubrey and Cathie Jones (High Altar)
Photographer: Kevin Aubrey

above This pillar hanging represents the architects who have been involved in the building of Southwell Minster.

Church: Southwell Minster
Arrangers: Nottingham Flower Club
Photographer: Toby Smith

Toby Smith
(on lighting)

- If you use spotlights ensure that the brightest part has a large surface area to ensure your subject is evenly lit.

- Florescent light gives a bluish cool tone, tungsten a red and warmer tone. To get a true tone use halogen or daylight balanced bulbs which are neutral and mix well with natural light.

- Do not mix bulb types such as different wattage or type of element (for example halogen, tungsten, florescent) as they have a different colour balance.

- Using a diffuser or shade over the light will give a softer feel by reducing the contrast and illuminating the effect of shadows.

- Up-lighting should be used with care. As the light source is so close to the subject it is easy to create distracting shadows or hot shots. Care should be taken to ensure the viewers cannot see the light source.

- Lighting should enhance the design but not be an overstated feature in itself.

- Care should be taken not to have plant material or fabric close to a light source. Particular care must be taken with Halogen bulbs.

Tom Sopko
Church of the Advent, Boston, USA

- Inexpensive pre-made Christmas wreaths are widely available in November and December in a vast range of sizes. Use one of these as a foundation and poke in small pieces of one or more contrasting foliage and then berries, cones, fruit and/or dried flowers. Add a bow and you have a lush, expensive-looking wreath with minimal work and expense.

- Heavy duty black nylon cable ties, available at DIY stores, are ideal for attaching mechanics to screens, posts and poles. They can be pulled very tight without scratching and hold more securely than wire.

- To keep the colour of dried moss, use yellow-green food colour diluted about 5:1 with water in a spray bottle to give an extremely effective 'colour rinse'. Be careful to keep the green spray off any surfaces that could be stained or damaged, including skin!

- Large, lightweight, strong columns can be made out of 15 cm (6 in) diameter PVC drain pipe, using PVC flanges to attach a plywood base and cap. Cover them with a sort of papier-mâché made from roughly torn pieces of heavy, brown Kraft paper soaked in water-based clear polyurethane varnish. When dry it is waterproof, very durable and will not scratch easily. It look rather like birch bark.

- Consider scale – soaring gothic spaces, whether medieval or Victorian, require large arrangements. Novices find this very difficult, and professionals cannot make an arrangement incorporating 5ft branches in their shop and then put it in a van for delivery to the church.

- Particularly in a high church make sure that the flowers are not in the way of processions, swinging censers, or any of the numerous clergy and acolytes, and that they do not block sight lines.

- Keep flowers off altars and tabernacles and out of fonts.

- Never obstruct the altar cross.

- Select flowers that coordinate with the colours of the altar hangings and vestments. Have extra flowers for feast days, basic pedestal arrangements during ordinary time, and nothing during Advent and Lent.

- Take a walk – remember that your designs will often be seen from across the church, so you need to assess balance and scale from a distance. It is especially useful to step away before placing your last few pieces of any one type of plant material, so you can fill any gaps that may not be obvious from up close. Also, arrangements in churches are often seen from the sides and from behind, and they should look finished and balanced from any vantage point.

- Do not move flowers once you place them – stems and blooms will break and the floral foam will disintegrate. It is easier to make adjustments by adding material than by moving it. Repositioning large branches is especially dangerous. Pruning them a bit once they are in place is a much safer alternative.

- Christmas greens will last for weeks if you wrap saturated floral foam tightly in dark green or dull black florist's foil (the stuff they use to wrap potted plants) before inserting the stems. Tape the foil-wrapped blocks securely into a waterproof tray to collect drips and provide stability, and add a length of steel pipe along the back if necessary to keep it from tipping. An advent wreath made this way can last for a month with just an occasional misting if you start with fresh greens.

- Collect a variety of containers. The brass altar vases sold by church supply houses are usually dreadful – too tall, too narrow and too shiny. It is good to have containers in a variety of sizes, shapes and finishes that will hold several blocks of floral foam and a reasonable amount of water. Cachepots, planters and lightweight garden urns can be very useful, and one of my favourite containers is a wide, low, footed copper dish with a natural brown patina that is sold as a birdbath.

- Invest in custom-made mechanics. Sturdy, well-proportioned pedestals whose design and colour compliment the architectural setting are invaluable. Low pans made to fit around the font, lectern, paschal candle, etc. save time, make arranging easier, and prevent water damage, and they can be completed off-site and then moved into the church quickly on Christmas Eve or Holy Saturday.

- Oasis® Raquettes® can be taped to steel plates which have been cut to fit window sills, lintels and other narrow ledges – a safe, easy way to place flowers in awkward spaces.

Grace Sumerton (aged 13)
St. Hilary's Church, in the Parish of Llanrhos, North Wales

- Although I have little experience on arranging flowers in church, I do have some knowledge of what to do and what **not** to do. During my school holidays I visit my grandmother who began her flower arranging by doing flowers in church. Naturally, I go with her to church when she is arranging the flowers there and have watched her on many occasions. Here are my useful hints.

- First learn the basic skills of flower arranging, which should include:
  - Use of tools and equipment
  - Use of a variety of mechanical devices
  - Care and conditioning of cut flowers and foliage

- Find out what type of church – is it in the traditional style or of a modern nature. This will determine what style of design is most suitable.

- Simple styles look best in church, adding to the beauty of God's house and also keeps the cost down.

- Remember that flowers are a source of welcome for visitors to church.

- Always ask the churchwarden when it is possible to enter the church to arrange the flowers. Nowadays most churches are locked when not in use due to burglary and vandalism, even in rural communities.

- When arranging a design it is important to take plenty of covers to place on the floor to eliminate any damage with water etc. Also, making sure that placements are made safe to avoid accidents.

- There are occasions during the church year that would best suit children to participate in. The festivals are the best time for families to get involved; they are Easter, Harvest time and Christmas.

- Depending on the season and time of year it is good to use garden foliage, especially if it is in a traditional setting. There is some plant material available all the year round in the garden. If your family does not have a garden ask friends and family if they can provide what you need.

- It is nice to be invited to arrange flowers in church, the atmosphere is so peaceful and the stillness makes you concentrate on the task. Do ask if you would like to do an arrangement, my grandmother says "one is never too young or too old to offer our gifts to God".

- It would be nice if we could arrange flowers in our school church, especially at Christmas, but this has not yet materialised. Maybe in a couple of years I could ask to do a design.

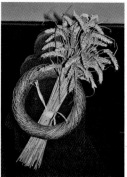

above Three pew end designs.
Church: St. Hilary's Church, Llanrhos
Arranger: Grace Sumerton
Photographer: Phyl Evans

Hilary Tupper
Chichester Cathedral, England

- If you have a patron of the festival do encourage them to get involved, to come to meetings, visit the wholesaler, and keep them informed of progress.

- Thank you letters and gifts, if appropriate, to everyone involved should be done immediately after the event. If organising the festival you will be tired but it is essential to do this. People are happy to help and really do appreciate a thank you at the end.

- Mark sure that your arrangers keep to the budgets you give them and remember to allow for extras such as foam, containers, hessian, staging, hire of equipment, lighting.

- Some of the arrangements at a festival should be at a level that wheelchair bound occupants can easily see and smell the flowers.

- Encourage the Festival Designer to have plenty of 'bonding' meetings with the arrangers. Communication and preparation is everything.

- Have posters of different sizes. Remember shops do not like all their window space covered with huge posters.

- Wear comfy shoes when flower arranging, standing for long periods on the floors of churches and cathedrals will often tire the legs greatly.

- Ask a local school to help the arrangers and get involved – good PR for both and will bring in visitors who might not necessarily come to the church or a flower festival.

- To encourage the young have a children's competition based on the theme of a festival and the flowers/arrangements in the church.

Graham Watts
St. Illtyd's Church, Llantwit Major, Wales

- Invest in a pair of good strong secateurs.

- Have a selection of containers to match the flowers and arrangement.

- A good wire cutter is essential if you are working with chicken wire.

- Collect shells, pebbles and driftwood from the seashore.

- If you are using drapes make sure that they have been properly ironed.

- Leave a space in the container to top up water levels.

Carolyn Yarbrough
Grace Episcopal Church, Charleston, SC

- When placing flowers in foam be sure you insert the stems deep enough so that they can get water. Be sure you do not let the stem come out of the foam in the back.

- When you finish the arrangement be sure to water thoroughly. Water should stand in the saucer. The first 24 hours are the most critical for your arrangement. Be sure you keep it watered as long as it is on the altar.

- If your design becomes off balance or wants to tip forward tie several heavy fishing weights together on the hook of a coat hanger. These can be used on the back of your container to balance the weight of your plant material.

- To obtain extra height, and to have access to a greater area of foam, use a plastic saucer on the top of your vase or container. Place the foam in the saucer, cover with chicken wire and tape the wire to the saucer. This gives you more room and is easier to move from place to place. The weight of the wet foam and the flowers help hold the saucer in place.

Organisations and suppliers

Organisations

Across the world there are organisations and private schools where information and courses are offered on how to arrange flowers in churches. Here are a few. If you can recommend any more do let me know so that these can be included in the next edition.

CEFAA
Church of England Flower Arrangers' Association

The Church of England Flower Arrangers' Association (CEFAA) was founded in 1981 in Liverpool to help and encourage all those who tend flowers in church and link them together in fellowship and friendship. It is open to all those baptised in the Christian faith. The aims are to expand interest in church flowers as part of worship. The Association is non commercial and non competitive. There is a junior section (8–18). A quarterly news booklet is sent to members.

For further information contact
Mr. L.W. Fielding (secretary)
Tel: +44 151 709 5116
Email: cefaa@eastquay.fsnet.co.uk

NAFAS
The National Association of Flower Arranging Societies

The National Association of Flower Arranging Societies (NAFAS), which has many member clubs throughout the British Isles and a number of overseas associates, has been and continues to be responsible for thousands of cathedral and church festivals. It encourages a very high standard of artistic beauty and meticulous organisation. Festivals have varied in scope from simple ones in country churches using only garden flowers to resplendent spectacles involving hundreds of flower arrangers in St. Paul's Cathedral and Westminster Abbey.
For more information:
Email: flowers@nafas.org.uk
Website: www.nafas.org.uk

St. Philips Cathedral, Atlanta, Georgia, USA

Laura Iarocci and Victoria Denson are the owners of Faith Flowers, a flower school specializing in arrangements for sacred spaces and the home. Faith Flowers offers demonstrations and hands on workshops for churches starting new Flower Guilds and those seeking to enhance their Flower Guilds. Laura and Victoria are the Chairs of the Cathedral of St. Philip Flower Guild in Atlanta, Georgia. They recruit, train and manage the Guild of 50 volunteers, which arranges flowers for three to five altars each week.
Please contact Laura or Victoria at Faith Flowers for more information.
Laura Iarocci:
Tel: +1 404 578 0950 Email: laura@faithflowers.net
Victoria Denson:
Tel: +1 404 213 6236
Visit their website: www.faithflowers.net

Washington National Cathedral, Washington DC, USA

Each year the Washington National Cathedral offers two Flower Arranging seminars for Holy Spaces. One is in January and the other in February. Classes and workshops are taught by Linda Roeckelein, Flower Guild Coordinator, and other Flower Guild instructors. Linda also offers flower demonstrations and workshops throughout the country.
To inquire, please contact Linda Roeckelein:
Tel: +1 202 537 6215
Email: Lroeckelein@cathedral.org

Judith Blacklock Flower School, London, UK

Two and three day courses learning about church flowers from basic design to working with large mechanics. Private lessons can be arranged. The school is located in a delightful London mews in Knightsbridge.
Tel: +44 207 235 6235
Email: school@judithblacklock.com
Website: www.judithblacklock.com

Useful products and suppliers

***The Flower Arranger* Magazine**
The Flower Arranger is the official magazine of NAFAS
and the world's leading flower magazine covering all
aspects of floral design and featuring festivals,
competitions and events.
Email: flowers@nafas.co.uk
Website: www.nafas.org.uk

Flower Dry Desiccant
Moira Clinch
Flower Dry
64 Hackney Road
Matlock
Derbyshire DE4 2PX
Tel: +44 629 581026
Email: moiraclinch@hotmail.com

*Mechanics and metalwork for
flower designers*

Harold Burns
2 Hamps Cottage
Leek Road
Waterhouses
Stoke-on-Trent ST10 3HN
Tel: +44 1538 308178

Roger Hardy
Tranters
The Common
Winterslow
Salisbury SP5 1PJ
Tel: +44 1980 862726

Pam Lewis
Wellaway
Close Lane
Marston
Devizes
Wilts SN10 5SN
Tel: +44 1380 728819

Photographers

Tom Allwood
info@tomallwood.com
www.tomallwood.com

Christina Bennett
christina@cmb45.wanadoo.co.uk

Valdis Breidis (USA)
valdisb@comcast.net

Robert Brown
mail@dr-bob.co.uk

Xander Casey
xander@xandercasey.co.uk
www.xandercasey.co.uk

Michael Chevis
info@michaelchevis.com
www.michaelchevis.com

David Connor
connor@nrauceby.fsnet.co.uk

Mark Finkenstaedt (USA)
mark@mfpix.com
www.mfpix.com

Adam Fox
adam@fox.eu.com

Oliver Gordon
ollygordon@lycos.com
www.olivergordon.co.uk

Richard Greenly Photography
mail@richardgreenlyphoto.co.uk
www.richardgreenlyphoto.co.uk

Chris Harten
chris.harten@btinternet.com
www.thegardener.btinternet.co.uk

John Holden
+44 1206 298 242

Patricia Howe
patricia.howe@tesco.net

Barbara Hurst
BarbaraHurst1@aol.com

Lynn Keddie
lynn@lynnkeddiephotography.com
www.lynnkeddiephotography.com

Jocelyn Knight (USA)
Jocelynkinghtphoto@yahoo.com
www.jocelynknight.com

Phillip Lawrence
phillip537@btinternet.com

Pam Lewis
cledwyn.lewis5@btinternet.com

David Lloyd
davidlloyd7@talktalk.net

Dick Makin Imaging
dick@dmimaging.co.uk
www.dmimaging.co.uk

Ash Mills
ash@silver.co.uk
www.AshMills.com

Ron McIntosh
camphillron@gmail.com

Mark Nixon – The Portrait Studio (Ireland)
info@theportraitstudio.ie
www.marknixon.com

Mike Pannett
m_pannett@sky.com

Lyndon Parker
lyndonparker@mac.com
www.lyndonparker.com

Graham Rodger
graham@rodger1.myzen.co.uk

Allen Rout
agrout@heathsidecrafts.co.uk

Matt Samolis (USA)
shoe4@verizon.net

Louisa Scott
info@louisascottphotography.com
www.louisascottphotography.com

Toby Smith
toby@roofunit.com
www.shootunit.com

Don Somner
photo@donsomner.com
www.donsomner.com

Benedetta Spinelli (USA)
info@benedettaspinelli.com
www.benedettaspinelli.com

Lee Thompson (USA)
leet@nc.rr.com
www.LeeThompsonPhotography.com

Acknowledgements

This book has been created not just by myself but with the contributions of many kind and generous people. Many have given their time, knowledge and talent to arrange the designs you see in this book – some intricate and complex, others simple and unassuming. Without their work – created to the glory of worship – this book could not have been published. Many of the designers are members of NAFAS (The National Association of Flower Arrangement Societies) who selflessly spend thousands of hours creating beauty in places of worship to generate money for so many valuable causes.

This book has taken several years in the making and my worst fear is that I leave out someone's name. If I have, let me know and the next version will include the omission – it could be a photographer, arranger or simply someone who has given me invaluable advice.

I owe a huge dept to Brenda Hall. I asked Brenda to look at one chapter and her advice was so sound that I ended up asking her to go through every chapter, which she did with speed and knowledge where mine was lacking. She told me what was wrong and what to do about it and I will always be grateful.

Laura Iarocci of St. Philip's Cathedral in Atlanta and Tom Sopko of Church of the Advent, Boston helped to advise me on the American content of the book and provided me generously with beautiful photographs of inspirational designs.

I visited flower festivals, big and small, across the country to learn more and to take photographs. What a marvellous way to fill the church with beauty and to give pleasure and to raise funds for the church. Michael Bowyer the designer at Salisbury Cathedral, Julia Legg and the arrangers at Sheffield, Clare Cowlin in Mortlake, Hilary Tupper and Georgie Macqueen at Chichester, Marilyn Williams, Lee Berrill and the wonderfully generous team at Southwell Minster are some of the distinguished people who have shown me their way of doing the flowers from which I have learnt an immense amount.

Grateful thanks must be given to the photographers across the world who have been so generous in letting me use their photographs – in particularly Wally Breidis, Bob Brown, Xander Casey, Mark Finkenstaedt, Richard Greenly, Chris Harten, Fotis Karapiperis, Jocelyn Knight, David Lloyd, Mark Nixon and George Westinghouse.

Stef Adriaenssens is not only a brilliant designer and has taken some magnificent photographs of his work in Alden Biesen that show a new and exciting edge to floral design.

Robert Koene, who lives and works in Athens, has allowed me to use several images from his book *Wedding Stories* (published by Stamoulis Publications, Athens). Together with his photographer Fotis, he has introduced a different aspect of working with church flowers.

Jean Taylor was the author of *Church Flowers* and *Church Flowers Month by Month*. She was one of the most respected writers in the world on the subject of flower arranging. The family of Jean kindly allowed me to use information from her book in the chapter on flower festivals.

I also want to extend thanks to the following people:

Susan Adams and members of the Flower Guild for their inspirational designs in St Mary's Church, Barnes.

Sheila Banks who has gone through all the photos submitted through *The Flower Arranger* magazine. As ever she has been a source of patience, efficiency and good humour.

John Beare and Tim Harris of The Flower Press. John for his good humour and efficiency in the production of *Church Flowers* and Tim for his belief in publishing it.

Hillary Brian for her tips and advice on the Church of England Flower Arrangers Association.

Harold Burns for his amazing engineering knowledge and excellent line drawings.

Christina Curtis for her wide-ranging and professional knowledge on botanical correctness.

Mary Daykin who advised me when starting out.

John Deards for his help on mechanics.

Mo Duffill and the editorial board at *The Flower Arranger* for allowing me use of the images that have appeared in the magazine.

Marion Gough who runs a mission entitled 'Orphans in the Wild' and who provided the photograph showing flowers in a church in Africa. Look at the website www.wildorphans.org for more information on this important charity.

Petal Harvill of Petal Designs in Boca Raton, Florida.

Tom Koson, Rachel Petty and Lindsay Richards for their support at the Flower School. Rachel is the person responsible for Bowel Cancer being the charity to benefit from sales from the book.

Wendy Smith for sound advice.

John Vagg for advice on illustration.

Hans van der Voort of Metz UK BV for advice on roses.

Jean Vernon for her words on composting.

Graham Watts for helping with the proof reading.

Louise Wheeler and the team at Bowel Cancer UK.

Nik at Peters and Zabransky UK Ltd. for the line illustrations and for his ease and charm.

And to all the generous people who have provided the wealth of tips that comprise chapter 17. Their knowledge and experience will pave the way for many more to enter the world of church flowers.

Amanda Hawkes the designer of this book has worked, when needed, 24 hours a day with style, patience and grace. I am honoured to count her as a friend.

Lastly my family who have supported me so generously in the creation of this book.
Joan Ward, my mother, who at 87 proof read the book, my husband David and children Charles and Jane who have each helped me with their skills.
I promise never to write another book!

Photographic credits

The publisher would like to thank the following people, companies or organisations for giving permission to use their photographs:

The Flower Arranger magazine (published by NAFAS) for the use of photographs on the following pages: 88, 123, 147, 221, 222–3, 275, 276, 277, 398

David Austin and Hilliers for providing photographs for chapter 3.

daisy_joy/iStockphoto.com for the photograph of *Laurus nobilis* on page 37.

Roger Whiteway/iStockphoto.com for the photograph of *Sorbus aria* on page 51.

David Hawkes for the photographs of *Buxus* on page 33; *Cymbidium*, *Lilium orientalis* and *Leucospermum* on page 63.

Stane Crnjak/iStockphoto.com for the photograph of spray *Dianthus* on page 63.

sad/Fotolia.com for the photograph of bloom *Chrysanthemum* on page 63.

anzeletti/iStockphoto.com; Flowers & Plants Association – www.flowers.org.uk; Metz and Scheurs for the photographs of roses on page 339.

Index